BUILDING
A WINNING
CAREER

BUILDING
A WINNING
CAREER

A comprehensive blueprint
for job hunting success
in turbulent times

WILLIAM COWAN

About William Cowan

William has a great deal of wisdom. He injects a quiet confidence and sense of fun into the process, while at the same time providing helpful encouragement and motivation to do the work. And, most importantly, his technique works! *Steve Clifford – CEO*

William is the master at building careers. He supports you to build your career ambition, increase your confidence and build a professional network. He's always there for advice, coaching or challenge to spur you on. *Madelyn Ring – CPO*

William provides his clients with insightful advice, disciplined decision-making and an understanding of the need for flexibility and resilience. He artfully combines wisdom and good humour in the support he delivers. *Fiona Reed – NED*

William is one of those rare individuals who has the ability to guide others without taking control or pushing his own agenda. He clearly loves seeing his clients push their personal boundaries to deliver more than they thought they could. *Philippe Etienne – NED*

William is a very thoughtful and capable individual. His background and experience mean that he can give even most senior of executives robust, insightful and supportive counsel. He excels in his field. *Peter Lamell – NED*

William has an incredible ability to unlock insights around your unique superpowers. He is both the stretch and the safety net as you reimagine your career. He brings a balance of sharp intellect and big heart ... and undeniable impact. *Nicole Sparshott – CEO*

William coached me to build a network for life. By building a deep understanding of me, William partnered with me to ensure every career decision was fully informed by optimising values, fit and family. *Tony Dunstan – CEO*

For more than 200 five-star reviews,
see www.goodreads.com and www.amazon.com
Average rating: 4.99 stars

If you find this book helpful,
please add your review at www.goodreads.com

About this book

A must read for senior leaders in finding the right new job or those wanting to take their career to the next level. It's highly engaging, yet practical, with home truths that you won't get from your family, friends or colleagues. *Kalpana Gee – Senior Banking Executive*

This book is outstanding and provides really insightful and valuable information that can be practically applied by any executive who wants to secure their ideal role and build a successful career. *Ian Nankivell – 35 years as a leader in executive search*

In a world of ever-increasing disruption, the navigation of one's own career will continue to be challenged in ways that we can't imagine. This book provides concepts, strategies and tactics that help in a way like no other. *David Nicolson – Senior Career Consultant*

How do you cut through the emotion when you are out of work? To be focused, rational, reflective, and successful, you need a great process based on expert experience. That is why you need this book! *Russell Parker – Global CEO*

This book offers precious pearls of wisdom for all to learn from and apply. It is guaranteed to become your trusted career companion, one you will consult for practical, transferable insights throughout your career. *Aimée Samuels-Meens – Senior Career Consultant*

Getting a great job is about so much more than being the best candidate. There is an art to being the successful candidate and this book provides straightforward and practical advice to help you get your dream job. *Julia Shtepa – Senior Financial Services Executive*

This book fills an important gap in the inadequately served field of career guidance. It provides executives – at all levels – with practical advice on how to re-position and significantly enhance career progression. *Alan Winton – Senior Search Executive*

I am fortunate to have successfully worked with William, embracing the principles, practical methods and purposeful disciplines in this book. The purposeful and practical path laid out in this book make the process less confronting. *Greg White – COO*

First published in 2021 by William Cowan
Reprinted May 2022
Reprinted with minor updates February 2024
Minor updates February 2026

A catalogue entry for this book is available from the National Library of Australia.

ISBN: 978-1-922553-50-8

Project management and text design by Publish Central
Cover design by Tess McCabe

This book is written in British English.

The paper this book is printed on is certified as environmentally friendly.

Contents

APPENDICES

NOTE ON THE USE OF AI

1. **Make sure you do not lose what makes you special if
you use AI to develop your CV and cover letters:** AI drafts
usually look polished, but they often miss the most critical personal
elements that make you special, including clear thinking, concise
language, consistent presentation, and catchy style.

2. **AI can help you greatly with the following:** Analysing
feedback you receive regarding your strengths to identify roles that
might suit you, identifying possible areas for further job research,
comparing your CV with job position descriptions to identify issues,
rehearsing for interviews, analysing offer letters to identify issues,
and so on.

3. **Observation:** It is possible that AI will make the CVs of many
candidates look similar. If this happens, it is likely that building
your network of personal connections – in the way suggested
in this book – will become even more important as you seek to
differentiate yourself.

About the author

William has over 30 years of experience in senior management positions. He has served as an advisor to boards and chief executives worldwide, and been the chief executive officer of a number of listed and unlisted companies.

For 20 years, William was Director, Key Executive Services, at Directioneering. During this time, Directioneering grew to be the leading career strategy firm in Australia and New Zealand. It provides individuals and organisations with tailored career transition, career coaching and leadership development services. While at Directioneering, William worked successfully with over 1000 senior executives from every industry, providing them with consulting and advice related to their careers.

During the late 1970s and early 1980s, he was a partner of McKinsey & Co, servicing major clients in Europe, North America, Asia and Australia. He led the development of a transformational strategy for the Australian Football League in 1982. In 1983 he led a leveraged buyout of Southern Cross Broadcasting, which grew to become the fourth largest commercial broadcasting network in Australia in the late 1980s.

During the late 1990s, William was the chief executive of Davidson & Associates, at the time the premier career management firm in Australia. Over this period, Davidson & Associates consolidated its position as a leader in South-East Asia, with offices in five countries. While leading Davidson & Associates, William worked with some of Australia's and Asia's most senior executives, providing them with career management advice and counsel. In 1998, the firm was voted the best service firm in Australia by readers of *BRW* magazine.

William was the chairman of various boards and committees in a number of not-for-profit organisations. These included Trinity College at the University of Melbourne, and the Australian International Opera Awards. He led the development of a strategy to strengthen Victorian Thoroughbred Racing as a world leader in 1995.

He was educated at the University of Melbourne where he obtained Engineering and Commerce degrees. He was awarded exhibitions in Economics. In 1970, he was awarded a Harkness Fellowship by the Commonwealth Fund in New York for study at Harvard Business School. This fellowship enabled him to obtain a Master of Business Administration with High Distinction in 1972 from the Harvard Business School where he was a Baker Scholar.

On 26 January 2015, he was awarded a Member of the Order of Australia for significant service to the community through educational, medical research and arts organisations, and to business.

Acknowledgements

With my special gratitude to the three people without whom this book could not have been written:

- Frederick Davidson – one of the world leaders in career transition, who brought me into this profession and taught me so much;
- Jannine Fraser – The CEO and Co-founder of Directioneering, which has been a very important part of my life for the past 20 years;
- Imogen Cowan – my talented daughter, who urged me to write this book, and gave me so much help along the way.

MY THANKS

Many hugely accomplished people have assisted me to bring this book to life, including:

- Kath Walters – who provided the wise counsel, the energy, and the continuing guidance to make sure I not only started, but also went on to finish, this project;
- Michael Hanrahan, Charlotte Duff, Anna Clemann and the whole team at Publish Central – for their unending patience and skill in shaping the book and publishing it;
- Steve Clifford, Steve Hrubala, Raj Khetarpal, Daniel King, Peter Lamell, Andrew Maitland, Laura Morse, Ian Nankivell, David Nicolson, Conor O'Malley, Russell Parker, Isaac Russo,

Aimée Samuels-Meens, Michael Symons, Andrew Thorburn, Greg White and Alan Winton — for important ideas to improve the book and valuable support and encouragement as the book took shape;

- My colleagues — who taught me most of what I know about career management; and

- My clients — who have been so supportive with advice and encouragement over the past 25 years.

Introduction

We hear much these days about how many jobs you will likely have during your lifetime. We hear less about how to make good job selections. And we hear very little indeed about how you should manage your transition between jobs to build a successful career and thrive. With so little guidance available, it is easy to assume that, if you are an effective individual, your transition between jobs will be straightforward. This is unlikely to be true. Whether you are a high performer or you aspire to be one, you need to make considered job selections and plan for successful transitions between them. If you have recently left your job, are unhappy in your current role, considering a portfolio career or entering the professional space for the first time, you need to work through a clear, structured process to identify and secure attractive career growth opportunities. In writing this book, I aim to help you understand this process and then use it to assist you to build a winning career. A career that could change your life. A winning career, by the way, is quite different from living a successful life. Your career is only one part of this much bigger challenge, but an important part for most people.

What is a 'winning career'? I am not talking about being successful because you are fortunate to be in the right place at the right time. I want you to capitalise, in an active way, on your special strengths. This means you need to stretch yourself, show some grit and take some risks. I want you to have a career where you can look back on your contributions and be proud that you have been engaged in your work and fulfilled in your relationships. Very few of us can plan our careers or our lives in any detail. But we can manage the process of seeking out work that we will find fulfilling and where we can shine. This book is intended to assist you to do this whenever you are facing a career transition.

The reason I use the word 'winning' is because I am suggesting an active process. I want you to apply your energy and brainpower to identify and secure the best outcomes for yourself and for those you care about. As a result, I take you through how to identify your special strengths and how to communicate these strengths in a compelling way. I suggest ways in which you can open up more opportunities for yourself. And I consider how you might maximise your chances of attaining a role where you can thrive – a role where you can add the most value and be the most satisfied. My purpose in writing this book is to set out in detail a practical process that has worked for my clients so as to help you. You do not need to design your own job transition process. You can learn from what has worked for others. I am confident that the process I describe here will have many elements that will work for you.

Many successful people, at all levels of their career, find it more difficult than they expect to seek out and secure exciting, fulfilling new roles – roles that will help them to drive their careers forward and to excel. Why is this the case? One key reason is that finding a new job requires entirely different skills from the ones you are likely to have developed as a successful executive. If you are a leader, you are likely to be comfortable with and used to being in charge. However, when you are looking for a job, your progress is almost entirely at the whim of others. This reversed power dynamic can be extremely disconcerting for you. Even calm, relaxed and highly effective individuals can become extremely anxious as they seek out new positions. If you feel this way, you're not alone. However, it is not only possible but also likely that you will move from a state of uncertainty to a state of confidence if you follow the process set out here.

In *Outliers*, journalist and best-selling author Malcolm Gladwell argues you need at least 10,000 hours of experience and practice to develop world-class expertise. Over the past 25 years, I have worked with over 1000 high-performing executives, as well as many graduates. As a result, I have spent over 20,000 hours coaching people transitioning in their careers! Fortunately, the outcomes have virtually always been excellent.

You will see that I ask many questions in this book. This is because I do not have specific answers for you; however, by being asked the right questions, you will work out the answers for yourself. Throughout this book, I have included anecdotes using my clients' experiences to illustrate many different situations that you might face. (Note that all names and identifying details have been changed to ensure the anonymity of these individuals.) These examples help to highlight that searching for a new job is more complicated than many people realise, but there is a process that works.

The overarching questions I discuss in this book are:

- What should you do to find a role that will be satisfying and fulfilling, and that will assist you in building a winning career?

- How can you be reasonably certain your jobs and your career will not damage the relationships that matter to you in your life?

This book takes you from the start point of looking for a new (or perhaps even your first) job to being established in a new role and evaluating whether you have selected wisely. Through the chapters in this book, I set out how to manage your job search process and how to address all the challenges that this presents. Some of the activities and ways of working that I suggest may seem counterintuitive to you. For instance, you may think it obvious that you should be clear with your friends, colleagues and everyone you meet that you are looking for a job. But this is almost always counterproductive if you are a senior jobseeker. People often freeze when you ask for their help in finding a senior role (or any role for that matter). Why? Because most people do not have a clue about how to help you to find a job. More often than not, they will provide naïve suggestions that do not help you. Rather than talking about finding a job, what you need to do is to ask them for *advice*. If you do this, and frame your request properly, you will make much more progress. My mantra is:

> *Seek a job, and you will get advice.*
> *Seek advice, and you will get a job.*

WHO WILL BENEFIT FROM THIS BOOK?

This book is written to provide guidance for senior jobseekers. If you are a senior executive, my aim is to set out and explain practical guidelines for successfully managing your job search and transitioning into a new role. You will see that senior executives face numerous complex challenges. You have a lot to think about if you wish to take active steps to maximise your success as a senior jobseeker – and, more than this, to position yourself for a successful subsequent career.

Despite my focus on helping senior jobseekers, it is clear that many of the central principles will help *anyone* who wants to take charge of their career. You may only be a few years into your first job. You may be happy in your current role but feel the need to rethink your career. You may want to change what you are doing or start a business. You may have had a busy and demanding role, but are now thinking of moving to a portfolio career or starting retirement. You may not have a job, and this could be for many reasons: You could still be at university or school, you could have decided to take a break, you could have other priorities, you could have resigned, you could have been terminated, you could have been made redundant, or you could have already retired.

Whatever kind of major transition you face, this book provides signposts to help you. All transitions have elements in common, even though the starting and finishing points, and the intensity of the various steps in the process, may be very different. Depending on where you are in your career, different parts of the book will be more or less important. If you are not yet a senior executive, you can take the parts of this book that are relevant to you and use them. If you are just starting out, you may possibly need to focus more on functional skills and less on management and leadership capability. And you will not have the same kind of network to call on as a senior jobseeker does. But whatever your starting point, I provide practical advice and processes that will help you find a new role – with detailed examples of how to handle both successes and setbacks. I describe a process that will help you find a role that maximises not only the value you can deliver but also your satisfaction and happiness. I also provide you with life skills that will enable you to position yourself for a long, successful career – helping you to be 'future proofed'. In addition, I include tips to help you to minimise the possibility of making career transition mistakes.

Most books on this subject have been written to help prepare relatively junior people, emphasising how to write CVs and cover letters for job applications. They also explain how to best present yourself in interviews, and how to respond to standard behavioural interview questions. At a more senior level, this kind of advice is not of great value. It is only a small part of the story. Whatever your situation, between 70 and 80 per cent of your underlying success in identifying and attaining roles will result from information originating from people in your network. As a result, your main focus needs to be on harnessing your current network and then on expanding your network significantly. You need to do this in a way that leads to success, not only for your next job but also, ideally, for the remainder of your career and for your life.

No matter what level you are working at or aiming for, this book will help you to be better equipped to address challenges as they arise. Unfortunately, these important life skills – the skills you need to 'future proof' yourself – are hardly mentioned, either at school or at university. This book is designed to remedy this situation. My hope is that, if you understand the process set out here and what is required to be successful, you will be forewarned and forearmed – before you find yourself stranded under pressure, without these skills!

NO JOB IS SECURE

These days virtually no-one has a secure job. You might be surprised to learn that, according to Dan Ciampa in the *Harvard Business Review*, more than 30 per cent of new chief executives fail within 18 months. Outstanding people are leaving, or being asked to leave, their jobs every day. Importantly, senior executives rarely lose or leave their jobs because they lack capability.

Your potential reasons for leaving are almost endless. Your values may not match those of your employer. You might be unlucky – in the wrong place at the wrong time. You might have been handed a poisoned chalice. You might be forced to leave for reasons beyond your control – such as a perception that you do not 'fit' in the organisation. You may have lost your sponsor. You may have decided to leave to start a family. Perhaps problems developed in New York that led to a downsizing in London or Sydney. Your new boss may be insecure and feel threatened by you. Perhaps you have outgrown your role. You may have identified problems that people above you are covering up and do not want aired. Or perhaps you have been transferred back from overseas, and no suitable role is available for you at home. A new CEO or Chair may want to bring in their own trusted team, not because they think the current management are incompetent but because they themselves are under extreme pressure to deliver results quickly. Therefore, they choose to bring in a team they know and trust. The possibilities are many and varied.

Despite the continuing likelihood that their jobs could be at risk, most senior executives are not well prepared to tackle the job search process successfully. Perhaps they have been fortunate enough to have had a dream run, being headhunted or promoted throughout their careers. As a result, they have never had to face the challenge of finding a new role. This is a common situation among the individuals I work with. As a result of their success to date, many effective executives assume that finding a new job cannot be too hard, and that they can work out what they need to do as they go along. In fact, this is not a wise strategy. The more senior you are, the less likely it is that an ad hoc process will end in the best result for you. Just because you have been a success in one role does not mean that you will automatically be a success in a new role.

HAVING A PROCESS CREATES THE BEST CHANCE OF SUCCESS

If you believe that all jobs are insecure, gaining a prior appreciation of the best process for finding a new job becomes a wise next step. This makes sense if only because, one day, you might need to put it into practice. If a proven process is available that increases your probability of success, you don't have to invent your own. However, the difficulty you face is that few, if any, sources are available to teach you what you need to know.

Most advice I've seen is high level and unhelpful in its generality – for example, 'You need to arrange some coffee meetings' or 'You need to meet some recruiters'. It is all very well to be told that networking or meeting recruiters is desirable, but how do you prepare to do this effectively? How do you become more visible in a positive and constructive way to people who might be able to help you? How do you get the most out of your meetings? And how do you restart if you hit a serious roadblock? This book is intended to fill these gaps. It describes an active and intentional process that works if you put in the effort and maintain your focus.

Four distinct steps are involved in my proven job search process. Each part of this book covers one of these four steps. These steps are shown in the following figure, along with the chapters that delve into each of them in much more detail.

Four steps in the job-search process

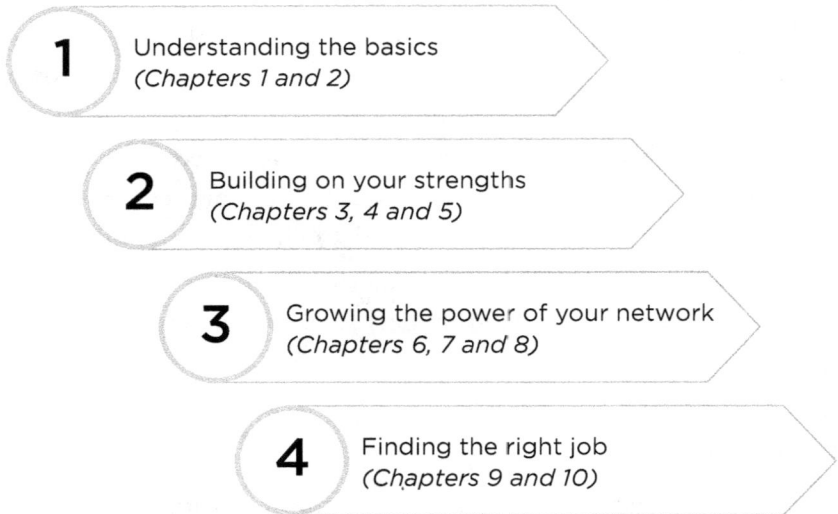

1 Understanding the basics
(Chapters 1 and 2)

2 Building on your strengths
(Chapters 3, 4 and 5)

3 Growing the power of your network
(Chapters 6, 7 and 8)

4 Finding the right job
(Chapters 9 and 10)

The process of finding a new job is not only complex but also uniquely personal. It involves much more than a routine set of mechanical steps and requires significant investment of your emotional energy. As I explain later in this book, building emotional connections with a series of new people outside your current network is key. Many senior jobseekers do not know how to tackle this challenge or feel very uncomfortable in attempting to do so.

Think of it this way. In Hollywood, you may produce a powerful, widely-praised movie, but you will not necessarily win an Academy Award. To win an Oscar, you need to gain the most votes from the members of the Academy of Motion Picture Arts and Sciences. Winning these votes involves managing a vote-seeking process that is totally different from managing movie production. For you to obtain a new job, you will require similar skills to those required to generate the votes needed to win an Oscar. If you want to be offered a job, you need to understand how to generate 'votes' from all those in the hiring process. The 'voters' in your process will include your colleagues, referees, recruiters and HR executives, along with members of the senior management and, maybe, the members of the board in the hiring organisation. To generate these votes, you will need to be visible and build emotional connections. How can you do this most effectively?

In the following chapters, I guide you through the process of improving your visibility and winning the votes you need to be awarded the role that you aspire to. I want you to aim high, and to achieve a role where you are happier, more productive and better paid than in the one you left. In my experience, this is quite achievable for most people. But to increase your chances of being a winner, you need to dedicate yourself to this process, through thick and thin.

WHY YOU MUST HAVE A STRONG FOUNDATION

This book is structured around the process I use when working with my clients. Similar to every great building, every effective career transition process must have a strong foundation. As you tackle the job search process, you are no exception. You need to prepare your own strong foundation before you begin to build your network. This is vital to your success. The first eight chapters of this book are designed to help you to build this foundation.

First, in chapter 1, I explain the seven guiding principles that underlie your future success. Keep these principles in mind as you conduct your search. In chapter 2, I show you why seeking and filling a senior job presents such significant challenges for most of us. Understanding these challenges will help you be better prepared as you progress.

Once you understand why these challenges are important, the next step is to critically think about your strengths and key competencies. Because each hiring process is usually competitive, you then need to go one step further - to identify, as clearly as you can, what makes you special. Everyone is special in their own way and identifying what makes you special deserves deep consideration. You then need to work out how best to communicate your unique skillset – with strength and brevity – both in writing and in conversations with your network. This is not as easy as you might think. Many people struggle to communicate briefly and with impact without first investing in serious preparation. The good news is that, if you can do this well, you will actually reinforce other people's perception that you are indeed special! These topics are covered in chapters 3, 4 and 5.

Following this, in chapters 6, 7 and 8, I discuss how to explore and evaluate your career options based on your strengths, how to launch your networking, and how to get the most out of your networking efforts. Finally, in chapters 9 and 10, I discuss how to generate attractive job offers and maximise your chance of continuing success when you start your new job.

In an effort to keep this book simple and clear, I have avoided detailed footnotes and complex references. Throughout the book, I touch on a number of individual topics, some of which fill whole books and research papers elsewhere. I often mention this work in just a sentence or two. Think of these specific topics as threads in the larger tapestry of life. Many of them are golden but understanding them in depth is not the purpose of this book. If you want more detail on the thinking in these sources, please refer to the books, articles, blogs, and videos set out in the Further Reading section at the back of this book.

As part of trying to keep things simple, I have included a summary of key points at the start of each chapter to signpost the information included. I have also set out some questions for you to consider at the end of each chapter, to remind you of the key questions you need to address as you go through this process.

Finally, three additional simplifications:

- I have used the term 'family' throughout this book as shorthand for any and all relationships you consider important.

- I have used the term 'CV' throughout this book, rather than differentiate between curricula vitae and résumés.

- I have used the term 'Chair' to cover Chairman, Chairwoman and Chairperson.

LOOKING FOR A JOB IS A JOB

While each person and each job search situation is different, one thing is clear: the challenges you will face are quite predictable. At least to begin with, you may be angry and upset, and are likely to feel isolated and defeated. The phone rarely rings – and even if it does, the opportunity may be unattractive. When things go wrong, you will be tempted to believe that you are the one who failed in some way. Of course, the setback might have had nothing to do with you, but you do not understand this and you think the worst.

Making progress takes longer and is more difficult than you expect. People who you presume will be most helpful do not seem to have anything useful to contribute. Others promise a lot but do not deliver. You find it impossible to obtain helpful, compelling, personalised advice. You cannot find anyone who provides rigorous help in testing and validating your thinking. You worry that you have run out of good ideas. You are concerned that others do not understand or value your unique background, your strengths or your special skills. People brand you in ways that you think are ill-fitting or inappropriate – too general or too specific. You start to be concerned that you might have reached your use-by date. The list goes on! That is why I've written this book: to reach more people facing the challenges of job seeking with a structured process that will help deliver a positive outcome.

Identifying the final outcome when you are just starting the process is almost impossible – the world is too complex for that. Never forget that your job search is an activity-based process, not an intellectual one. You do not know what you do not know. Opportunities exist out there that you cannot imagine and overthinking where you might end up early on in the process is a mistake. The key is to focus your energy and activity using a structured process to generate attractive opportunities. Once you have developed a strong foundation, you need to work hard to create ideas and new possibilities. You need to be a good explorer – and to be a good explorer, you must leave your base camp and find out what is over the next ridge. In fact, you may have many ridges to climb before you reach your destination!

Some luck is required too! But remember the words of the great golfer Arnold Palmer (and many others who have been credited with these same words): 'The more I practise, the luckier I get'. This will be true for you too! You will find a job if you remain committed.

The great thing about my job is that I work with outstanding people. I learn something new every day. Even better, I help to change people's lives in a positive way. In some ways, I am similar to a personal trainer who wants you to build your physical fitness. When we work together, I try to stretch your thinking to be as creative as possible. I take this same approach in this book, encouraging you to always consider more than your next job. Where will the next job lead? If you live to the age of 80 or more, how will you lead a long, productive life and be part of a happy family? When you reach 80, will you be able to look back on your transition experience and say, 'Even though the job search process was much tougher than I expected, it turned out to be a worthwhile experience and it helped to change my life for the better'? Helping my clients answer these questions in a positive way is why I have never tired of my work.

CLARITY CREATES OPPORTUNITIES

One key message I want to reinforce is to be brief and clear in your communications with others. I have taken this to heart for myself. Even though I cover many different topics in this book, in each area I have sought to be brief and clear. Perhaps my focus may seem too dogmatic to you – but the advantage of writing in this way is that it permits me to keep things simple. The trade-off is that I do not detail every conceivable job-search context or the full complexity of all the issues you may face. Life is complicated and I have no doubt that you will need to modify my recommendations to reflect the specific situation you face at any time.

For instance, I suggest that you should not accept any not-for-profit board positions while searching for a new job. My reasoning is that I do not want you to be distracted from your networking. Others might take an alternative view, suggesting that such a board position would be a wonderful idea. No doubt they will have their own rationale for taking this view. You will need to make up your own mind, depending on your situation. I also provide ideas that I hope will work in many different cultures, though I recognise my own intercultural understanding is limited. I, therefore, want to be clear that I recognise my advice may not be applicable or appropriate in every cultural context. If necessary, please adapt my recommended approaches to your own specific situation.

THIS RECIPE WORKS IN ANY CAREER TRANSITION

While adjustments may be necessary, I am confident this framework can be applied in any career transition. I sometimes hear comments along the lines of 'If you are over 55, you have no hope in finding another good job'. This is definitely not true. Anyone who suggests this does not understand how to search for a senior role. As in most things in life, your preparation, commitment, energy and skills are what count. Your age, or any other attribute, may be an element in the mix but it should not stop you making a successful transition. Present yourself as a leader, with a track record of success, with lots of positive energy, and with great commercial judgement.

Whatever your age, you will struggle to find a job if you tackle the job search challenge in the wrong way. Recently, I helped a young refugee find his first professional job. He did not learn English until he was 16 years old, yet he went on to achieve top grades at high school and university. He was a superstar! Alarmingly, despite applying for 500 jobs, he had received absolutely no offers. I couldn't understand it. Happily, after using the approach set out in this book, he found a superior job, beyond his wildest dreams, within three months. Whatever the stage of your career, this book provides strong pointers to the best way to plan and progress your job search.

When I began writing this book, I imagined that it might allow you to manage the job search process by yourself, without a coach. I soon realised this is unlikely to be the case. This book is a bit like the books you read when you are about to learn to ski or to play tennis or to play a musical instrument or sing. These books, no matter how well they are written and illustrated, will not make you a good skier or champion tennis player or a fine musician or an outstanding singer. To be good in each of these areas, you also need help from a competent instructor or coach – and a lot of practice.

As I wrote this book, I realised nothing can replace an effective career coach. These coaches can be a valuable sounding board, and can provide help and guidance that no book can communicate. Having said this, this book is intended to help you whether you have a coach or not. If you do have a coach, this book will assist you to ask smarter questions and to manage the transition process better. If you do not have a coach, you will be better positioned to tackle the job search process on your own.

Finally, even if you are not involved in a job search right now, you will find some pointers here that will help you to be well prepared, if and when the time arises for you to make a career transition.

As you are no doubt aware, jobs for life are virtually non-existent these days. A more likely scenario is that your career will be a series of four- or five-year 'chapters'. Given this situation, it makes sense to understand, in advance, how to make successful transitions between these 'chapters'. In other words: 'It is best to dig the well before you think you will need to drink!' This book is written to help you to be prepared, ahead of time, to be in a position to make these transitions in the best possible way

The keys to your success, whatever your situation, will be to identify and validate what makes you special and to have a strong, well-thought-out process to follow. Of course, you will need to modify this process and apply your own personal interpretation, to make it work best for you. Underpinning the career building process that I set out in this book are the seven guiding principles that I explain in chapter 1. So let's get started.

PART I

UNDERSTANDING THE BASICS

1

Seven guiding principles for job search success

If there is time to reflect, slowing down
is likely to be a good idea.

Daniel Kahneman, awarded 2002 Nobel Prize
in Economic Sciences

IN THIS CHAPTER:

Seven guiding principles underlie job search success:

- Leave well
- Aim high
- Prepare thoroughly
- Build warm relationships
- Don't seek a job; seek advice
- Expand your network
- Validate your thinking

MANY SENIOR JOBSEEKERS have experienced previous career success. If you are one of these people, you may not have had to search for a role since the very beginning of your career. Perhaps you have been fortunate enough to have been promoted or head-hunted, time and time again. As a result, if you happen to lose your job and do not seek proper help, you may think taking immediate action is best. You might want to dive in to attack your job search without delay. You could have a high sense of urgency and virtually no preparation. Because you have been successful in your career, you might assume you don't need help to plan and prepare for your job search.

Unfortunately, more often than not, this ad hoc approach does not work well. Being successful in your day-to-day job does not mean you will be good at searching for a role. Different skills are necessary. If you decide to go it alone, the results could be extremely disappointing. As a simple example of what can go wrong, my client Julia lost her CEO role after her company was acquired. She decided she wanted to find another comparable role without delay. So, she immediately called her friends and various recruiters.

Unfortunately, she could not provide a good answer to the one simple question that everyone asked her: 'What do you want to do, Julia?' As a result, the advice she received was superficial and not particularly helpful. In fact, her friends told her she looked very tired and should take some time off. This was not the advice she wanted to hear! Once she stepped back and tackled the challenge of finding a role in a more measured and thoughtful way, however, she began to make much better progress.

The approaches that work for senior job-seeking individuals are quite different from the ones that work for those seeking junior positions. Many of the approaches that work for senior executives are not obvious and some are counterintuitive. Before I dig deeper into the detailed approaches that will help you in your job search, you first need to understand the seven guiding principles for success if you are a senior jobseeker. These seven basic building blocks may seem self-evident, but it is surprising how often they are overlooked or forgotten. I return to these principles again and again through this book. This is because they are fundamental to the overall success of your job search project. Continually remind yourself of these seven principles, and strive to use them to underpin your work as you search for a role.

This chapter explains why each of these seven principles is so important and what can go wrong if you do not apply them. The following chapters then take you more deeply into how to put these seven principles into action as you plan and execute your job search. With these seven principles firmly in your mind, you will be well equipped to work your way forward to a successful job search outcome.

LEAVE WELL

Leave your previous job well if at all possible. You need to invest all your energy in your future, so it is best for you if you can be a 'good leaver'. Do your utmost to negotiate arrangements that allow you to take your time as you search for your next job. You should be seeking a job that is as good as, or better than, the one you are leaving. Finding such a job often requires having enough financial capacity to survive for several months, maybe up to a year, while you conduct your search. Part of this is setting yourself up so you can concentrate on your search without major distractions. In this regard, ongoing disputes and legal actions should be avoided – they rarely work and might damage you. They could, for instance, drain your energy and your financial resources. Of course, in some situations legal action may be warranted, but these are relatively rare.

Why it is best to be a 'good leaver'

When leaving your role, you may be tempted to take the view that you have been treated very badly. Perhaps you were. But the best way forward is usually to move on without a fight. A surprisingly common problem is exemplified by Jay's experience. He faced a situation that he could not believe when he was told he was being made redundant. Only one month earlier, his boss had given him a top rating in his annual performance review. Also, he had been praised in front of his peers for being an exemplary employee who was a role model for others. How could he be treated so badly after all this positive feedback? His friends agreed that his treatment was totally unacceptable and urged him to seek legal advice. He went to a lawyer who, not surprisingly, was keen to assist him and wrote to the company threatening to sue. Although Jay later decided not to initiate legal action, the damage was done. His reputation in the company as a good leaver was trashed, and he was not able to obtain a good reference for his next role.

By being a good leaver, you increase the probability that valuable contacts – including your previous boss and colleagues – will want to support you to make a successful transition to another role. If it comes to the crunch, your resources and staying power will likely be much less than the resources and staying power of your ex-employer. So, despite any other advice you receive, be extremely reticent in taking legal action against a previous employer. Sometimes, family members are especially aggrieved that their 'superstar', who has given everything to the company over his or her career, has been treated in such a 'despicable' way. Be careful that their anger and distress does not unduly influence your thinking.

Of course, taking legal action may have merit on some occasions. This is usually only where the odds of success for you are very high. Seek experienced and balanced professional legal advice from an employment lawyer. Do this immediately – without any delay – if you believe you have a strong case. It is important to obtain this advice before you move to take any action privately or publicly. Perhaps you have been significantly wronged and the possible reward of taking successful action outweighs the risk of damage if you fail. But, as with all legal action, recognise that a head-to-head fight in court can lead in all sorts of directions that you might not foresee when you initiate the action. Some of the risks you might face if you precipitate legal action include being distracted from the process of moving forward, being very bruised psychologically, and having your brand damaged in the marketplace. Be sure you are on strong ground, and put yourself in the best possible position from the beginning.

Another tip: in any final agreement between you and your ex-employer, make sure a clause is included that holds both parties equally responsible for non-disparagement. (Non-disparagement clauses ban parties from saying anything negative about the other party, in any form of communication.) Otherwise, you may find yourself with greater accountability for this than your ex-employer.

What to consider when leaving a role

Unless yours is a very special situation, moving on and getting as much help as you can from your previous employer and your ex-colleagues is best. Invest your energy in finding the right role for yourself as you move forward, not getting bogged down in leaving negotiations.

To help you move on quickly and successfully, ten practical factors need to be considered. Each of these factors deserves proper detailed consideration. I provide a few initial thoughts in the following sections to help start your thinking.

Negotiating your financial arrangements

No doubt you have an employment contract that includes severance arrangements. Many people don't realise, however, that these arrangements, particularly the payouts, are negotiable. In fact, it is a good idea to assume, as a starting position, that the first offer you receive is not the last. Most employers want to assist you make a successful move and will be willing to negotiate your arrangements in light of your particular circumstances. This should include paying for career transition consulting services. If you are not aware of these services, you need to explore what is on offer. Employers retaining career transition consultants do so not only to help employees who are leaving them, but also because they wish to send a positive message to remaining employees that, if they find themselves having to leave, they will receive proper support. These employers want to show that they will do everything they can to assist leavers to make a successful transition to a new job. Be aware, however, that some providers are selected by your ex-employer on price rather than quality of service. Not all career transition consultants are the same, so do your research before you make a selection.

Managing the timing of your exit

You may have a three- or six-month termination clause. You may be asked to work out this period. This is not a good idea. You will move from 'rooster to feather duster' almost immediately. If your previous role has been eliminated or reassigned, the situation is difficult for both you and your ex-colleagues if you remain in the office. Ideally you need to move on to 'garden leave'. In this situation, you continue to receive your salary and remain available to answer relevant questions as they arise, but you do not come to work. This enables you to start the preparation needed without delay, before you launch your networking activities. It also avoids the difficulties you will face at work, where your colleagues are embarrassed and don't know how to involve you, and where you're there with virtually nothing to do.

Negotiating your non-compete restrictions

Your employment contract may include extensive, and sometimes onerous, non-compete restrictions. These are usually written by lawyers who are trying to cover every possibility where you might compete with your previous employer, or might take intellectual property or try to attract customers or staff away with you. Some of these restrictions, in my experience, can be unreasonable. Try to renegotiate some basic arrangements, including time frames, that make sense. Courts are generally not supportive of extremely onerous non-compete restrictions. As a result, unreasonable non-compete restrictions are likely to be difficult for your ex-employer to enforce. Whatever you do, you need to be ethical and reasonable when you leave a job.

Preparing formal exit communications and leaving events

Importantly, any formal communication prepared by your ex-employer should not damage you or your brand. Most employers will involve you in the drafting of any formal announcement. Usually, employers like to keep these announcements brief. Ideally, the internal announcement should set out your achievements and contributions to the organisation, and your ex-employer should thank you for your contributions and wish you well. If these thoughts are not included in the draft presented to you, seek to add them. External announcements, particularly to the stock exchange, are likely to be very brief and may seem to be totally lacking in empathy, but you can probably do little about this. Finally, having a proper going-away event is important, not only for you to say goodbye to your colleagues, but also for them to say goodbye to you and see that you are okay.

Preparing your informal answer when asked why you are leaving

Your friends and ex-colleagues may ask you why you're leaving. Perhaps they are interested in whether you jumped or were pushed. You should not be drawn into answering these kinds of questions. Frankly, why you are leaving is none of their business. Instead, comment along these lines:

- You are proud of what you have contributed to the organisation.
- You think the time is right to make a move (ideally setting out some reasons).
- You are looking forward very much to the future.
- You intend to use the next few months to meet senior people to seek advice.
- Your ultimate goal is to generate excellent job options, and this will take time.

You may respect the person you are talking to, and would welcome their advice. If so, let them know that you would be grateful for the opportunity to test your thinking with them in a month or so, after you have had time to prepare your thoughts.

Identifying referees

Some companies refuse to provide written references. In any case, written references rarely carry any weight if you are a senior job-seeker. Recruiters and future employers want to speak directly to your referees and other people who may know you — because they are trying to identify not only your strengths but also your weaknesses. In particular, they want to know how you behave under stress. Some people are brilliant while the going is good but fall to pieces under pressure. Learning to sail in calm seas is unlikely to make you a good sailor in rough seas! It is important to involve your key referees in your preparation process as soon as you have completed your initial thinking. They can help you in several positive ways — well beyond simply providing you with a reference when you have been offered a job. For instance, they can help validate your special strengths. I discuss involving your referees from the beginning in more detail in chapter 6.

Selecting a career transition coach

Many organisations will pay for a career transition coach to assist you when you leave. Some organisations allow you to choose between accepting the career transition program or taking the cash equivalent. Hopefully, once you have read this book, you will see clearly the ways a professional coach can increase your chances of a successful career transition. Even the best golfers depend on a caddie who knows them well and can give them independent coaching advice. You will benefit from this too – providing, of course, you have the right coach. Looking for a job can be a very lonely process, with extreme highs and lows. Individuals who are not closely involved in the process with you are unlikely to provide useful or comprehensive advice. So, it is helpful to be working with someone who understands what you are going through.

In some editions of his popular book *What Color is Your Parachute?*, Richard Bolles takes the view that you should be very suspicious of career transition coaches. If you are a junior jobseeker paying the coaching fee yourself, you should definitely be careful to understand what help you will receive and how much it will cost. If you are relatively junior, you may not need a coach at all, particularly after you have read this book. If you are a senior jobseeker and the service is being sourced and paid for by your ex-employer, the situation is quite different. But, in making a final decision to work with a particular career transition coach, you need to be very clear about the service you will receive, and who you will be working with. The most comprehensive programs involve working one-to-one with an experienced coach and provide a raft of other services including:

- help with your financial planning
- a personalised health assessment

- advice on your personal presentation
- help with writing your CV
- public relations advice
- research assistance
- assistance with reviewing your offer letter for your new job.

If you are a senior jobseeker, look for programs that are not time-limited. Otherwise, you may run out of time just when you need the most support.

Managing your emotions

For some, being told they do not have a job comes as a tremendous shock. Even the toughest people generally feel very bruised when they lose their job. If this is your situation, you may not want to show any weakness but you may be very hurt and your confidence may have taken a beating. Losing your job is in the top four shocks experienced by most people, up there with divorce, major illness and death in the family. Many psychologists use a seven-stage model, originally developed as a five stage model by Elisabeth Kübler-Ross in the late 1960s, to identify the sequence of feelings you are likely to experience when dealing with a significant loss. One version of these seven stages is shown in figure 1.1.

The key thing to remember is that you, like virtually everyone else, will work through these stages and come out the other end in one piece. Some people transition more quickly than others. You will move at your own pace, and you will not necessarily go through all the stages shown in figure 1.1. Things might be very tough at the beginning, but you will likely reach a very positive state of mind as the transition progresses. Your coach will be a major asset to you in managing these feelings and emotions as you move forward.

Figure 1.1: Seven stages of grief when dealing with a significant loss

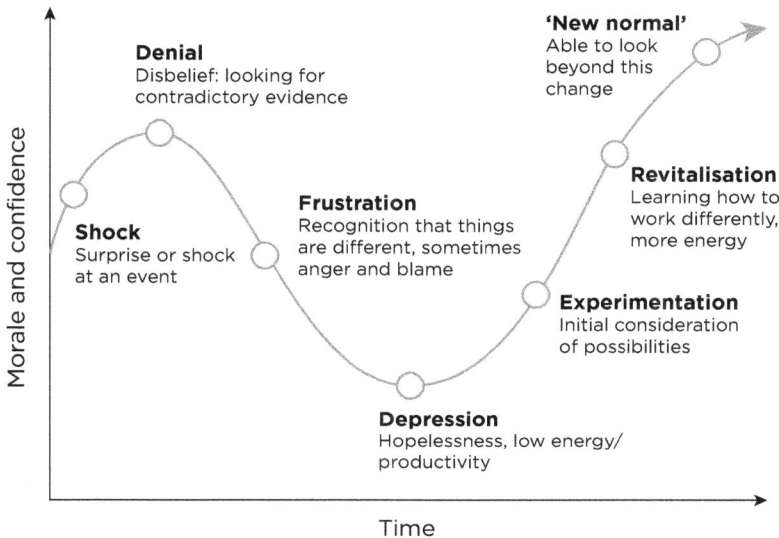

Addressing your family's emotions

When you lose your job, the members of your extended family – and particularly your parents – often experience more shock and distress than you do. Your parents may have expected their superstar child to hold down any job permanently. *How could these appalling people treat you this way?* Alternatively, they or other members of your extended family may ask something like, *'What did you do wrong to lose your job? I kept mine for 45 years!'* The main thing to remember with family, relatives and friends is the importance of setting the right expectations. They must understand that the job-seeking process takes many months, no matter how good you are. Virtually nothing is worse than members of the family and your friends coming to you with job suggestions. They may have the best intentions, but most of them have no idea of the jobs that will suit you or how to find them.

Actually, come to think of it, one thing is definitely worse than your family and friends bringing you job suggestions. The worst situation is when they start suggesting you are taking too long to find a role. They may even begin to suggest that you should aim lower or take any job offered. Do not follow this advice! Anne was a highly capable senior corporate lawyer, admired by all, who left her job as the general counsel of a major industrial company. Her friends had no idea that roles at her level only come up a few times a year. Therefore, after six months, they tried to be helpful by suggesting that she should take any job, even a secretarial role. This was absolute nonsense!

Moving from 'unconscious competence' to 'conscious competence'

After losing a job, your confidence begins to return when you let go of your past role and begin to invest your energy in the future. If you set high standards and then measure yourself against these standards, you can easily become super critical and dwell on any failures – even, in fact, if these failures have little or nothing to do with you. Many high performers are not aware of just how capable they are. They have never had to measure their level of competence outside their own workplace. Perhaps you've heard of the theory developed by Noel Burch – that, as you become more accomplished, you move from 'conscious competence' to 'unconscious competence'. This process needs to be reversed for you. You need to become aware of the strengths you have taken for granted in your previous role. In other words, move from unconscious competence back to conscious competence. This helps you to become 'match fit'. Once you do this, your confidence lifts. Your coach can play a big part in helping you move in this direction.

I do not discuss how to be a good leaver any further in this book. My assumption is that you and your ex-employer will work out a mutually acceptable exit arrangement. If this is not possible, your situation is not disastrous – just not as happy and encouraging as it would be if the arrangements are jointly agreed.

AIM HIGH

When looking for your next role, set your sights high. Try to aim for the stars – and then be happy if you hit the moon. By aiming high, I mean identifying the kind of position you would want to have in three to five years if you could wave a wand and remove all barriers. Unless your aspirations are moving in a different direction, this role is likely to be a step up for you. Once you've worked out your ideal future role, you can work out the roles that will be pathways to this future role. Try not to aim for an exact repeat of the job you have just been doing, but be realistic. Richard, a young client who worked with me, said he wanted to be a CEO (Chief Executive Officer) of a top global corporation. This goal made no sense at all for Richard in the medium term – maybe in 20 years, but not in three years. This idea did not reflect well on his judgement. Another common situation I see relates to a CFO (Chief Financial Officer) looking for a new role. The basic question he or she must answer in setting their goals is whether they wish to work out their career as a CFO, or see their current role as a pathway to CEO. If they see the CFO role as a pathway to CEO, they will be looking for a very different next role, and having very different conversations, than a CFO who wants to remain in the CFO role for the rest of his or her career.

Keep the following ideas in your mind as you start to think about what it means to aim high.

Set a stretching goal

Stretching your thinking to visualise what might be possible for you in three to five years may end up being more difficult than you think. Indeed, many people struggle with this. They are tempted to identify a whole range of jobs they could be doing in three to five years. Instead, do your best to set one clear goal and then test whether this aspirational goal makes sense to your colleagues and the people you trust. Do this as part of your networking. If your goal makes sense to your partner, friends and/or colleagues, you can then test your thinking when speaking with others, including recruiters. Make it clear that you might need more experience before you are ready for this aspirational role. As in golf, you may achieve a hole in one, or you may need a couple of shots to achieve your goal. These discussions might feel both exciting and scary. However, all you are doing is testing a concept; you are not saying this is the only job you will take. It is the stretch goal. A key idea to test is whether the people you have worked with and who know you agree that your aspirations make sense. If they think you are aiming too high – and if they can convince you they are correct – you can always recalibrate. If not, keep your sights high!

Understand the role of recruiters

In simple terms, recruiters are in the risk-management business. To oversimplify, they are generally keen for you to accept the same role you have just left, but in a new organisation. Aiming for the stars makes little or no sense to them. So, if you set a high goal, you are likely to be told by recruiters, and others in your network, that aiming high is much too risky for you. But remember, you are in a different business from recruiters. You're in the marketing business, because you're marketing yourself. You're not in the risk-management business. Ideally, you need to show you are a leader with a great deal of energy, very good commercial judgement, and a track record of success. I cover how you should prepare for and conduct meetings with recruiters in chapters 7, 8 and 9.

The problem is most CVs don't usually demonstrate any of these attributes in any compelling way. Instead, CVs are often very administrative, largely because individuals tend to focus on describing their previous roles. Recruiters tend to focus on your job history too. If you can convince people that you are a leader with energy, great judgement and a track record of success, however, who knows what might be possible? Of course, progression in your career tends to be a step-by-step process. It is risky – and almost impossible – to be successful if you change a lot of variables, such as employer, role, and location, all at once. For more on this, see chapter 6.

Aiming high — avoiding the risk-management approach of recruiters — is made more difficult if you suffer from 'imposter syndrome'. Maryanne applied for five jobs on the internet and received a rejection email for each one. This confirmed in her mind that she was not good enough — and that others could see this too. Nothing could be further from the truth. Once Maryanne prepared herself using the process outlined in this book, it became clear that she was a high performer with many strengths — she was just approaching the challenge of job search in completely the wrong way. Once she was properly prepared, her job search ended in great success.

Avoid aiming low, even if you are tempted

If you aim low, you may miss important opportunities and may even damage your brand by appearing to be too conservative. I was approached by Jerry several years ago. He had been a very senior executive on a salary of over $1 million per annum. Jerry had been conducting his own search before he approached me, and it had not gone well. He had been rejected for several jobs and was extremely worried and depressed. As he described his situation to me, it became clear that, as a result of these rejections, he had lost his nerve. Because he had made no progress with jobs equivalent to the one that he had left, he began to apply for smaller roles with salaries of about $250,000. He was shocked to find he was rejected for these roles too. I told him this was no surprise — in fact, it was entirely predictable. The recruiters involved would have been assuming one of three things:

1. He was damaged goods.
2. He was parking himself until he found a better job.
3. He really wanted the boss's job.

Once we worked together, he recalibrated himself, prepared himself properly, and aimed high again. In a few months, he found a better job than the one he had left, at a higher salary.

Be courageous

Many executives are concerned with the possibility of failure if they aim high. This seems to be a particular issue for senior women. Tara Mohr, a coach for senior women and author of *Playing Big: Find Your Voice, Your Mission, Your Message*, explores this issue in depth. Mohr has coached a series of extremely successful women in the United States, and highlights that each of these women, without exception, told her they wished they were more confident. Mohr argues that more confidence is the wrong thing for women (and men) to wish for – sitting back and waiting for your confidence to grow is pointless. Confidence will not grow by itself. Instead, you need to learn to live with your lack of confidence and consider how to develop more *courage*. In her view, with sufficient courage anything is possible. As she argues:

> *Confidence is faith in our abilities and ourselves. Courage is going forward even when we don't feel that faith. We talk a lot to women about their finding more confidence, but it's time we put more attention on courage, on taking action in the* absence *of certainty that we can do a task well.*

Take Rachel. She had had a number of senior executive roles reporting to CEOs and was highly regarded. She had never considered the possibility of actually leading an organisation, however. When she tested this idea with her colleagues, they all said it was obvious she could be a CEO, and wondered why she had not figured this out for herself. During her networking, she tested this idea further and, as a result of positive input, became very confident that she should aspire to be a CEO. After further networking, she was offered a COO role and, once she was established, excelled in it. It was then just a matter of time before she became the CEO of the business.

How do you set your sights high, even if this seems too ambitious? It is challenging for most of us to consider this by ourselves. Very often, a strong supporter, who trusts you and has seen you in action, needs to help you think this through. I explore this important area in much more detail in chapter 3.

PREPARE THOROUGHLY

Rushing into a senior job search process is a mistake. As with any complex major project, it is better to prepare carefully in advance, and then to take a measured approach. Rarely will you find a major role in less than six months, and it may take you a year. You will find that proper preparation pays off. The hiring process is usually extremely competitive for top jobs, and those who are not prepared struggle to rise above the other applicants. Most of the time, those who have taken the trouble to be well prepared will prevail. Remember – even if you are fortunate enough to reach the short list of five for a particular role, you still only have a 20 per cent chance of being selected for that role. So, taking a month to prepare yourself will usually put you in a much better position and pay off handsomely as you progress. And, in my experience, the likelihood of missing your dream job because you have taken a month to prepare is extremely low.

Dr William Bridges has developed a helpful model for explaining change. He argues that every significant change has an Ending, a Neutral Zone transition period, and then a New Beginning, as shown in figure 1.2.

When you leave a role, you might experience a number of the emotions set out in figure 1.2 related to the Ending period. These emotions can include shock, stress and anger. Then you will move into what Bridges calls the Neutral Zone. Some of the emotions you might experience in this zone are anxiety, impatience and confusion. Don't rush through this Neutral Zone. As Bridges argues, 'Supporting people through transition rather than pushing forward is essential if the change is to work as planned. This is key to capitalizing on opportunities for innovation'. At this stage, use the luxury you have of time, not only to restore yourself but also to prepare and then start your networking. Likely you're very anxious to start meeting people. You want to hit the accelerator. My job is to slow you down and to make sure that you will be well prepared when you begin to have meetings, maybe earlier. After you have had about 50 meetings, you will start to see signs of a New Beginning. This is when you usually begin to receive calls and people come up with job suggestions that are a good fit for you.

Figure 1.2: William Bridges' transition model

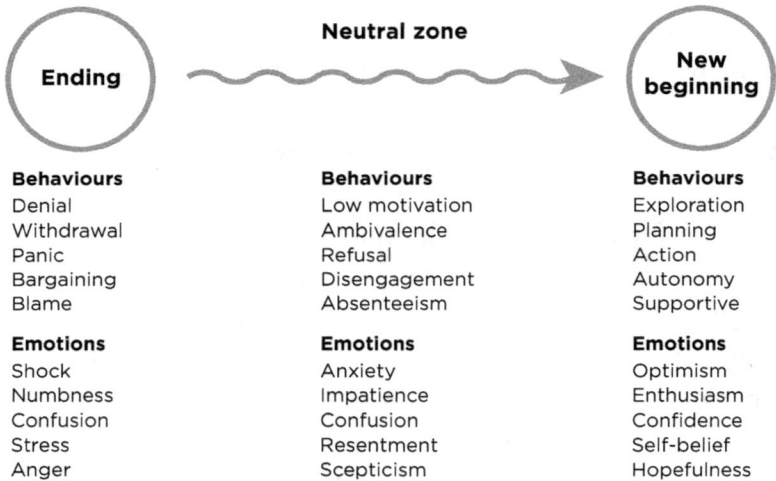

Ending	Neutral zone	New beginning
Behaviours	**Behaviours**	**Behaviours**
Denial	Low motivation	Exploration
Withdrawal	Ambivalence	Planning
Panic	Refusal	Action
Bargaining	Disengagement	Autonomy
Blame	Absenteeism	Supportive
Emotions	**Emotions**	**Emotions**
Shock	Anxiety	Optimism
Numbness	Impatience	Enthusiasm
Confusion	Confusion	Confidence
Stress	Resentment	Self-belief
Anger	Scepticism	Hopefulness

Be careful not to fall into the reverse trap of saying, when you finish a job, that you are too tired to do anything. Because of this, you decide to do absolutely nothing for three months, apart from resting and relaxing. This is not a good use of the Neutral Zone. You should not send the message you are exhausted and, as a result, suggest you lack drive and energy. It is better to say you're taking a month to think and to prepare, before you start meeting people. Use this time to rest and restore yourself, and to do the preparation required before you start networking. Once you have prepared your thoughts, you can then start building your network and using your established and new contacts to test your thinking. In these early days, clarify with everyone who invites you to coffee for a chat that you would prefer to hold off for a bit – because you are in the process of preparing yourself to have productive meetings with senior people. Let them know this preparation will probably take at least four or five weeks. Then you would be happy to meet them. If a recruiter calls you early on, tell them the same thing: you need some time to prepare and you will send them your CV in a month. They are likely to praise you for doing this preparation. If they really need you for something urgently, they will tell you.

Three things are vital to prepare yourself properly for building your network, and the following sections outline these in more detail.

Look sharp, and be in good physical and psychological shape

The people you will meet have a great ability to size you up, sometimes in seconds. Look and act as though you are a leader with energy and great judgement. Rarely can you look and act like this if you start to involve yourself in meetings as soon as you leave your old job. You are likely to be stressed as a result of not having a job. Very often when you leave a job, you are exhausted physically and mentally, and you have not looked after your body properly. You are not as fit as you should be. You look worn out. You are not at your best. If you don't look at your best when you start meeting people, you're starting from behind. Take some time to ensure you have a genuine spring in your step and a bright sparkle in your eye. I cover this topic in more detail in chapter 7.

Some people will suggest you take the next three to six months off to rest. This is not usually good advice. I am all for rest, but you should also use this time constructively to prepare for networking. Preparing adequately to network is impossible on a beach in Bermuda or Bali. If you want to take a holiday, do this after you have completed your preparation, and before you start intensive networking. Then, if you meet someone on a beach, or an unexpected opportunity arises early on, you will be fully prepared to have a productive conversation about your career!

Be properly prepared and rehearsed

You need to be able to clearly explain to everyone you meet what makes you special, how you add value in your work, what level of a role you wish to explore, and what areas you intend to research. To do all this takes serious thought, hard work and dedicated rehearsal. You are likely to prepare better when you are working with someone who can test and stretch your thinking. Not only must you be clear and confident, but you also must be able to explain your strengths very simply and in a memorable way. If you are not prepared you will generally speak for too long and your story will be too complicated. For most of my clients, developing and rehearsing a strong, clear story with impact takes about a month of work. I discuss the need to rehearse more fully in chapter 5.

Have a strategy for moving forward that can be tested

Your initial ideas must have been tested with your confidants and with your prospective referees. Once you are clear about your strategy, you can discuss it with others who you do not know but who have been introduced to you. You need to be able to explain what kinds of people you would like to meet in your networking and what you wish to talk to them about. You need to know what materials you will leave them with. You also need to think through what questions you will ask them. Effective meetings generally involve conversations rather than you simply answering questions. To start useful conversations, you must ask good questions. You will sell yourself more by asking intelligent questions, rather than by explaining how good you are. Asking intelligent questions requires proper research, focused on identifying the important issues facing the individuals you are meeting and possible emotional connections with them. I discuss the kinds of research you need to do in chapter 7.

You may think getting on with your job search without any delay is important. If you think this way, you are not alone. Many senior people want to kick off meetings immediately. This is usually a mistake, however. In reality, you are most likely to do well when you are at your best, when you are properly prepared, and when your strategy is clear. If you are seeking the best long-term career outcome, you will do much better once you are confident and well prepared.

Very rarely, the ideal job is presented to you early in your job search, perhaps before you have completed your preparation. If this occurs, it may make sense to accept this job, providing you have done thorough due diligence. My test in this situation is to ask yourself, 'Is this so good an offer that I can't refuse?' The obvious risk is that you do not know what other opportunities might be available. Also, you will miss out on building a better lifetime network for yourself. You will have to think carefully before you make this early call because, all too often, people later regret moving too fast.

BUILD WARM RELATIONSHIPS

As Eleanor Roosevelt suggested, 'To handle yourself, use your head; to handle others, use your heart'. You need to understand and utilise the power of building warm, enduring relationships as you network. If you can do this, you will be well positioned to seek future meetings and future assistance. Warm relationships are important because you never know when an individual might be able to help you. It could be right away, or it could be years from now. If you believe the Pareto Principle – that roughly 80 per cent of results come from just 20 per cent of your actions – about 20 per cent of those you meet will be most likely to help you at some stage going forward. Some of my clients seem to believe that a single meeting, where they explain their thinking, is sufficient to build a relationship. They regard each meeting as a one-off transaction. This is a mistake. A senior recruiter once told me that only three out of 10 individuals who came to meet him through introductions thanked him for taking his time to meet with them. And even fewer attempted to stay in touch or keep him in touch with their progress. He made the point that these people missed an important opportunity to build a relationship with him that could have benefitted them longer term.

How do you begin to build warm relationships with people who can help you? I discuss the ways of doing this in the following sections.

First, you need warm introductions

When you are introduced to someone who might help you with advice, being given a warm introduction is important. Cold calling rarely works. People will trust you if you are introduced by someone they trust. So, it is vital that you are properly introduced. Simply having your name circulated to an email list is a bad idea. Sometimes partners in large accounting firms, for example, will offer to circulate your name to other partners. Do not accept this invitation. You do not want to be shopped around. Meeting three partners through trusted personal introductions is better than having your name circulated to 100 partners by email. Similarly, a recruiter may offer to circulate your name to his or her clients. Do not permit this to happen unless you provide this recruiter with specific permission in advance. Make sure you control who is seeing your CV. You need personal introductions rather than to be part of a list of individuals sent to prospective employers who have absolutely no emotional connection with you. The danger of permitting yourself to be shopped around is that people may presume you are desperate, and this could damage your reputation and your personal brand. I discuss this in more depth in chapters 5 and 7.

Second, you need a story that resonates

As I mention briefly in the Introduction, I was recently introduced to a young man who was a refugee. He was a remarkable young person who had endured great hardship. Despite this, he had learnt excellent English in a detention centre, when he was 16 years old. He then went on to perform in the top 1 per cent of students in Year 12. After that he won a scholarship to a top university. There he received First Class Honours in his undergraduate degree. When he graduated, he applied for 500 jobs through the internet. He received 20 interviews. Not one of these interviews progressed to a job offer. I could not believe this, given his incredible story. It turned out he was embarrassed to tell his full life story since he did not think it would help him find a job. Once he started to meet various relevant people face to face, with warm introductions, and explained what he had been through, the whole situation turned around. He started to build helpful relationships that led to him being offered a number of excellent positions. His personal story, the one that he had been too embarrassed to discuss, was actually the key piece of the puzzle that made others want to help him.

Third, you need to find supporters who will 'vote' for you

I mention in the Introduction the need for you to be able to attract 'votes'. If you treat a meeting as a transaction, rather than an opportunity to begin to build a warm relationship, you may be missing out on an important future opportunity. Try to build a relationship where the other person will seek to help you and, as time goes by, 'vote' for you. You will need people to vote for you throughout your job seeking process – from the time you begin networking, through to the final hiring decision.

To win votes, Peter Gruber, the well-known Hollywood producer and author of the article 'What do the Oscars Mean For You and Your Success?', has pointed out that you need to build a special connection with those who you want to vote for you. His model for doing this is TALENT, the acronym for:

- *Team:* Put together a team to help you win votes

- *Audience:* Tailor your message to appeal to your target audience

- *Likeability:* Be likeable to the potential voters
- *Emotional connection:* Build warm connections with voters
- *Negativity:* Be positive and avoid any sign of negativity
- *Tenacity:* Remain committed and do not give in

The idea that you must build warm relationships works in many areas of human endeavour. In *Outliers*, journalist Malcolm Gladwell tells the story of two men with IQs that were off the charts. One grew up in a troubled family in a deprived environment and he had no social skills. The other had parents who involved him in their cocktail parties in Manhattan. The man who had no social skills was continually expelled from high school even though he was a genius who was begging his teachers for more knowledge. The other was permitted to stay on at university even though he stepped way out of line. Why was the man who begged for help expelled, while the one who had broken all the rules permitted to stay? The short answer is all about social skills! One had the ability to persuade and convince, while the other did not.

You might think that building relationships will take too long. You might also think that individuals involved in the recruiting process are only interested in your skills and competencies. This is wrong. In my experience many individuals who are not – when you assess their specific capabilities – the best candidate for a particular job are actually offered the role. They may have had longer experience. They may have managed to build more trust and greater rapport with those making the recruiting decision. They may have been seen to be a better fit with the team. Maybe, they have been introduced by someone held in high regard by the recruiting team and so had a trust advantage. Or, possibly, they may have had a more engaging story. How do you build warm relationships and avoid being transactional? This is a big topic, and one that is so central to my approach that I cover it in much more detail in chapter 7.

DON'T SEEK A JOB; SEEK ADVICE

Never approach people saying that you are looking for a job. As noted in the Introduction, your mantra must be: 'Seek advice and I will get a job. Seek a job, and I will get advice.' People generally do not know how to help you find a job, but they are usually more than willing to provide you with advice. If you are a driven person and used to taking charge and getting results, this mantra may seem strange to you. You might think that you should be clear with others that you are seeking a job. Asking for advice may seem to you to be much too circumspect. 'Why not get to the point?' you might ask. However, remember that most people do not have the slightest idea of how to assist you to find a job. And the better they know you, oddly enough, the less likely it is that they can help in this regard. In some ways, they know you too well. More than 70 or 80 per cent of the time, jobs come from new people you have been introduced to as part of your networking.

Asking for advice moves you forward in various ways, as I discuss in the following sections.

Helps you identify attractive opportunities

It may be tempting to explain that you have left your job and are looking for a new one. But this is usually the worst possible move you can make. The people you are speaking to will feel helpless and intimidated when asked to help you find a job. They are likely to have no idea of how or where to begin. They close down. You, too, will feel disempowered because you are vulnerable and will be, in effect, rejected if someone says they cannot help you. Then, your feeling of helplessness will only get worse.

Asking for advice works much better because doing so draws on their knowledge, expertise, experience and creativity. The people you meet can talk about themselves and their career. They can come up with ideas. If you explain that you are trying to learn more about a particular industry, for example, or understand better how they managed their own career, or who might be a good role model for you, they will usually be delighted to help you. If you say you are looking to find a CEO role in a mid-sized company with strong growth prospects in Asia, they are likely to tell you that is a wonderful idea. This will be quickly followed by the comment that they cannot think of any opportunities right now, but, of course, if something comes up, they will let you know. You can be almost certain you will never hear from them again. Obviously, it is more desirable to build continuing relationships that will assist you in the future, rather than being told by people you meet that they cannot help you.

Makes building emotional connections easier

Making emotional connections with the people who might be able to help you with advice is important. In the famous *How to Win Friends and Influence People*, which has sold 30 million copies in over 200 languages and, amazingly, is still available in bookshops more than 80 years after it was written, Dale Carnegie lists six things likely to encourage people to like and help you. His six recommendations, which seem quite obvious really, are:

1. become genuinely interested in other people
2. smile
3. remember that a person's name is to that person the sweetest sound
4. be a good listener and encourage others to talk about themselves
5. talk in terms of the other person's interests
6. make the other person feel important – and do it sincerely.

By asking for advice, you are well on the way to achieving Dale Carnegie's six techniques for encouraging people to like you and want to help you! I recently surveyed some of my previous clients to discover what they remembered most vividly about our work together. What did they feel was most helpful to them? The most important lesson, they all said, was the idea that you need to focus on seeking advice. This allowed them to build warm connections with people who subsequently helped them. In fact, many of my clients said they had gone on to use this approach successfully in all sorts of other situations where they were seeking to persuade others. When you seek advice, you begin to build a warm emotional connection. Some of these connections are likely to benefit you throughout your career.

Minimises the risk of analysis paralysis

Some of my clients want to work out what their next role should be as soon as I meet them. I tell these clients that we will not be able to identify where the next role will come from by sitting in my office thinking – no matter how much we deliberate. Finding a role is not an intellectual exercise! It is an activity-based process. You need to get out to meet people. Seek their advice. You will be amazed how roles start to emerge after your network reaches a critical mass. Importantly, though, before you begin to meet other people, you must prepare and articulate the hypotheses you wish to test. You need to be clear about the level of seniority you are seeking, the scale of your role, and the sectors where you are likely to be able to add real value.

To use another analogy: you need to work out what ponds you want to fish in. This will depend on what kinds of fish you wish to catch, where these fish are likely to be, your skills as a fisherman, and the fishing equipment you have available. Going out into the ocean with a simple line and a hook and no preparation to catch a fish is extremely unlikely to be successful. If you are vague and uncertain, and you do not appear to know how to frame the problem you are trying to solve, even the people who really want to help you will not know where to begin. Determine what you want to investigate, frame the problem and then start networking to test your ideas.

To be effective in seeking advice, make sure you prepare and rehearse. Then decide who to meet and when. This will be covered in more detail in chapters 6 and 7.

EXPAND YOUR NETWORK

As I mentioned earlier, statistics show that 70 to 80 per cent of offers that lead to a role will come through your network. Often these jobs are in the 'hidden market' of roles that are available but not advertised. Only about 20 per cent of roles come through recruiters or job sites. Jobseekers who do not know what they're doing spend 80 per cent of their time trying to speak to recruiters – despite recruiters only sourcing 20 per cent of the roles. On the other hand, jobseekers who do know what they're doing will work to expand their networks and build warm connections. They will not apply for jobs online. Ideally, you should meet at least 50 new people – which is actually quite easy to do. In fact, I have had clients who put a huge effort into networking and met over 250 new people. Your expanded network will be a life asset, a group that you can call on when you need them in the future. As one recruiter explained to me:

> Your client is better off expanding his or her personal network rather than meeting me on the off-chance I might have a suitable role. When a role comes up, I call 10 people asking for ideas about who might fill a role. If your client's name comes up twice, I will definitely make contact.

As you can see, this recruiter uses his own network to identify opportunities. You need to do the same. I discuss some ideas related to expanding your network in the following sections.

Being unemployed is an advantage when it comes to networking

Expanding your network quickly with warm connections is almost impossible to do while you are working in a full-time role.

Arranging each meeting, doing your prior research and meeting face to face might require three or four hours. If you have five meetings in a week, this will therefore require 20 hours or more each week. If you have a job, you do not have this kind of time to spare. So, oddly enough, being unemployed is a huge advantage when it comes to finding time to expand your network. Once you do have networking momentum, you should have the goal of meeting with at least 65 people over three months – with a mix of 15 people you already know, and about 50 new people. If you have a demanding job, there is no way you can build a new network this quickly.

Some argue that it is better to look for a job while you are in a job. They might also argue that your network is not really particularly important. Neither of these views is correct. The facts are quite the reverse. If you are unemployed:

- you have more time to prepare yourself to be a more effective jobseeker
- you are more flexible and available to meet other people, including recruiters
- recruiters like the fact you are more available than someone with a job.

If you do not have a job, avoid the mistake of taking a full-time consulting contract while you are looking for a new role. Doing so will likely cause you to lose networking momentum. If you need to accept an interim contracting role, commit to only three days per week, or less.

Identifying and benefiting from super-networkers

Some individuals are born networkers. One of my clients calls these people 'Energiser Bunnies'. They help you expand your network and, just as importantly, they also energise you in a really positive way. Brian Uzzi and Shannon Dunlap, in their *Harvard Business Review* article 'How to build your network', describe the potential power of super-networkers. The authors tell the story of Paul Revere who, at midnight on 18 April 1775, managed to sound the alarm to a large group of American colonists that units of the British Army were approaching Concord. Another man, William Dawes, also went out on the same night but went in a different direction. He only managed to alert a handful of people. What was the difference? Revere was a trader and information broker with a large network of clients and friends, each with their own networks. So, Revere's message went out to a large interconnected group. Dawes' network was small and interrelated. Because members of his group only knew people within their own small group, Dawes' message did not go far. The stylised differences in Revere's and Dawes' networks are shown in figure 1.3.

Figure 1.3: Closed networks versus super networks

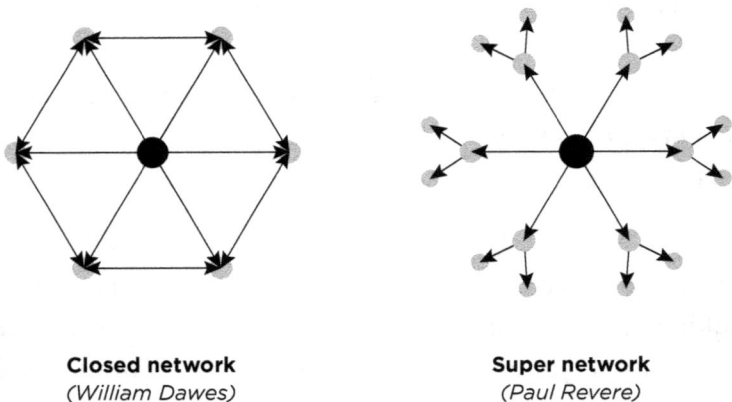

Closed network
(William Dawes)

Super network
(Paul Revere)

You need people like Revere helping you to meet others, prefer-ably 'energiser bunnies', rather than people like Dawes. You may hate networking. If so, check out 'Learn to love networking' by Tiziana Casciaro, Francesca Gino and Maryam Kouchaki (from the *Harvard Business Review*). In this article the authors argue that networking can be a positive experience if you see it as a process where you and the person you meet are both helping each other in a mutual way.

Start your networking by meeting individuals who know you and who, ideally, have extensive networks. When you are thinking about who you should meet, an important test is whether they are natural networkers. You never know who they know, or who will ultimately help you. You may be concerned that you have a limited network, probably mainly related to your work. This is not necessarily a problem. I have worked with clients who knew virtually no locals, because they had just moved to a new city or country. These clients were able to use their lack of local contacts to their advantage, explaining how much help they needed to meet super-networkers to help them build a better local network. The few people they did know went out of their way to help them and, before long, they were able to build strong local networks.

Think of yourself as being at the centre of three concentric circles

The way to plan your networking is to think in terms of three concentric circles. I call this approach your 'ABC Network'. Use this approach to expand your network. You are in the middle, at the bullseye. Your goal is to build your ABC Network from the inner circle to the outer circle, as follows:

- *The inner circle includes your A-List:* People who you already know.

- *The next circle includes your new B-List:* People introduced to you by your A-List.

- *The outer circle includes your new C-List:* People introduced to you by your B-List.

To summarise, you want to test your thinking with people who you already know, your A-List. Once you have done this, you want your A-List to introduce you to people they think can provide you with good advice. These new contacts become your B-List. Then you want your B-List to provide warm introductions to people they know in the third circle. These new contacts in third circle become your C-List. Think of this as a three-step process, where

people you have met give you a warm introduction to contacts
they have in the next circle, as shown in figure 1.4.

Figure 1.4: Building your ABC Network

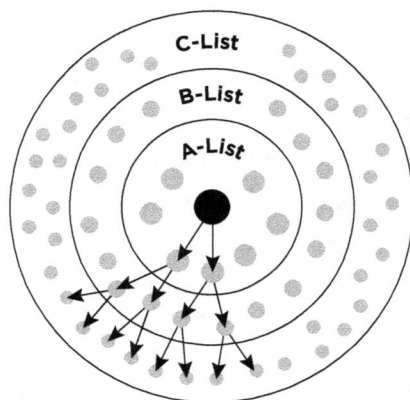

The people in your A-List are important in validating your thinking and your materials before you move on to meet your B-List.
Your A-List is composed of 10 to 20 individuals who you know
and who are likely to be happy to assist you. Ideally, they will have
strong networks and be willing and able to introduce you to at least
two new people each. Your A-List may have been colleagues from
previous jobs, individuals who went through university with you,
or people you know socially. If you are working with a career transition consultant, they should be included in the A-List, since they
should be able to introduce you to some of their alumni group.

Say you now have 15 people in your A-List and each one
introduces you to two new people to create your second circle,
or B-List. This means you now have 30 additional people in your
network. If each member from your B-List introduces you to two
new people to create your third circle, or C-List, you now have an
additional 60 people in your network – making 90 new people in
total in your extended network. Of course, achieving this success
rate is not easy because not everyone will introduce you to two

new people. I discuss how this process works in more depth in chapters 6, 7 and 8.

An important point to remember is that your job offers are likely to come via people in your C-List. The phenomenon involved here was first researched by Mark Granovetter at Stanford University. In his article, 'The strength of weak ties', Granovetter shows that the diversity introduced through connections of connections markedly increases the opportunities available. The problem with strong ties is that the people in the group with strong ties all know each other (like the people in William Dawes' network), so they're not necessarily exposed to new thinking or new opportunities. Granovetter points out the importance of weak connections in the job-seeking process. He researched a random sample of individuals who changed jobs in a suburb of Boston. He determined that over 80 per cent of the participants in his survey found jobs through contacts they saw either rarely or occasionally. His research supports the idea that weak links – in other words, individuals in your third circle – can be crucial for success in the job seeking process. This view is supported by my own experience and the experiences of my clients.

The following story about Don also shows the power of networking, and how trust can be transferred easily through a network if each individual in the chain trusts the previous connection. A Chair of a major private electricity utility approached the audit partner of his business, and asked whether he could recommend someone from another state, where his utility had substantial business operations, to be a director on the company's board. The Chair wanted someone who had an engineering background, who had already worked in an electricity utility, and who had experience in a major strategy consulting firm. The auditor called a partner in his firm in the other state and asked for a recommendation. This partner called a leading local banker seeking a recommendation. The banker recommended Don. The Chairman met Don for lunch and, at the end of the lunch, offered the board directorship to Don. This series of events was possible because the Chairman defined the kind of person he was seeking quite precisely, and because of the transfer of trust between the three individuals involved.

Another example is Annabelle. She lost her job and immediately circled back to a previous boss she had stayed in touch with. This ex-boss introduced her to a consulting firm he was using on a project. This firm introduced her to one of its clients, and she was interviewed by this client. After doing a contracting assignment for the client of the consulting firm, Annabel was made a permanent offer. Again, trust was the important factor in this three-step process.

When my clients finish their work with me, they often say they now realise they have neglected the challenge of building their personal network in their previous jobs. They make a firm commitment to do better in their next role! This sounds easy, but once you are in your new role, you will find it extremely difficult to build your network outside your business associates. In fact, expanding your network is a luxury that is tough to achieve while you are employed, even if you have set this as a key personal priority. Effective networking is vital for your success as a senior jobseeker, and I discuss this further in chapter 7.

VALIDATE YOUR THINKING

Unsurprisingly, when you are seeking a role, people generally want to help you if they can. They may see this as the right thing to do and also, possibly, because they realise that they may need reciprocal help one day! A potential problem is that they may not want to hurt your feelings, and so tend to be very supportive and avoid appearing critical. Well-meaning colleagues and friends may provide advice that is superficial, unrealistic, unhelpful and, even, counterproductive. An example of this is the suggestion that you should 'meet some recruiters'. Another example is being told you will have no trouble finding a job 'because you are so good' and that 'the phone will ring off the hook'. Don't assume this advice is correct. Similarly, if someone offers to introduce you to a recruiter before you have prepared yourself properly, realise that this is likely to be counterproductive. In my experience, meeting with a recruiter before you are well prepared and confident is a mistake. The best time for you to meet recruiters is when you have met with a series of senior people (those in your A-List) who have validated your thinking. In the sections below, I set out some of the things you need to consider in order to validate your thinking, before you move into the networking phase.

Test your hypotheses with your A-List

So, how do you obtain honest, clear, supportive feedback that helps you to be authentic and grounded? The answer is by developing a series of hypotheses to test with your trusted A-List. You are much more compelling when you can state the framework of propositions you are testing rather than vague assertions about jobs that might be good for you. These hypotheses must build on the advice of your trusted advisors. For instance: 'I have spoken to 15 senior executives who I have worked with during the past few years. They believe I should be aspiring to lead a family business in retailing [or manufacturing or logistics] with 500 employees that has a strategy of expanding overseas'. To be specific is important because, if you are aiming high, you must be authentic, realistic and believable. Believe in yourself. If you present a vague idea about what you are seeking or cannot explain your goal, you lose credibility. If this happens, most people will have trouble providing you with useful advice.

Take the story of Sangiev, a senior CFO who thought, perhaps correctly, he could probably do well in pretty much any CFO role, in pretty much any company. When he met his network, he said he could work anywhere and did not describe specific areas where he could add value. As a result, he was seen as unfocused and lacking commitment. People who met him while he was networking thought he was low on energy and uninspiring. One day he visited me full of energy and enthusiasm. 'What on earth has happened?' I asked. Sangiev told me, 'I have found a job advertised that I really want.' It turned out he had grown up in a rural area, living next to a well-known vineyard. He had spent all his spare time while he was a child in that vineyard, and when he was older had worked there during his vacations. He'd loved it. The job he'd seen advertised was CFO of a vineyard. He applied and showed how enthusiastic he was, and how he had an emotional connection with the business. He was selected for this CFO job!

I discuss the challenge of building your hypotheses and validating them in much more detail in chapter 6.

Do not be complacent – work hard on the subtleties

Some senior jobseekers have strong communication and interpersonal skills. They know they can be very persuasive. They have a reputation for being able to sell anything. Although this is usually a strength, it may lead them to become complacent. They might think that looking for a role is relatively easy. They, therefore, take the view they can be quite nonchalant. Nothing is further from the truth. Lack of preparation is likely to lead to failure. I once sat through a masterclass of half a dozen singing students with Dennis O'Neill, CBE, the great Welsh/Irish tenor. O'Neill learned from Pavarotti. He spent a 20-minute coaching session with each opera student. Each of the students performed just one single line of music, repeating it more than 10 times for Dennis. The remarkable thing was how much could be learned about each line of music. The words and the notes were only a small part of the story. Also vital to being a good performer are your intonation, your facial expression, the way you hold your body, your breathing, your physical movements, your timing, and more. This was a tremendous learning experience for each student. And also, for me, as an observer!

You can learn a great deal when you are taught by a great teacher! And, very importantly, they can validate that you are properly prepared. In fact, great teachers will not allow you to take part in a competition until you are ready. They know their own reputation is at stake if you do not perform well. The same goes for coaches in career transition. A common error to watch out for is the assumption that you do not need to rehearse. Thinking that you can just be natural and make it up as you go along is unlikely to be the best strategy! You will be much, much better when you have tested your thinking with people who know what they are doing and who you trust – and also, of course, when you have actually rehearsed out loud. What is in your head and what comes out of your mouth, particularly if you are under stress, will rarely be identical. The need to rehearse is covered more fully in chapter 5.

Do not arrange coffees – arrange working meetings

Many people encourage you to have coffee meetings. However, you need to regard networking as more purposeful than this. Asking for a coffee meeting sounds too vague, and seems to indicate you want to have a chat. What you really need is a working meeting to test your thinking. Your meeting may involve coffee, but coffee is secondary to its real purpose. Your question to your network should be, 'Can I test my thinking with you, and seek your advice?' not, 'Can I have a coffee with you?'

The story of Kaley Chu is illuminating in this context. Kaley, born in Hong Kong, was so shy that she was unable to say anything in a client meeting after she graduated from university. She and her boss decided that she needed to do something to improve her ability to work with people she did not know. They came up with the idea that Kaley should organise 100 lunches with strangers. As a result, she approached strangers through LinkedIn and about 25 per cent of those she approached agreed to help her meet her goal. She has now met over 200 strangers for lunch, and says she is a totally different person. She has even written a book and given a TEDx talk about her experience and what she learned. I think having a clear goal and a clear purpose, which she could explain to the people she approached, was why people agreed to help her. People wanted to help her meet her goal of having 100 lunches with strangers. This clarity of purpose was a key to her success and enabled her to build an emotional connection with those who wished to help her meet her goal. You need to have this clarity of purpose too. As you will see in chapter 7, I suggest you set yourself a goal of meeting at least 50 new people through your network.

★★★

In this chapter, I have outlined how you are likely to be much more successful if you understand seven fundamental principles for success. In my experience, if you remember these seven principles and use them as you conduct your search, you will be well on the way to a successful outcome. Many of the approaches that work for senior jobseekers are not obvious, and some are counterintuitive. Most senior jobseekers have experienced career success and have little experience in job search. As a result, they often attack the problems related to job search the wrong way, sometimes with disappointing results.

In the next chapter, I explain the four main challenges for senior job-seeking individuals. These challenges are broad and deep, and knowing about them in advance is worthwhile. If you are aware of these challenges and how to tackle them, you will be well ahead of most of the individuals who you are competing with for a position.

SOME QUESTIONS FOR YOU TO CONSIDER

- How can you make sure you get the best leaving arrangements?
- Can you obtain advice without delay to address any exit issues?
- Do you understand the value of a good career transition coach?
- What role do you see as your goal in three to five years' time?
- What roles are likely to be pathways to this future role?
- Are you prepared to build emotional connections?
- Do you understand the ABC Network approach?
- Who are the best 10 to 20 people to be on your A-List?
- How can you prepare yourself to seek useful advice?
- Who will be the best people to validate your job-seeking hypotheses?

2

You face four distinct challenges

**Imagination is more important
than knowledge. Knowledge is limited.
Imagination encircles the world.**

Albert Einstein

The four challenges you face are:

- Challenge #1: Managing your job search process effectively
- Challenge #2: Securing a potentially attractive job offer
- Challenge #3: Deciding whether the job offer is right for you
- Challenge #4: Completing due diligence before you commit

IF YOU'RE LOOKING for a senior role, this could well be the first time you've ever had to do so. Therefore, you may not understand what is required for success. First, you may not know how to attack the initial job search process. Second, when you are actually selected to be part of a formal recruiting process, obtaining a job offer involves jumping over many hurdles. Selecting a preferred candidate is a complex process, not only for you but also for the recruiting team. Even when you have been offered a role, your third challenge will be to decide whether the job as described is right for you and your family. Assuming it appears to be a good choice, your fourth challenge will be to complete thorough due diligence to verify your decision. You need to ensure you understand precisely what you are getting yourself into. In our lives we often refer to the concept of 'buyer beware'. If you have been offered a role, the reverse is the case: you – the seller of your services – must beware.

An example helps to illustrate the problems you might face as you begin the job-seeking process. Robert lost his high-level job in a corporate restructure. He was an ambitious senior executive in his mid-fifties. He'd had a dream run previously with a series of promotions. This was his first major career setback. He did no preparation in advance of losing his job. He immediately called all the recruiters he knew and asked whether they had any jobs that might suit him. The answer from each was, 'No, not right now, Robert. But something might come up during the next year.' He was confused, depressed and worried. The key question troubling him was: What should I do now?

These kinds of situations occur every day. A common problem for senior individuals who have lost their jobs is that they don't see their job loss coming and they're not prepared. I have worked with many CEOs who were the last person in the organisation to see that they were about to be terminated. They had been too busy – not only doing their jobs to the best of their ability, but also looking after their families. If you are one of these senior executives, you may not have invested in understanding your personal strengths and weaknesses. And you may have a relatively limited, or relatively narrow, network to call on.

Whatever your situation, there is a good way forward. My experience reinforces that, if you tackle the challenge in the right way, you have a good chance of finding a better, more satisfying role. Also, you may find a higher paying job than the one you just left. The process I set out in this book works. But there is one significant problem: you have no way of knowing, when you kick off, how long it will take you to find your new role. This, of course, can be extremely disconcerting!

Conceptually the challenge you face is illustrated in figure 2.1. You need to focus on, first, what makes you special, second, what you actually like to do and, third, what roles are available. These three areas naturally overlap. Your challenge is to expand the area at the intersection of these three circles by taking steps to maximise your special strengths, what you like to do, and what is available to you. The larger the overlap, the more likely you are to have a successful outcome. The preparation and networking parts of the process described in this book (in chapters 3 to 7) are designed to help you expand each of these circles – particularly the circle representing what roles are available – and to maximise the area intersected by them.

Figure 2.1: Expanding the area of overlap between what makes you special, what you like to do, and the roles available

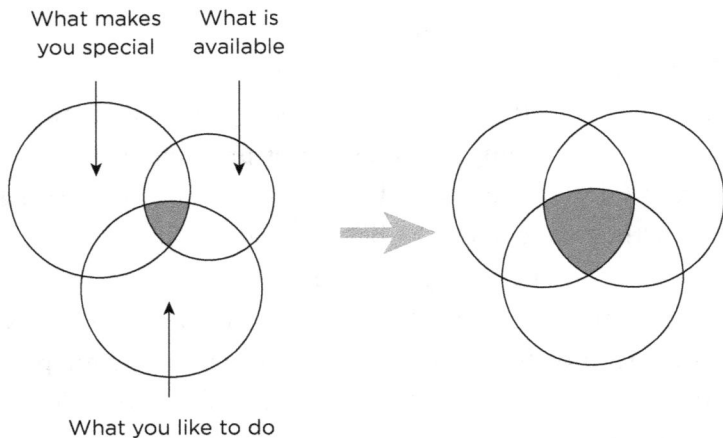

What makes   What is
you special   available

What you like to do

As a senior jobseeker, you face four challenges:

1. *The job search process:* How should you prepare for, and then conduct, your search?

2. *The hiring process:* How do you maximise the probability of receiving a job offer?

3. *Evaluating the offer:* Is the job being offered likely to be the right one for you and your family?

4. *Completing due diligence:* Are you aware of all the significant potential problems you and the business might face?

Each of these challenges can be complex, particularly if you do not have any job search experience to draw on. This chapter explains these challenges and why it is important that you prepare in advance to meet each of them.

CHALLENGE #1: MANAGING YOUR JOB SEARCH PROCESS EFFECTIVELY

Job searching at any level is difficult for most people. But the challenges for senior jobseekers are particularly varied and complex.

Those who expect the process to run smoothly are normally perplexed when it doesn't. If you are one of these people, you're used to pressing your foot on the accelerator and your car moving forward. Now you press the accelerator and nothing happens. You do not anticipate the amount of work you must do, or the lack of clear feedback you will receive. The uncertainty involved can generate significant anxiety for you and your family. At times, this increasing anxiety can be transmitted to others. As a result, even good friends and colleagues can pull back from helping you.

The process involved in senior job searching can be likened to farming. You need to prepare the ground, select the seeds and then plant them. Some seeds germinate, and others do not. Some of the germinating seeds flourish. Others do not. Some of the plants that flourish may be damaged or destroyed by freak events. But if you plant enough seeds in the right places, you're highly likely to achieve an excellent harvest. In fact, many candidates are surprised to find that they receive several job offers as they progress in the process. The outcome depends on the energy you invest and your activity level. You cannot sit by the phone and expect good results. In fact, if you do this, you will be fortunate to make any progress at all.

One important difference separates senior job searching from farming. It is much more involved than sowing seeds because it is all about successful relationship building. This is more important at a senior level than at a junior level. Juniors are largely hired on technical competence. The skills required at a senior level are much more sophisticated and difficult to evaluate.

Consulting firms are a good example of how this works. When you start out in management consulting, the question is whether you are hard-working, smart and able to fill out the spreadsheets. As you progress, the skills required relate to your ability to manage a project team. Later, the question becomes whether you can manage multiple teams and relate successfully to clients. At partnership level, you need strengths in negotiating with clients and ensuring that work is priced correctly. You also need to ensure that outstanding and valuable results are delivered to your client, usually under extreme time pressure. At the highest level in a consulting firm, your ability to become a trusted advisor with your clients becomes paramount. In addition, to be effective you must be able to draw on the resources of your firm and your partner colleagues worldwide.

For a consulting firm, hiring new people from outside at each level becomes exponentially more complex. As a result, most of the leaders in professional management consulting firms are promoted from within. What is true in consulting firms is also true in many large organisations seeking to hire senior people. These organisations are trying to evaluate complex and subtle skills. This presents a series of significant challenges − not only for those doing the hiring, but for you too, if you are a senior jobseeker. How do you prepare and then present yourself at your best? How do you differentiate yourself from other candidates in a positive way? How can you be sure that your preparation is as complete as possible, so you are well prepared when a good opportunity is presented to you?

As you prepare to tackle your job search, eight factors need to be considered. I cover these in the following sections. Each of these areas will be revisited and covered in more detail in the rest of this book.

Assessing the stage you have reached in your career

Careers evolve. Most breakthrough innovations come from young individuals who are specialists. In the early 1940s, the British psychologist Raymond Cattell introduced the concepts of fluid and crystallised intelligence. In the article 'Your professional decline is coming (much) sooner than you think' (published in *The Atlantic*), Professor Arthur Brooks from Harvard University has this to say about fluid versus crystallised intelligence:

> *Innovators typically have an abundance of fluid intelligence. Fluid intelligence is highest relatively early in adulthood and diminishes*

starting in ones 30s and 40s. This is why tech entrepreneurs, for instance, do so well so early, and why older people have a much harder time innovating … Crystallized intelligence, in contrast, is the ability to use knowledge gained in the past. Think of it as possessing a vast library and understanding how to use it. It is the essence of wisdom.

As Brooks notes, crystallised intelligence is developed by using our accumulating stock of knowledge. This means it tends to increase as you reach your 40s, and does not diminish until very late in life.

Starting out, many of us excel because of our specialised expertise, our drive, and our willingness to question conventional wisdom. You could be a great innovator in an intellectual field, a revered chef, or an extraordinary athlete. The difficulty that many of us face as our careers progress is transitioning from specialised functional expertise to more general management. Many people leave their timing for this transition too late. In some ways, the more skilled and gifted you are, the more difficult it is to transition to a broader role. How many great researchers make great university presidents? How many great chefs make successful restaurant owners? How many extraordinary athletes go on to successful careers after they retire from their sport? Very often societal barriers are blamed for failure to make this transition. What might be happening, however, is a failure to reinvent yourself as a more general contributor, using your crystallised intelligence.

Brooks argues that those who are best able to synthesise and explain complicated ideas – that is, the best teachers – tend to be older, in their 60s, 70s or even late-80s. Brooks writes of the different ways Charles Darwin, famous for his breakthrough theory of evolution, and Johann Sebastian Bach, the musical genius, managed their careers:

When Darwin fell behind as an innovator, he became despondent and depressed; his life ended in sad inactivity. When Bach fell behind, he reinvented himself as a master instructor. He died beloved, fulfilled, and – though less famous than he once had been – respected.

If you want to make the transition from specialist to generalist, start thinking about how to achieve this early on, evolving your career so that you can exploit your crystallised intelligence. To do this, you will need to find ways to use your experience, judgement and wisdom. For instance, through:

- *Teaching and coaching:* Drawing upon your knowledge to connect the dots of the past with the future.

- *Senior management:* Using your experience to make measured decisions that will be the right combination of risk and reward.

- *High-level consulting:* Bringing an outside perspective to help managements solve complex issues or validate challenging decisions by consulting or mentoring.

- *Directorships:* Leveraging your experience and judgement to provide measured insights on how to solve complex problems.

Part of the challenge you face is figuring out where you are in your career and how you would like your career to evolve.

Determining the complexity and scope of a role

Senior roles are difficult to calibrate because they involve a high level of complexity and subtlety. Most senior roles involve articulating a vision and purpose, leading cultural change, thinking strategically, setting priorities, allocating and reallocating resources, holding people accountable in multiple areas for delivering results, motivating teams to deliver what has been promised, and co-ordinating with a variety of stakeholders who often have conflicting goals. These senior roles involve many complex responsibilities and decisions including the evaluation of strategies, the selection and motivation of people, setting expectations, allocating responsibilities, and evaluating performance.

This kind of complexity requires broad-based judgement and wide influence rather than a focused approach. To clarify the difference, let's look at a classic example of related but different roles – those of a sales representative and a sales manager. Successful sales managers love to manage and motivate sales teams. Successful sales representatives love to sell and are motivated by individual sales success. According to Dr Bruce Sevy in the *Forbes* article 'Why great sales people make terrible sales managers',

> *Only one out of every six candidates who are a strong fit for a sales role is also a strong fit for a sales management role. Perhaps equally surprising, as many as five out of every seven candidates who are poor fits for sales roles are strong fits for sales manager roles.*

Make sure you are searching for a role that plays to your strengths. Sometimes people who blame outside factors for failing to progress do not understand that they have been successful in a focused role but are yet not equipped with the wider perspective required in a broader management role.

The difference between the wide and narrow focus is shown in figure 2.2. This concept, known as the T-Shaped Influencer concept, originated in global management consulting firm McKinsey & Company in the 1970s. The firm wanted consultants with a combination of deep subject-matter expertise in certain areas and the business and relationship capacity to tackle problems with a wide commercial perspective. The vertical bar on the letter T represents the depth of related skills and expertise in a single field, and the horizontal bar represents the ability to collaborate across disciplines with experts in other areas and to apply knowledge in areas of expertise other than one's own. Individuals with a strong horizontal capability strengthen collaboration within their teams and between teams. They're able to allocate resources, break down silos and increase the flexibility and agility of their people.

Senior general managers and executives are likely to have a strong horizontal bar and may actually have several vertical legs on their Ts. In other words, in addition to having multiple areas of deep expertise, they will have broad overview and management skills. A remarkable example of this mix of general management and specialist skills was Ford's mass production of B-24 heavy bombers during World War II. Over 1,225,000 perfectly machined parts were needed to manufacture each individual four-engine aircraft. Ford, using techniques it had honed in car production, assembled a workforce of over 42,000 workers. This team was able to deliver a complete working heavy bomber every 55 minutes, almost ready to fly away. Managing and coordinating the thousands of skilled specialists in the plant was a large team of general managers who had to plan and synchronise all aspects of this hugely complex production facility. They did this without computers! In total, over 8,600 B-24 Liberators were delivered by Ford's facility at Willow Run in three years.

Figure 2.2: T-Shaped Influencer - wide versus specialised

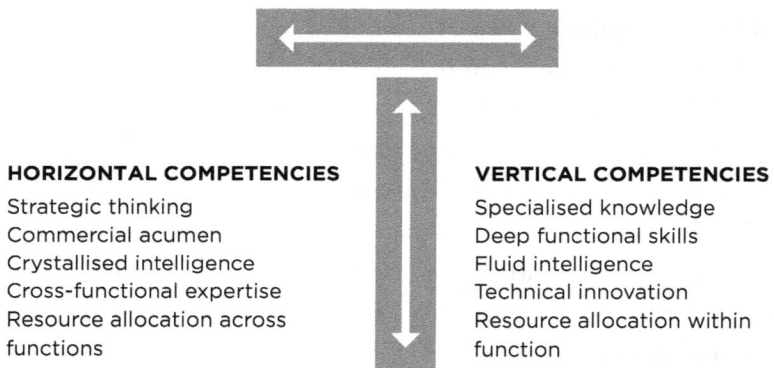

HORIZONTAL COMPETENCIES
Strategic thinking
Commercial acumen
Crystallised intelligence
Cross-functional expertise
Resource allocation across
functions

VERTICAL COMPETENCIES
Specialised knowledge
Deep functional skills
Fluid intelligence
Technical innovation
Resource allocation within
function

The complexity of senior positions means formal position descriptions prepared by HR executives or recruiters for senior roles can also be complex – often much too complex! A certain number of years of experience are often required, and finding 10 to 20 functional skills listed as prerequisites is not uncommon. In addition, another 10 to 20 competencies, traits and soft skills might be listed as desirable. These might involve your leadership qualities, such as being calm under pressure and being a visionary leader. Despite all these details and requirements, what is required to be successful in a role is often far from clear. In fact, the specified requirements are often extremely confusing. Often, the emphasis is on process and outputs (like preparing the monthly accounts), with little or no discussion of desired outcomes and impact of this work (like changing the way the business operates).

Your fundamental challenge is to determine the real requirements for the job. What value needs to be added by you and how? What needs to be achieved by you, by when? What challenges must be addressed? How will success be measured? The position description is merely the glamorous shop window on the street. What is going on behind this window, in the storeroom, is often totally different from the presentation in the window. In one situation, Tim asked the CEO of the hiring organisation (which happened to have a hugely complex position description with over 40 requirements) what he must do to be successful in the job. The answer provided by the CEO was simple – manage the successful merging of a newly acquired business into the parent business. Tim then understood what his job would be. As a result, the conversation going forward was much more constructive. How can you work out the real complexity of a role and show that you have the capacity to excel in the face of this complexity? I discuss this topic in more depth in chapters 8 and 9.

Displaying your leadership attributes

At senior levels, the capacity to be a leader, as well as a manager, becomes a key attribute in many searches. You need to show you are a strong, proven leader with lots of positive energy, and great commercial judgement. Most CVs fail to make these attributes explicit. They tend to be administrative documents that provide a list of the jobs you have undertaken with some achievements related to each job. In *Thinking, Fast and Slow*, Nobel Prize winner Professor Daniel Kahneman says his favourite two equations are 'Success = talent + luck', and 'Great success = a little more talent + a lot of luck!'

Figure 2.3 captures the increasing competence and requirements as leadership evolves. Aim to be a successful leader, no matter what level you might be in the organisation. Even entry-level people can be leaders! How do you show that you are an effective leader at your level? How can you show that you are a leader who can excel even when things are not going smoothly, and that you can manage stress effectively? How can you show that you have a history of success and that your achievements were not simply due to good luck?

Figure 2.3: The evolving requirements of leadership

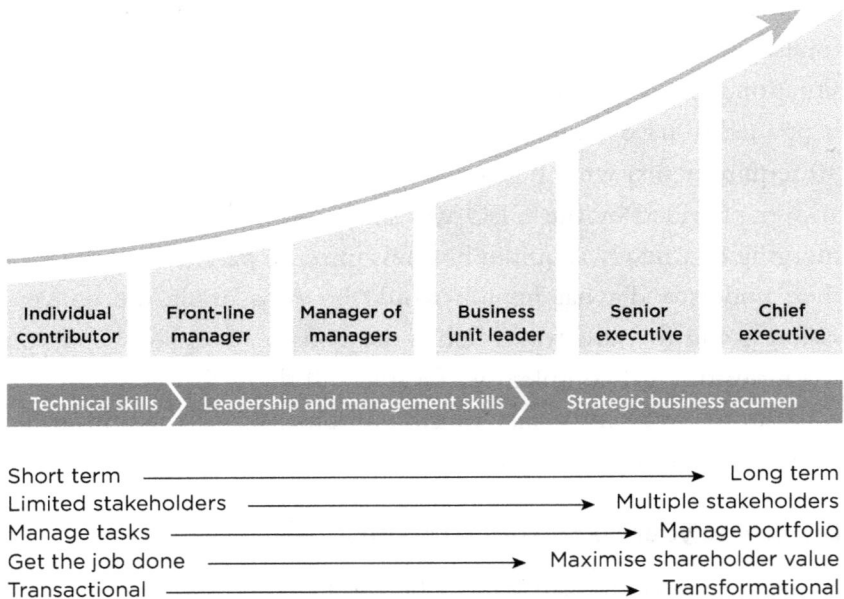

| Individual contributor | Front-line manager | Manager of managers | Business unit leader | Senior executive | Chief executive |

Technical skills 〉 Leadership and management skills 〉 Strategic business acumen

Short term ———————————————————→ Long term
Limited stakeholders ————————————→ Multiple stakeholders
Manage tasks ————————————————→ Manage portfolio
Get the job done ——————————————→ Maximise shareholder value
Transactional ——————————————————→ Transformational

Source: Charan, Drotter and Noel (2011) six passage model

Providing proof of your capability

Some experts argue that only about 40 per cent of your success in a particular role is due to your own skills and attributes. If this is true, the remaining 60 per cent of your success is due to the organisation and situation in which you work. We all know people who have thrived in one role but struggled in another. In his talk 'Most leaders don't know the game they're in', author and inspirational speaker Simon Sinek describes a young man, Noah, he met who was a barista in a hotel in Las Vegas. This young man impressed Sinek as one of the most delightful, service-oriented people he had ever met. He gave him a 100 per cent tip. Sinek asked him whether he liked his job. The young man replied that he *loved* his job. But he also said he worked in another hotel where the reverse was the case. He hated his job at that hotel. The reason he gave to Sinek was that, in the hotel where Sinek met him, he was motivated and encouraged to be his best by all members of management. In the second hotel, he was micromanaged and management were constantly on the lookout for any mistakes.

My point is, even if you have been a high performer in one organisation, you should not assume that you will automatically be a high performer in a new organisation. And, of course, the reverse is true too!

Another issue is that apparent high performance in a role may have nothing at all to do with your relative ability. Professor Kahneman researched the performance of currency traders in one of the leading firms on Wall Street. He showed that the results achieved by those identified as the high performers by top management – those who received the biggest bonuses – could be explained purely by chance. In other words, the big bonuses were going to the traders who just happened to be lucky. They were in the right place at the right time. The question for you is how can you provide strong proof and support for the idea that your previous success was due to your capability rather than luck? In addition, how can you show that you are likely to be a high performer in the new organisation? I cover the topic of identifying your strengths and communicating them in chapters 3, 4 and 5.

Demonstrating your management skills

Thoughtful observers point out a difference exists between managing and leading: we manage *things* and we lead *people*. A major issue in selecting between senior job candidates is how well they will both manage and lead – not only downwards with their direct reports, but also sideways and upwards in the organisation. Some executives are superb upwards managers but they fail when it comes to managing downwards or sideways with their peers. Some boards have been lulled into complacency by CEOs who are experts at managing upwards. For some reason, these boards have not bothered to obtain 360-degree feedback to evaluate their CEOs. If they had done this, they might have been shocked and surprised to find that the CEO, who was so effective when reporting to them, was actually a bully and a control freak who had their teams living in fear. If you are a senior executive, how would you show that you are capable of managing your team well, while at the same time also interfacing effectively with all relevant stakeholders? I outline a way of identifying your special strengths in the next chapter.

Exhibiting your personal resilience

Recruiters may wish to understand your resilience under continuing pressure, your capacity to handle stress and maintain your principles under challenging conditions, and the strength of your code of conduct in ambiguous situations. They will also be interested in your ability, among others things, to find appropriate and highly principled solutions to tough, complex ethical problems.

In addition to your resilience in a job, your resilience during the search process will be important. Will you have the commitment and tenacity to keep going through a long, demanding and opaque job-seeking process? If you become more anxious as the process continues, you will almost certainly appear less attractive and less desirable. You will need to find ways to maintain your confidence and morale. To do this, you must have reasonable expectations about the time it will take you to find a new role. You will also need to make these expectations – that a senior job search is usually a long-drawn-out process, no matter how capable you are – clear to those close to you.

Dirk, an accomplished senior executive, is an example of this. Dirk arrived in my office and told me that he wanted to obtain a fantastic job within eight weeks. He stated that, if I was any good at my job, I would find him this job without delay. I explained that he did not understand my job. He was the one who had to do the work, and I was there to provide guidance. I was his personal trainer and he was the one on the treadmill. I also pointed out that, unless he was well down the path of negotiating a role, he had only one chance in 1000 of achieving his eight-week goal. In the end, he took nearly 10 months to secure a job, but the outcome was excellent because this was the perfect role for him.

When thinking about timelines and resilience, I always remember a wise client of mine when I was a young consultant. When I was pushing him to move more quickly, he used to remind me, 'It takes nine months to make a baby.' Some things cannot be rushed. Mohammed Ali put this same idea another way (as you might expect): 'I hated every minute of my training, but I said to myself don't quit, suffer now and live the rest of your life as a champion.' You too need to put in the effort and training time. How can you prepare properly and maintain your resilience and your calmness under ongoing pressure? Your career transition coach or other mentor will be an important asset to you in setting sensible expectations. I suggest various ways of maintaining your positivity in chapter 7.

Attracting active supporters

An important part of preparing yourself for a job search is to build a strong network of supporters. These people will be vital in providing you with advice, assistance and support. For best results, as I outline in chapter 1, you should aim to meet at least 50 new people through warm introductions. These new acquaintances will be vital in stimulating your thinking and identifying possible opportunities. One of my clients, Neil, was offered four jobs by companies in his third circle – his C-List. Each of the four companies that offered him a role was initially introduced to him via a single individual in his second circle – his B-List. The amazing thing, as far as I was concerned, was that Neil had never met this B-Lister.

This key individual had been given some background material and a glowing reference by a supporter of Neil from his first circle, a member of his A-List. Not only did the four companies meet Neil, but each of them subsequently offered him a role. This shows the power of transferring personal trust from someone you know to someone you don't know. The person who you are meeting will trust you too, if they trust your recommender. How can you generate trust in members of your network and have them transfer this trust in a positive way to others? I tackle this issue in chapter 5.

Pacing yourself

Many of the success factors in senior job seeking are complex, and some are counterintuitive. Approaching your job search the wrong way is easy if you are not experienced in seeking senior roles. The preparation for the process of seeking senior roles cannot be rushed. Rushing in will likely make you look unprepared and, as a result, lacking in gravitas and credibility. This then compounds, as uncertainty and lack of progress generates increasing anxiety, not only for you but also for your family and friends. As a result, you may not get a job at the right level, or you may get a job where you will fail to thrive.

Compare these two stories:

1. George had lost his role as a senior executive in a public utility. Given the economic turndown, the state where he lived was investing huge amounts in building new infrastructure. George assumed that it would be easy to find a job. He called his ex-colleagues to ask whether they were aware of any jobs suitable for him. His calls were not returned. He became very anxious and had no idea what was going wrong. He had broken a fundamental rule: Do not ask for a job.

2. Amanda was proud of her CV. She had written down every job she had ever had and described everything she had done in each job in detail. The document was about ten pages long. She was disconcerted when none of her colleagues or the

recruiters she knew even wanted to read it. She had broken another fundamental rule: Be clear and brief.

Critics might say that George and Amanda were not savvy enough. This is not necessarily true. The problem is that capable people have not generally had to look for jobs during their careers. Throughout their previous careers, they have been approached with opportunities. As a result, they are not equipped to launch a job search that will deliver the best results. Their immediate responses are often misconceived, and their assumptions are often wrong. As Thomas Edison, the great US inventor and founder of General Electric, is quoted as saying, 'Our greatest weakness lies in giving up. The most certain way to succeed is always to try, just one more time.' What is the right approach to pacing yourself and refusing to give up? I discuss this in chapter 7.

The ideas in the preceding sections help to illustrate some of the complexities of setting yourself up for a successful job search at a senior level. Going into the process with your eyes open will reduce the possibility of disappointment! In particular, you need to avoid starting to believe you are a failure because the process takes longer than you could ever have imagined. Next, I describe some of the significant challenges faced by those who will have to make a decision to offer you a role in a senior position. They too are under pressure!

CHALLENGE #2: SECURING A POTENTIALLY ATTRACTIVE JOB OFFER

Deciding to make a job offer to you is an extremely challenging decision for a future employer. Your future employer knows that any mistakes could be very costly financially and may affect their reputation. If you do not work out in the new role, additional financial costs will be incurred as a result of having to find someone else to fill the role, and possibly significant resources will be required to fix problems that you caused. In addition, time and energy will have been wasted in the failed recruiting process. And a more subtle issue is that a mistake could also reflect badly on the individuals involved in the hiring decision. Their judgement will now be suspect. Finally, a failure to make a good hiring decision may even reflect poorly on the hiring organisation itself, particularly if it is a publicly traded company with announcements to the stock exchange. A great deal is at stake. Consequently, a hiring mistake at a senior level is a big deal.

According to Elena Botelho, Kim Powell, Stephen Kincaid and Dina Wang in their *Harvard Business Review* article 'What sets successful CEOs apart', 'superior business leaders' have four attributes. These attributes are:

1. *Deciding with speed and conviction:* These leaders make decisions easily, despite ambiguity.
2. *Engaging for impact:* They get prior buy-in and support from relevant stakeholders.
3. *Adapting proactively for change:* They adjust early to rapidly changing environments.
4. *Building and maintaining momentum towards goals and delivering reliably:* They maintain a steady trajectory and do not chop and change.

These attributes may be relatively easy to assess in retrospect. But the problem with these attributes is how to measure them in advance. If you were being interviewed, how would you convince the interviewer you could operate as a 'superior business leader' in their particular organisation? What questions would they ask you to try to identify that you would be able to display these four behaviours? And, how would you successfully display these attributes if you were a candidate for a role? A difficult challenge for the recruiter and for you!

As a result of this complexity in evaluating senior people, your prospective employer is likely to be very conscientious in managing the hiring process. Part of the problem they face is that the attributes they are attempting to find are not easy to measure. Also, analysing these attributes often involves judgements that are not clear cut. As a result, some companies go to great lengths to socialise senior hiring decisions. It is common, for instance, for professional consulting firms to put senior job candidates through 10 or more interviews and case study assignments, a battery of psychological tests, and maybe an assessment centre evaluation. To try to mini-mise the risk of a failure, recruiters for senior roles will often also informally approach a series of senior executives, above and beyond those submitted by you as your formal referees, for input before they make a hiring recommendation.

In the following five sections, I outline the kinds of questions those in the recruiting team will be considering as they conduct the search process, and what you should be thinking about when you answer them. Keeping these questions in mind is worthwhile as you prepare for interviews, as discussed in chapters 8 and 9.

First: Are you trustworthy and will you command respect?

Those in charge of recruiting for a role want to know whether you can be trusted. Professor Amy Cuddy, in her book *Presence*, points out that human beings will nearly always make a judgement about you based first, on whether they can trust you, and then, on your level of perceived competence. She argues that someone who is trusted will generally be preferred to someone who is more competent but less trusted. You could be less trusted just because someone has no previous relationship with you, or because your trustworthiness cannot be easily validated.

Humans also make these judgements super quick. In her TED Talk 'Your body language may shape who you are', Cuddy states,

> *Alex Todorov at Princeton has shown us that judgments of political candidates' faces, in just one second, predict 70 per cent of US Senate and gubernatorial [state governor] race outcomes.*

Cuddy postulates human beings developed amazing pattern recognition skills as we evolved. When we were cave-dwelling hunter-gatherers, we wouldn't invite someone into our cave who we thought might injure or kill us. Warmth, gravitas, presence, judgement and calmness under pressure are all important markers in the trust equation. How can you convince the hiring team that they can trust you, and that you will be respected by your future colleagues?

Second: Do you have potential for growth in the organisation?

A recruiter's focus when hiring a senior person will usually be on whether you can do the present job. But, if they are good at what they do, it will go well beyond this. They will take a view on whether you have future growth potential. Figuring out whether you can do a complex job is difficult enough. But determining whether you can grow to more senior roles is even more challenging. Years ago, many leading multinationals invested heavily in the development of their senior people. They used to have strong executive leadership programs that tracked the performance of their senior executives, and assessment centres and many development programs were in place. Those executives deemed to have high potential were exposed to a variety of roles and different business challenges internationally. Today, this seems to be much less common. We have moved to a process favouring the survival of the fittest. How can you show that you can not only do the job, but also thrive and grow, and take on additional responsibility?

Third: Will you fit our culture?

Recruiting teams must determine whether you will be a good fit with the people you will be working with in their organisation. Also whether you will help the established teams perform better. They will be asking, 'Will the members of our current team want to work with you each day, and will you help lift the team to a new level? Will you complement the people we already have in place better than the other candidates for this role?' As a general rule, I take the view that an external candidate needs to be 50 per cent better than an internal candidate for a role in order to be hired. Why? It comes down to risk management. The company knows more about the intellectual attributes and interpersonal skills of an internal candidate, including how well they already fit into, and contribute to, the culture of the organisation. These attributes are tough to measure in an unknown candidate from outside. How can you convince the recruiting team that you will be a good cultural fit and that you will be an asset working in the established teams? Will you be 50 per cent more capable than the internal candidates you are competing against? How will you be able to convince the recruiting team of this?

Fourth: Are you committed to the job being presented to you?

Another key question for the recruiting team is whether you genuinely want the job and whether you will stay. How enthusiastic and committed are you? This is not as easy to gauge as you might think. In an interview process everyone is on their best behaviour. Naturally, a candidate for a job will express enthusiasm for the role. Even if you are committed when you are given the role, might you prove to be 'too big' for the job once you arrive? If so, will you soon work this out and move on?

This is an important issue for those doing the hiring and for you. If you know you are too big for a job, the only reasons to accept it are:

- if you are repositioning yourself for a future promotion in a new industry where you are learning
- if you need a job badly, for the income
- if you are planning to work at lower intensity.

You need to ensure that accepting such a role is a smart decision. How do you work out whether you are really committed to a particular role, and will not be too big for the role once you have taken the job?

Fifth: Will the members of the recruiting team look good?

The last thing the recruiting team wants to do is to make an obvious hiring mistake. As mentioned earlier, the financial, cultural and reputational consequences of a mistake in a senior hire could be substantial. In addition, a bad decision might affect the career progression of any members of management involved in the decision. Their judgement will now be suspect. For these reasons, mistakes are not always identified or dealt with quickly. Organisations may take time before they face the reality that they have got the hiring decision wrong. Many organisations and hiring teams do not want to deal with this issue head-on because of concerns about their own reputation. The temptation is to give the new hire more time to prove themselves. Boards, in particular, may not want to admit that they have made a CEO hiring mistake. So, they tend to allow time for the new CEO to evolve and to be successful in the role, even though it is clear that he or she is not performing well.

Remember, one reason executive recruiters are able to maintain such high recruiting fees is their ability to convince boards and senior management that the costs and risks of a hiring mistake are huge. Recruiters argue that they maximise the probability that their clients will avoid these costs and risks. The question for you is how can you make sure that the recruiting team are likely to see you as a high-performance, low-risk hire who will make them look good?

To show how subtle the hiring problem can be, here is an example. Bob was widely recognised as a high calibre and high-performance CFO. He was selected as one of the last two candidates for five different senior CFO roles in a row. Inexplicably, he failed to be offered any of these roles. I could not see how this could happen and approached the recruiters involved. I wanted to know why Bob had fallen at the last hurdle five times in a row. It turned out that the Chair of his previous employer had subtly implied that he had serious doubts about Bob's capability when approached by the recruiters for an informal reference. Once Bob understood what was happening, he was able to explain rather easily the reason behind the Chair's adverse input to the recruiters. As a result, the recruiters understood they were likely to receive a negative assessment from this Chair, and why. The next reference checking process went very smoothly, and Bob was hired without delay.

You might be thinking that the issues related to offering a senior job cannot be this complex – after all, people have been hiring for senior roles for many years. Unfortunately, however, the process of finding the right person at the right time – and of minimising the risk of failure in the new role – is not at all easy. The issues being explored go well beyond your ability to do the job. By the time you reach the short list, you are presumed to be able to do the job well. The key issue then is your fit with the culture of the organisation and with the people in it. Remember, even when recruiters present five good candidates to a client as a 'short list', four of these will be rejected. You only have a 20 per cent chance of being hired, even when you have made it to the short list! A fundamental question for you is how can you increase your odds of success from 20 per cent to, say, 60 per cent if you are selected to be on a short list?

Your key challenge, of course, is to understand the relevant issues related to the particular role you are seeking. Then you can prepare yourself in advance to address any recruiting team concerns. As a senior jobseeker, if you are aware of the particular issues facing the recruiting team, you will enjoy a major strategic advantage over those who have not prepared. You can position yourself effectively, maximising the upside and minimising the risks. I tackle this issue in much more detail in chapters 8 and 9.

In the next sections, I discuss the issues you will need to address when you actually receive a job offer.

CHALLENGE #3: DECIDING WHETHER THE JOB OFFER IS RIGHT FOR YOU

When you are offered a role, you need to be certain that it will be the right career move for you, before you accept. When you analyse the situation in detail and step back after the interviews, the job may not be the right one. It may have become obvious that your personal values are not aligned with those of the management of the business. Or you may realise that you're unlikely to be able to add significant value or the risks of failure are just too high. Your reputation may be at risk of being damaged. You might decide the job will not lead to greater opportunities and could be a dead end. Or that the likely stress on you and your family will be excessive. Perhaps the compensation being offered is not appropriate.

I realise that it may not be easy for you to decide to refuse an offered role. But doing so may save you a great deal of future anguish. Your decision to refuse a particular offer will, of course, be much easier if you are being offered a number of different roles. Having more than one offer is surprisingly common if you conduct your job seeking process along the lines I suggest in this book. With more than one offer, you will be much more able to evaluate in depth the relative trade-offs involved in each role. Also, because you have the luxury of having options, you will have more negotiating power!

Investigate the five questions outlined in the following sections before you decide that a role is the correct one for you and your family. This is a brief overview. I discuss these issues more deeply from various angles in chapters 7, 8 and 9.

First: Are my values aligned with those of my new employer?

If a mismatch exists between your values and those of your future boss and/or your future employer, this could be a knockout for you. In his *Harvard Business Review* article 'How will you measure your life?', Professor Clayton Christensen makes the point that it is much easier to maintain a strict set of values rather than allowing yourself to diminish or modify your values because of situational pressure.

He provides a series of stories from his own life to support his view, and he points out that various catastrophes have resulted when values have been compromised. One was the massive failure in the US of Enron Corporation in 2001. Enron's failure then pre-cipitated the failure of the global accounting firm Arthur Andersen LLP. Enron's failure was the result of sophisticated accounting fraud initiated by its top management, and Arthur Andersen was its auditor. This fraud occurred because the values of Enron's leaders became more and more compromised over time. Obviously, this is an extreme example, but the question of values is still important. How can you work out whether your values are aligned to those of your future boss and the new organisation that wishes to hire you?

Second: Can I add real value ... and will I be permitted do this?

Do not accept a role where you will be treading water or shuffling paper. You need to believe that you have the potential to have a real impact and add considerable value as a result of your role. For instance, while a management consultant, I always set myself a goal of delivering 10 times the value of the fees that I charged to my client.

If you can do this, you are likely to be a great success and your career should flourish. The 'if' is important here. You may well have all the strengths needed to make a big difference to your employer. The problem is generally not so much whether you can theoreti-cally add substantial value, but whether you will actually be given the opportunity to add this value by your new employer.

Some of the things that will reduce your ability to add value could include: lack of a clear direction from top management, a complex organisational and decision-making structure, the board's or top management's unwillingness to take risk, budget constraints, systems weaknesses, unclear accountabilities, and cash flow issues. How do you determine whether you are likely to be given the opportunity to add substantial value before you accept a job offer?

Third: Where will my job lead in the future?

Your aim should be to take a job that will be a stepping stone towards an increasingly challenging and fulfilling career. Don't accept a role where you are likely to be up a creek without a paddle in two or three years. Two questions to ask during the interview process are:

1. 'How might my career evolve over the next three to five years?'
2. 'How will I be assisted to develop professionally as I move forward?'

You need to be given roles that stretch you and help you to grow. In this regard, you are likely to benefit from attending courses that expose you to a wider range of problems and permit you to expand your professional network worldwide. Ideally, the recruiting team will provide you with positive advice about your likely way forward in the organisation. If not, this omission could be a significant issue – and one that needs to be addressed before you accept the role.

Therese was a high performer in her role. She was becoming bored and felt she was not being stretched or developed. She discussed this with her manager and was told that she was doing so well in her current role that the business could not afford to move her. Her manager took the view that no-one else in the organisation could do this role as well as she could. As a result of this failure to help her develop and grow, Therese decided that she needed to leave the organisation. It turned out a number of other employers were really impressed with her and she easily found a better job. By failing to assist Therese, the business lost her. How will you work out where your job might lead and what your new employer will do to assist you to grow?

Fourth: How might this move affect my family?

No doubt you're hoping for a successful, productive and happy career. At the same time, you will want to have a successful relationship with your family as your career evolves. And here, as I explain in the Introduction, I have in mind whatever 'family' means to you and whatever relationships you care most about.

If this role is likely to damage your family — by the work hours involved, the amount of travel, the time living away from home, the stress of succeeding, midnight phone calls, or for any other reason — do not take it. I have seen families disintegrate. I have experienced situations where an adverse outcome was totally predictable, but my client took the role despite my advice not to go forward. The usual reason for not taking my advice was, 'It won't be that bad, and, in any case, I can manage the situation.' Be wary! The question for you is: How can you understand and minimise the stresses that this role might put on your family and your personal relationships?

Fifth: Will I earn enough?

Think very carefully before you accept a role that involves a reduction in compensation. You should be seeking to find a role where you can add sufficient value to justify your current salary, or higher. Sometimes roles can be redesigned to make them larger and, therefore, able to deliver more value and justify a higher salary. Salaries are negotiable. The first offer is rarely the last. Obviously, a salary negotiation where you are asking for higher compensation can be difficult for you — especially if you only have one role on offer. When you receive two or more offers, negotiating becomes much easier. It is often amazing what can be achieved if more than one organisation wants to hire you!

Private equity situations are different from the usual compensation arrangements in traditional businesses because of the equity component. Not-for-profits are different too (and sometimes can offer various advantages through different tax treatments). In this case, you may agree to accept lower compensation because you wish to invest your efforts in improving society. Whatever the role, you need to work out ways to add sufficient value to justify the salary you want. Before you decide to accept a role, you need to ask, 'Have I negotiated a suitable salary?'

Thinking through these five questions is important. I discuss them in more depth — and how you can formulate questions to explore them further – in chapters 7, 8 and 9. In the next section, I discuss the need to complete thorough due diligence before you commit to a new role.

CHALLENGE #4: COMPLETING DUE DILIGENCE BEFORE YOU COMMIT TO A NEW ROLE

For senior roles, you need to find out as much as you can about the organisation and your particular role before you accept the job offer. Sometimes problems are lurking beneath the surface that you are not aware of. For instance, a business might have paid too much for an acquisition and, although the deal was publicised as a triumph, it was in fact a mistake that is dragging down the performance of the whole business.

Thorough due diligence is particularly important if you are being offered shares or options as part of, or in addition to, your base compensation. In effect, you are becoming an owner in the company. In these situations, you need to complete comprehensive due diligence as if you were a professional investor being invited to invest in the business. You should complete an in-depth analysis of all aspects of the company before making a decision to go ahead and 'invest'. If you are asked to invest your own money in the business when you join, thorough due-diligence analysis is even more vital. You should never invest up-front on the basis that you trust the information provided by the management or other investors, no matter how well you know them. Wait until your probation period, usually six months, has passed, before you actually transfer your own money into the company. During this period, working inside the company, you will find out more about the business and the way it is run than any external analyst can do. Armed with this additional information, you can then decide whether risking your own money in the business is wise.

Why due diligence is important

If you do not conduct proper due diligence, all sorts of unexpected issues might arise that make accepting the role damaging. You may accept a role where you will fail. Or you may find yourself in a situation where you're unhappy, or where your personal brand is damaged. You may also face the risk that you will not reach your potential because the role does not take you forwards. You may accept a lower salary than necessary. And, finally, you may face the risk that your family and relationships will be damaged because you are so involved in work that they never see you. Although I may be too cynical, I think you can usually safely assume, when you take a new role, that, 'Things will generally be worse than they appear on the surface'. Of course, this will not always be true but, in my experience, it pays to be alert and wary! I discuss these issues in more detail in chapters 9 and 10.

Although proper due diligence is vital, senior jobseekers often fail to ask even the most basic questions about the role being offered and the enterprise making the offer. Position descriptions can be superficial or misleading, or can fail to describe the problems in the business with governance, stakeholders, systems and cash flow. When jobseekers do ask questions, the answers provided are not always frank, transparent or honest. Sometimes boards and senior management are out of touch or distracted.

Three examples of what can happen if you accept a role without proper due diligence are as follows:

1. Frieda really liked the CEO of a business who interviewed her for a role. He was charming and enthusiastic. The CEO offered Frieda a senior job, reporting to him. She decided to accept the role without delay. In her view, due diligence was unnecessary. Six weeks later, she resigned, saying she had made a terrible mistake. The company was in deep financial trouble and, although he was charming, the CEO was an incompetent manager. This was a great learning experience for Frieda.

She decided that she would never accept another role without conducting comprehensive due diligence!

2. Charles was offered a CEO role in a small business that was publicly traded and headquartered in another state. As part of the hiring process, he was shown the Annual Accounts for the prior financial year (which had concluded 10 months earlier). He did not identify any significant financial issues in these accounts. When he arrived to take up his new role, he was told that the company was nearly out of money, and only had sufficient funds to trade for two more months. The board was clearly either incompetent or had withheld vital information from him. The question facing him, of course, was whether to stay to try to fix the problems, or to leave straightaway given the board's failure to inform him of these problems.

3. Alex accepted a CFO role without understanding the immaturity of his team in his new employer. He came from a global company where he had been the regional CFO for Europe. He managed a highly competent accounting team of over 200 people who delivered high-quality work for him to take to the regional board. When he left the global business, his new CFO position was in a much smaller company. His team was small and very junior. He failed to thoroughly check the numbers presented in the board papers at his first board meeting, and was shocked when a board director pointed out several important errors in the accounts. He was terminated on the spot.

Perhaps you're thinking you would not fall into these kinds of traps. You might think that these executives were naïve or too trusting. I can assure you that plenty of people make these mistakes. Whatever the case, one thing is clear: these individuals did not do sufficient due diligence, either during the recruiting process or after they were offered the role. Carrying out due diligence is very difficult without a significant effort to meet people who work in the organisation or who have previously worked there. You face a particular problem if those involved in hiring you are not transparent or are not honest with you. Remember that both you and your future employer are on your best behaviour during the hiring process. Problems might be skirted around.

Rather than being too accommodating, try to act more like a 'reluctant bride'! The good news is that you are usually more attractive when you show some reluctance or hesitation, and try to understand the situation you will face in more detail.

Finding out as much as you can about the organisation

Always 'trust but verify' before you accept a role. Advice from someone whose judgement you trust can help raise the issues you should explore before you accept a role. The people you could approach to throw light on the actual situation you will face, if you join the organisation, are:

- people who work in the organisation, or have worked there recently
- those who know people who work or have worked in the organisation
- advisers, consultants, suppliers, customers and competitors
- industry experts and individuals who have been on industry committees and boards
- stock analysts, bankers, auditors and other financial people who may have insights
- board directors or ex-board directors, and members of board committees.

A considerable amount of information can usually be found by searching information and articles related to the organisation on the internet. Another important resource is LinkedIn, which can allow you to identify people who can help you. This is possible by approaching your 1st and 2nd connections who have the organisation's name in their LinkedIn Profile. LinkedIn is a powerful tool for you. I discuss this in more depth in chapters 4 and 7.

Let's look at an example of a situation that might signal possible problems. Joe was approached to take on a CEO role in a key part of a large, diversified family business. He was told that the negotiations were in confidence because the person he would be replacing was still in charge. During the discussions related to the role, it became clear that the person he would be replacing was widely considered, both inside and outside the business, to be incompetent. Joe tracked down a number of ex-employees and they all confirmed this. And yet the family owners of the business had permitted this person to stay in the role for the past 18 months. During this time, many business opportunities had been lost and much damage had been done. Joe's concern, of course, was why the owners had permitted this situation to continue and whether they were the right people for him to work for, given their failure to take more decisive action.

In the end, of course, you will need to make the final decision and, if appropriate, take the leap. You will not find out what the job is really like until you take the position. But having a rigorous checkpoint review with your coach at the one-, three- and six-month marks in your new role is wise.

Two examples show how you can benefit if you do your homework properly:

1. Genevieve was careful to do her due diligence. She was offered the CFO role in a newly listed, fast-growing, publicly listed company. On searching LinkedIn, she found that the company had employed three CFOs over the previous five years. She checked with senior partners she knew in the 'big four' accounting firms, and was advised by all, in clear terms, not to accept the CFO role at the company. They questioned the reputation of its board and its senior management. She decided not to accept the role. Six months later the company struck severe financial problems. In the meantime, Genevieve

had secured a much better role in another growth company. If she had not rejected the initial offer, she would undoubtedly have been publicly saddled with the problems in the company, and her brand would have been badly damaged.

2. Tom was joining a successful business with a strong position in a growing industry as COO. The business was about to go public. Tom was aware that the current private owners were regarded as bullies, and that the business experienced 60 per cent turnover in staff each year. Tom believed he could change the culture and transform the business once it became a public company. As a backup plan, Tom negotiated an exit clause where he would receive one year's salary if he decided to resign should the public listing fail to go ahead. As it turned out, the public listing did not proceed and Tom decided to resign. He was very pleased to have negotiated the 'Golden Parachute' to protect himself!

An experienced career transition coach will help you identify what due diligence is required and the best way of completing the analyses required. More discussion of how you can conduct due diligence is provided in chapters 9 and 10.

★★★

In this chapter, I have explained that senior jobseekers face a complex series of challenges. These challenges relate to, first, how you conduct your search; second, how you maximise the probability that a hiring team will make you an offer; third, once you have received an offer, how to evaluate whether the role will be the right one for you and your family; and, fourth, ensuring you do sufficient due diligence to understand and evaluate any possible problems you might face. The question for you, of course, is how best to meet and address each of these individual challenges. The remainder of this book sets out my advice in this regard.

In the next chapter, I discuss the importance of understanding and focusing on your strengths. You need to develop this understanding before you begin to search for a role or approach your network.

SOME QUESTIONS FOR YOU TO CONSIDER

- Have you considered what actions you would take if you were to lose your job?
- Do you understand the role of career transition consultants and what they offer?
- Can you articulate what you have to offer in terms of being a T-shaped influencer?
- If you are a specialist, have you given any thought to how your career should evolve in the future?
- How would you present yourself as a 'superior business leader' and what evidence could you provide to support this?
- Are you building a diversified network of individuals who might help you in the future?
- Do you have strong relationships with a number of recruiters in your industry and area of expertise?
- Have you given any thought to how your career might evolve and progress?
- Should you be taking any initiatives to accelerate your personal development?

PART II

BUILDING ON YOUR STRENGTHS

3

Framing your special strengths

Always bear in mind your own
resolution to succeed is more important
than any other one thing.

Abraham Lincoln

Before you begin to meet the people in your network or recruiters, you need to identify and frame your strengths, and to consider whether you are sufficiently visible to relevant decision makers. To do this, you need to:

- Understand why you must discover what makes you special

- Consider how you can perform from strength

- Identify the attributes that make you special

- Find out what others think makes you special

- Structure your thinking about what makes you special

- Create a strong personal brand

- Be visible in a positive way to relevant decision makers

WHEN YOU'RE SEEKING a job, you're in the business of marketing yourself. To do this well, you need to differentiate yourself from any others seeking the same role. And the best way to differentiate yourself is to be able to explain your special strengths, simply and clearly. In other words, you should explain what makes you special. This sounds easy. But very few people can easily explain their strengths and what differentiates them from others. Often, they have not given deep enough thought to identifying and describing their strengths. Even if they have considered what makes them special, they may not have validated their thinking by testing their view with other people who have worked with them. They are, therefore, basing their analyses on their own intuition. Often, their intuition is incorrect. Because they have not really validated their strengths, senior jobseekers can also make their story far too complicated and too long. They mistake quantity for the quality of simplicity and clarity.

At the same time, many high performing jobseekers do not want to be seen as self-promotional. They take the view that selling themselves is not what senior people do, and the thought of this makes them uncomfortable. They say that they want to be authentic and understated. The danger with being understated – even if you think you are being more authentic – is that you are likely diminishing and down-playing your achievements. In my experience, even when senior jobseekers think they are being too self-promotional, their colleagues often tell them they are actually underselling themselves. The risk of overselling yourself is low, while the risk of underselling yourself is high.

WHY YOU NEED TO DISCOVER WHAT MAKES YOU SPECIAL

Knowing what makes you special permits you to express your brand more clearly. Each of us has a brand, whether we like it or not. But few of us have taken the trouble to develop a way of describing our brand in a clear, simple and strong way. What we say about ourselves is marketing. What others say about us when they talk to others is our brand. To be seen as authentic, these two differ-ent perspectives – what others say about us and what we say about ourselves – must be consistent and self-reinforcing. If a mismatch occurs, our credibility will be in jeopardy. Ideally, our brand should relate to our long-term performance rather than to a particular one-off success. For example, 'David is always reliable. He never fails to deliver what he promises!' is better than, 'David is a great guy!' As a senior jobseeker, you need to develop a clear, compelling brand. Do not underestimate the challenge involved.

Unfortunately, most CVs fail to show you are special in any compelling way. They are usually merely an administrative docu-ment, setting out a list of jobs with some description of the roles you have had. Perhaps you've heard the comment (commonly mis-attributed to Mark Twain), 'I didn't have time to write you a short letter, so I wrote you a long one'. The same approach goes for the materials most often prepared by senior jobseekers. They prepare their materials too quickly, and don't spend enough time and effort thinking through and abbreviating what they have to say. They ask the reader to do too much work. When you prepare your written materials, you need to assume that most people will not take the trouble to read what you have written. Even if you can actually entice them to read what you have written, they will not want to invest time to think or analyse ideas that are not clear. Your story needs to jump off the page and be simple and clear.

Depending on who you ask, most CVs are read in somewhere between six and 16 seconds. This seems incredibly quick but, time and time again, those involved in recruiting confirm this with me. So, what does a reader of a 10-page document learn in fewer than 16 seconds? Not much. Unless you can explain what makes you special succinctly and in a memorable fashion, you are severely diminishing your probability of success. In the worst case, you will be removed from a list of prospects for a particular role that you could well have been selected for. Give recruiters one compelling reason to hire you, not a long laundry list of fairly random thoughts. I once saw an advertisement on a billboard I have never forgotten. It showed the backlit silhouette of a European sports car with nothing else except the corporate logo and one word in large white print: *Remarquable!* I was fascinated that such a complex machine could be described in one word, made particularly memorable by it being in French and also because it refers to the idea of an automobile *marque* (brand, type or make). Working out how to prepare your own version of this one idea takes time, energy and deep thought.

Without clarifying what makes you special, you are likely to miss opportunities to succeed in the job-seeking process. You could severely limit your probability of success. In this chapter, I describe how to identify the strengths that make you special, and how to use these strengths to help define your brand. Then, in the next two chapters, I'll explain how to prepare your written and verbal communications. Remember, communicating your strengths and brand concisely and clearly will further enhance the perception you are indeed special. Most people mishandle this communication process.

Anyone making a hiring decision wants to confirm that your special attributes are likely to be important in adding value in their organisation. As I explained in the previous chapter, those involved in the hiring decision want to be able to trust you, to be convinced that you can do the job, to make sure you fit the organisation, to see that you are enthusiastic about the role and, most importantly, to make sure that they actually look good themselves when they hire you. You must be special and you need to communicate this specialness in a special way. Most CVs do not do this!

Ensuring your brand and speciality are not too narrow

One quick caution here. A potential problem for some senior job-seekers is that they are too strongly branded to a particular industry or company. They may certainly be perceived to be special, but not in a way that is necessarily attractive if they are seeking another type of role. This specific branding can severely limit them as they look for new roles. A classic example is a senior partner in a major law firm hoping to change career direction. Senior lawyers have a huge number of important transferable skills and competences but most people, including recruiters, are fixated on their legal career. This is usually reinforced by their CV, which starts with their tertiary law qualifications, goes through a series of promotions in a law firm, and then culminates in their role as a partner in a law firm.

If you are strongly branded in a narrow way, you may be boxed in and limited in your options. How you describe and communicate your brand needs to be addressed before you meet with and expand your network, especially recruiters. Recruiters in particular tend to simplify your brand. They often describe you in terms of your most recent job. Be prepared for this. If you have a narrowly defined brand, you will probably need to think through how to position yourself more broadly when you begin networking. You do not want to be a "one trick pony". How do you explain the breadth of your horizontal bar if you are a T-Shaped Influencer?

Part of what makes you special is whether you look and act the part. For example, unless you look like a CEO and express yourself as might be expected of a CEO, you are unlikely to progress in an interview where they are seeking to hire a CEO. As noted earlier, in her TED talk 'Your body language may shape who you are', Professor Amy Cuddy says that when other people first meet you, they form an impression of you very quickly, often in as little as a few seconds. This can be good or bad. For example, Fred came from the big end of town. He was invited to an interview with a successful start-up, and turned up wearing a formal dark business suit, a silk tie and cufflinks. As soon as the interviewer saw him, he told Fred that his company did not hire executives who dressed that way. No ifs or buts. The interviewer terminated the interview before it started. This was a big learning experience for Fred! The next time, he checked out the employer expectations in advance.

In the next section, I describe the importance of identifying your true strengths, since these will be what make you special. Everyone from the most junior person to the most senior person has strengths, but most jobseekers fail to identify and articulate these. I often think of a mailroom attendant I once worked with. He was superb at his job, including his attitude, his initiative, his responsiveness and his reliability. But when we first met, he introduced himself by saying, 'I'm only a mail room attendant.' He had much to offer but could not see this.

PERFORMING FROM STRENGTH

Peter Drucker, in his *Harvard Business Review* article 'Managing oneself', points out that 'a person can only perform from strength. One cannot build performance on weaknesses, let alone something that one cannot do at all.' Drucker states that most people do not know their strengths or what makes them special. I agree. Most senior jobseekers I work with cannot describe their strengths in any compelling way when we first meet. A typical example was Don, a top commercial lawyer, who said that he thought he was pretty much like every other senior lawyer in his field. This was not a great way for Don to sell himself! In fact, when we worked through his capabilities, experience and leadership abilities, it became obvious that he was very special in a variety of ways — including how he had excelled as a leader in his firm, his reputation as one of the best commercial brains in the country, and the fact that he had been an exemplary coach and mentor to young lawyers, particularly women, coming through his firm.

Despite struggling to explain what makes them special when asked, people tend to overestimate their own specific capabilities in relation to others. For example, in the *Harvard Business Review* article 'Delusions of success', Dan Lovallo and Daniel Kahneman point out:

> *Most people are highly optimistic most of the time. Research into human cognition has traced this overoptimism to many sources. One of the most powerful is the tendency of individuals to exaggerate their own talents—to believe they are above average in their endowment of positive traits and abilities.*

Lovallo and Kahneman then go on to quote findings from a 1970s survey of one million students, including that 70 per cent of those surveyed rated themselves as above average in leadership ability in comparison to their peers, and only 2 per cent rated themselves below average. In terms of their social skills and getting along with others, 60 per cent rated themselves to be in the top 10 per cent — with 25 per cent considering themselves in the top 1 per cent.

Various other studies have come to similar conclusions. Most of us suffer from this 'illusory superiority'. For example,

- 96 per cent of leaders said they have above average people skills compared with other leaders, in a study by Stanford Business School
- 94 per cent of the faculty of the University of Nebraska rated themselves as above average for teaching ability
- 88 per cent of American students believed they had above average skills as safe drivers, in a study by the College Board.

This seems to indicate that, although we cannot articulate our strengths well when asked in general terms, we overestimate our relative strength when asked about a particular attribute. As shown by the research, most of us are vastly overconfident when it comes to our own abilities. We believe we are smarter, more dependable and better than others when asked about specific skills. As a result, many senior jobseekers tend to be cavalier when it comes to describing their strengths.

As you have read, I am a great believer in focusing on, and using, your strengths. You need to concentrate on moving from good to great. I do not believe in spending your time focused on trying to fix your weaknesses in this process. Even if you succeed in making progress in fixing your weaknesses, chances are you will only move from mediocre to average. Tom Rath, author of the bestselling *StrengthsFinder 2.0*®, has the same philosophy. He also adds another dimension:

> *Our studies indicate that people who do have the opportunity to focus on their strengths every day are six times as likely to report having an excellent quality of life in general.*

Some of Rath's research findings are shown in table 3.1.

Table 3.1: Effect on employee engagement if manager focuses on strengths

If your manager primarily ...	Your chance of being actively disengaged are ...
Ignores you	40%
Focuses on your weakness	22%
Focuses on your strengths	1%

Rath also points out, 'Perhaps the most surprising is the degree to which having a manager who focuses on your strengths decreases the odds of your being miserable on the job.' Great sports coaches know this and keep accentuating the positive. As Alex Ferguson, one of the greatest coaches in English football, puts it,

> *No one likes to be criticized. Few people get better with criticism; most respond to encouragement instead. So I tried to give*

encouragement when I could. For a player – for any human being – there is nothing better than hearing 'Well done'. Those are the two best words ever invented. You don't need to use superlatives.

You need to be able to answer a key question: How can you be more confident, clear and authentic about your true strengths? For instance, are you a visionary leader with gravitas who energises your teams to deliver beyond expectations? Are you highly principled? Do you have good commercial judgement and great negotiation skills? Are you an effective communicator with individuals from the shop floor right up to the board? Can you motivate people when you speak? Do you deliver what you promise? Can you manage stress and stay cool in a crisis? Can you be trusted to keep your word?

As you consider what makes you special, use the following areas to hone your thinking.

Sell hope

You are not selling a physical product. What you are selling is the promise of providing a valuable future service to an organisation. You are being hired on the basis that the employer thinks you will add value as an employee in their organisation in the future. In *Selling the Invisible*, best-selling author and lecturer Harry Beckwith states that invisible services are sold on the basis of hope. He quotes founder of Revlon, Charles Revson: 'In the factory, we make cosmetics; in the store, we sell hope.' Unlike a physical product, personal services are not delivered with any guarantee of performance. The likelihood of convincing someone to commit to buy the service you will provide in the future will depend on you building the trust of those making the hiring decision. They need to take the view that you will deliver value in the future. How do you address this issue of building trust and selling hope in a compelling way?

In order to hire you, those involved in the hiring decision must 'vote' for you to be hired. Being competent and authentic is not enough. How does someone seeking a new employee sort between five apparently equally competent and authentic people, and select just one? A key factor will be that they feel an emotional connection with you. This connection could cause them to commit to you rather than to another talented person. To develop this emotional connection, they must have something in common with you and believe you are special. Think back to my earlier analogy of you being a movie maker trying to win an Oscar. You are a talented individual who is trying to generate votes from those involved in your hiring decision. Winning votes for yourself during a recruiting process will involve more than presenting yourself as an accomplished individual. The question then becomes how to generate the most votes by engendering trust and hope?

Be distinctive, with valuable 'signature strengths'

Beckwith points out that, if you are selling the invisible, it is best if you 'stand for just one distinctive thing that will give you a competitive advantage. The more alike two services are, the more important is each individual difference.' You need to stand out. As you go through a hiring process, your goal should be to differentiate yourself effectively from other talented applicants. Some people try to do this by demonstrating that they have a broad range of skills and can do virtually anything well. This approach is rarely successful because they appear to have no special differentiator. They can come across as too general and, as a result, bland. It may seem as though their application has been prepared without much thought. Positioning yourself as a broad generalist who can do everything well is not usually a good way to impress a recruiting team! It is better to focus, as sharply as you can, on the specifics of what make you special. What are your signature strengths?

I will always remember a friend of mine who worked for a used car dealer while studying at university. Although hopefully this would not happen today, this dealer took the view that a used car only needed one good feature for an effective salesman to make the sale. So, if a car had a good engine and good tyres, he would remove the tyres and replace them with older tyres. I tell this story not to support the approach of this dealer, but to reinforce Beckwith's idea that you must stand for one distinctive thing.

Even if you can show you are special, the hiring process can be difficult because you generally do not know anything about your competitors in the process. So, you don't know what strengths and skills these other candidates have, or how they compare to you. This can make the application and interview processes extremely challenging for you. A further issue is that the thinking of the hiring team will evolve as they meet more candidates and develop new insights into what talents and skills individual candidates might bring to the job. The way to differentiate yourself, given this situation, is often to be the one who asks the most thoughtful and probing questions. You can use these questions to clarify where the enterprise is headed, why your role will be important, and how you might deliver outstanding results. This starts a conversation that enables you to show that you are a probing thinker and a positive contributor. What questions can you ask that make you distinctive, and highlight your signature strengths?

Find out what is needed

The challenge facing you is how to discover what the recruiting team is looking for and the requirements of the job in as much depth as you can. If you do not identify these requirements as part of the interview process, the conversation with the recruiting team will be all about your competences at a high level. This is not likely to be helpful to you. You should be doing everything you can to convince the interviewers that, if they hire you, you will make a strong, positive impact in the new organisation in specific ways. To do this you must understand the challenges and be able to explain how and when you will make a difference. As mentioned above, in addition to you not knowing the competition, an additional complication for you is that the thinking of your interviewers will evolve as they meet more candidates. So, you may well seem very attractive one day, but not so attractive once they have met other candidates. How can you stand out from the crowd and maintain this positioning through a drawn-out hiring process? How can you continue to convince the recruiting team that you will be the best at delivering what they're looking for?

As I have already explained, most formal position descriptions do not describe the actual job that must be done. They tend to describe the role in an abstract way. Usually, the challenges you will face are not at all clear. (Incidentally, if the recruiting team does tell you the problems you are likely to face, this is usually a good sign!)

Take, for instance, the example of Ned. He was considering applying for a role where he would be in charge of operations in a large complex company. The position description provided by the recruiter made the job look routine, except from one sentence: 'This job is not for the faint hearted.' Ned researched the role in more depth, and tracked down and interviewed a number of people who knew the company. He found it was facing many severe issues that made the job almost impossible. In particular, the organisation structure was complex and difficult to navigate, and a number of the top management team were new and were struggling. Finally, a recent major multi-year IT program had failed so badly it ended up being cancelled and a huge amount of money written off. The position description was routine, but the job was anything but routine. A few words in the position description were the only hint of potential trouble.

As you think about what makes you special, don't make a formal application for a role without finding out what is really involved in being successful in the job you are applying for. If you possibly can, discuss the role with the recruiter and, preferably, with the person you will be reporting to – before you apply. You have to find out as much as you can about the role and the kind of person they are looking for. If you do this effectively, you will achieve four important things:

1. build rapport with the recruiter and your future boss

2. identify which of your attributes will make you special in the role

3. determine how to match what you offer with what they need

4. decide whether you should progress with your application or not.

Being aware of the exact requirements of a role is a huge advantage to you as you progress through the hiring process. Having a clear understanding of the challenges you will face, and what success will look like, allows you to be much more impressive in interviews. Different styles work in different situations. You may be perfect as a change agent if there is a burning platform, but become bored when everything is running smoothly. You may be very good with routine tasks, but become anxious in a rapidly changing environment. You need to understand what is needed to make you successful in the role you are investigating. You also need to decide whether the way you work will help you make a significant positive impact in the new role. Does your style suit the situation you will face in the job?

Table 3.2, adapted from Daniel Goleman's 'Leadership that gets results' (published in the *Harvard Business Review*), outlines different leadership styles and the situations where the particular leadership style works best. The question for you is, what style is required in the job you are seeking, and does this style suit you?

Table 3.2: What style is required in the situation being presented to you?

Style	The style in a phrase	When the style is required
Commanding	'Do what I tell you'	Demanding immediate compliance in a crisis
Visionary	'Come with me'	Mobilising people towards a new vision
Affiliative	'People come first'	Creating harmony and building emotional bonds

Style	The style in a phrase	When the style is required
Democratic	'What do you think?'	Forging consensus through participation
Pacesetting	'Do as I do now'	Setting high standards for performance
Coaching	'Try this'	Developing people for the future

Once you understand the situation you will face, you can tell stories during the interview process explaining how you handled similar situations in the past. This, in turn, makes it much more likely that you will progress through each stage in the process.

Internal candidates for a role already know the issues they will face if they are selected. They will be able to be quite specific about what they would do in the role. If you provide very general answers or waffle, because you do not know the precise challenges you will face, you will struggle to impress the interviewers. You will probably fail to convince the recruiting team you are a superior candidate in comparison with a good internal candidate or someone else who really understands the company and the issues it faces, such as someone who works for a competitor. How can you get a good handle on exactly what is needed to be successful in the role? I discuss this in more depth in chapter 9.

Make the recruiting team feel good about you

The content of what you write or say is one thing, but how you express it is likely to be even more important. Maya Angelou, the iconic American poet, is perhaps best known for this often-repeated – and misattributed – quote, 'People will forget what you said, people will forget what you did, but people will never forget how you made them feel.' (Carl W Buehner should be credited with this adage.) Whatever the source, remember this idea when you are thinking about what makes you special. The real question is not only the content of your message, but also the feeling you elicit in those involved with the recruiting decision.

In *Thinking, Fast and Slow*, Daniel Kahneman describes just how fallible we all are. His research shows that judges in court make different judgements in the afternoon when they are tired. Medical doctors provide different diagnoses depending on previous prompts and patient experiences. University academics score exam answers differently depending on how well the student answers the first question in the examination. These less-than-perfect human responses occur in professions where we expect the professionals involved to be absolutely consistent. How do you position yourself in a recruiting process where those involved, and the process they use, will be much less scientific and much more open to individual personal judgement than expected from the professionals above?

Many senior jobseekers list a series of competencies in their CVs to describe what makes them special. Often, they think the more competences they list, the better. This may work in junior jobs where hiring is decided largely on the basis of demonstrated functional skills. But it is the wrong way to approach explaining what makes you special in a senior role. Listing a series of functional key competencies will likely make people lose interest right away – they may not even read what you write. You're asking them to do too much work. So how do you identify your signature strengths in a way that your hiring team will not be turned off and will want to understand them and get to know you more? Read on …

IDENTIFYING THE ATTRIBUTES THAT MAKE YOU SPECIAL

Everyone is special. But most people find it extremely difficult to answer a question about what makes them special in a simple, clear and compelling way. The answer, when you are senior, relates less to what you can do, and more to how you do it. A diamond has a certain size, colour and clarity – and these attributes can be measured precisely. As a human being, you have many attributes that are much more difficult to understand, let alone calibrate.

For instance, the simple question of how you manage other people under stress is difficult for recruiters to explore and assess. Part of the reason for this is that every situation is different.

You may have many strengths but a single setback may confuse the picture. As a result, an issue of concern might be identified by the recruiter and then probed until it becomes a knockout. You might argue that a particular setback in your career was an excellent learning experience and you are better for it. You may be correct and some recruiters might agree. Others may not see it this way. Raising negative issues and addressing them on the front foot is best. How do you best illustrate your relevant strengths and turn your setbacks into strengths in a convincing way? If you do not quite meet the specified requirements for a role, you should face this head-on. I recommend you be clear with recruiters. Ask them whether it is a knockout or not if you do not have this skill or attribute. Often, they will say no and you can keep going. But if the recruiter says that the lack of this skill or attribute is a knockout, he or she will probably take you out of this process. It is best to resolve this early on. I discuss these issues further in chapter 9.

I always remember a class at Harvard Business School many years ago that explored a case study related to Damien, who was starting a new business. The case study was presented to us in three sections. Damien was starting his first business. After a quick description of this business, the professor asked who in the class would invest in it. About 80 per cent of the class said they would invest. The first part of the case did not end well. The business failed, Damien went bankrupt, and the investors lost all their money. Damien was undeterred, however. In the second part of the case study, he decided to start another business. Only 10 per cent of the class said they would invest this time. Once again, the outcome was bad, and this business also failed. Damien was bankrupt again, and the investors lost all their money. But Damien decided to have another go. No-one in our class was willing to invest this third time. At this stage, the professor introduced Damien. He was sitting at the back of the class.

According to our professor, Damien was now a billionaire. He had achieved this success by learning from his previous failures. This was a big lesson for all of us students about continuing to learn, and never giving up! Of course, another lesson was to be careful not to judge a person by a particular event or series of events.

On the other side of the coin, just because you have been through certain elite experiences does not necessarily make you an attractive hire. Physical products can be tightly specified, and measuring whether a product meets its specification is relatively easy. But just because you graduated from Harvard Business School, worked for a top consulting firm, were a manager in a big four accounting firm or were a university professor does not mean that you will be a good manager. Your previous experience and education does not mean you will succeed in a different situation or that you will be right for a particular job. If university credentials are so important, how is it that so many of the most successful entrepreneurs in the digital age have dropped out of university? Bill Gates, Larry Ellison, Michael Dell, Steve Jobs, Mark Zuckerberg ... the list of college dropouts who have been successful in business goes on! As a general rule, I would argue that a fine education is desirable. But it is not a prerequisite to – or a guarantee of – success.

As part of the recruiting process, a recruiter is likely to ask you to describe what makes you special or to describe your 'signature strengths'. A good answer to this question will tend to focus on five attributes or classes of strengths: your values, behaviours, competencies, experience, and your energy/drive. To answer this question well and with high impact, you must match your strengths with those the recruiter is looking for.

The content of your answer is important, but so too is how you structure your answer. Barbara Minto, who set out the rules for effective presentations in her book *The Pyramid Principle*, suggests that, to be an effective communicator, you need to communicate each of your key ideas at the same level of abstraction and impact. Describing one monumental strength and two weak ones doesn't work. Instead, identify three to five classes of strength that each carry about the same weight and impact. Government judicial enquiries — where they report with 200 recommendations involving totally different levels of importance — invariably fail the Minto test of grouping ideas into a limited number of areas of equal weight. I discuss how this works further in the next chapter.

How do you determine what attributes might make you special? First, let's consider what kinds of signature strengths might be important for senior people in senior roles. This is a big topic so, following Minto's advice, I have divided it into the five areas: your values, behaviours, competencies, experience, and energy/drive.

Your values

Your values are a fundamental part of who you are, and your values must be compatible with those of your future boss and the business you are proposing to join. In the article 'Managing oneself', Peter Drucker explains that values go well beyond ethics. Ethical behaviour is well-defined and does not change depending on where and how you work. Your values, on the other hand, might be different from those of your employer. Despite this, the values of each of you may be acceptable, just different. Drucker provides the example of a CPO (Chief People Officer) to illustrate this. The CPO believed strongly in promoting talent from within the business if at all possible. But her business was acquired by a business where the board had a strong philosophy that all key jobs must be filled with fresh talent from outside the business. Neither approach is necessarily right or wrong but, in the end, this executive resigned because her values were incompatible with the values of her new board. Another example from Drucker himself was where he believed in coaching and developing people. He joined a business where he found that making money drove all decisions. Drucker resigned because of a profound mismatch between the values of the business and his own personal values. You need to find out all you can about the values of an organisation you might join, and the values of your future boss, to try to avoid any possible values mismatches.

Your behaviours

I divide this section into two types of behaviour: your general behaviours and your leadership behaviours.

Your general behaviours

To enjoy your work and be truly fulfilled and engaged, you need to work on something that interests you. In *The Birkman Method*, Sharon Birkman Fink and Stephanie Capparell outline the work-place psychological assessment method created by psychologist Roger Birkman. The authors state that,

> *Interests are important for us to know because they say much about what satisfies us over the long haul. When an employer can connect what a person truly loves to do with that person's job, employee retention skyrockets … Your interests will be a source of your energy and well-being.*

The Birkman Method™ approach groups occupational interests into four areas:

1. *Doer:* Directing, building, high energy.
2. *Communicator:* Persuading, selling, coaching.
3. *Thinker:* Innovation, design, strategic thinking.
4. *Analyser:* Detailed work, working with numbers.

The world and most enterprises benefit from involving people with occupational interests across each of these areas. Doers like to build things, see finished products, work outdoors and solve problems. Communicators like to sell, promote, persuade, motivate and work with people. Thinkers like to be creative, visualise possibilities, read and write, and involve music at work. Analysers like to schedule activities, work with details, develop policies and procedures, and work with numbers.

The Birkman Method, however, goes well beyond your occupational interests and is a powerful tool for understanding the three important dimensions of your behaviours, in addition to your interests:

1. *Your usual behaviours:* The way you work when you are happy and effective.
2. *Your underlying needs:* These needs are your preferred prerequisites for you to be effective.
3. *Your stress reactions:* How you behave if your underlying needs are not met.

Each of these behaviours differs in each quadrant of the occupational interest groups, as shown in figure 3.1.

Figure 3.1: Overview using Birkman Map summaries

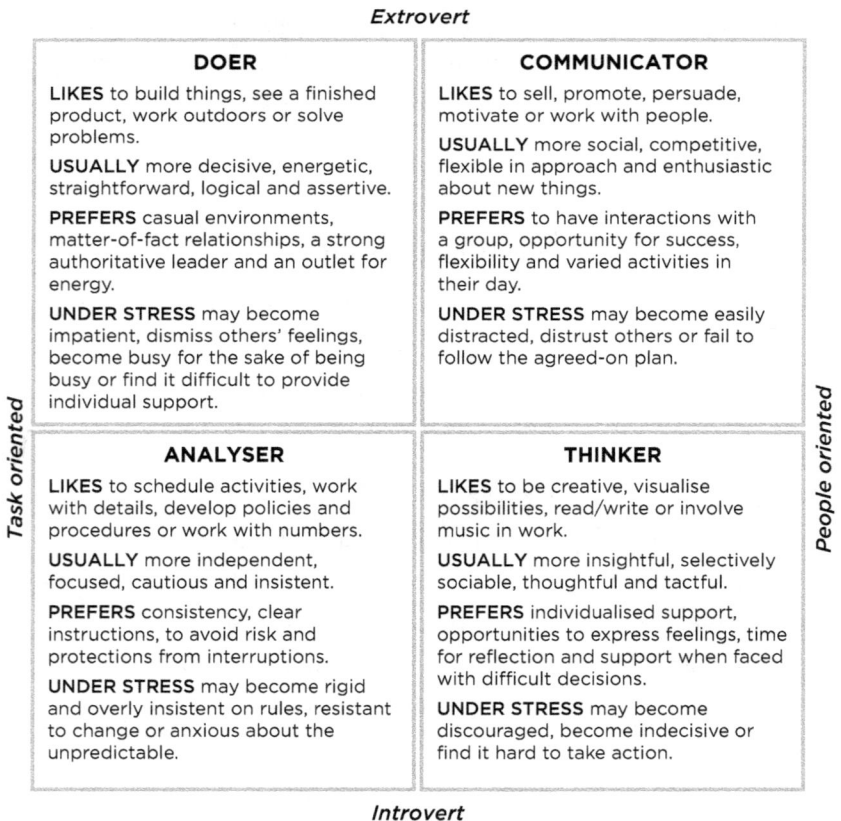

Extrovert

DOER	COMMUNICATOR
LIKES to build things, see a finished product, work outdoors or solve problems.	**LIKES** to sell, promote, persuade, motivate or work with people.
USUALLY more decisive, energetic, straightforward, logical and assertive.	**USUALLY** more social, competitive, flexible in approach and enthusiastic about new things.
PREFERS casual environments, matter-of-fact relationships, a strong authoritative leader and an outlet for energy.	**PREFERS** to have interactions with a group, opportunity for success, flexibility and varied activities in their day.
UNDER STRESS may become impatient, dismiss others' feelings, become busy for the sake of being busy or find it difficult to provide individual support.	**UNDER STRESS** may become easily distracted, distrust others or fail to follow the agreed-on plan.
ANALYSER	THINKER
LIKES to schedule activities, work with details, develop policies and procedures or work with numbers.	**LIKES** to be creative, visualise possibilities, read/write or involve music in work.
USUALLY more independent, focused, cautious and insistent.	**USUALLY** more insightful, selectively sociable, thoughtful and tactful.
PREFERS consistency, clear instructions, to avoid risk and protections from interruptions.	**PREFERS** individualised support, opportunities to express feelings, time for reflection and support when faced with difficult decisions.
UNDER STRESS may become rigid and overly insistent on rules, resistant to change or anxious about the unpredictable.	**UNDER STRESS** may become discouraged, become indecisive or find it hard to take action.

Task oriented (left side) · *People oriented* (right side)

Introvert

One of the key differentiators between the Birkman Method and other assessments is that almost half the questions in the Birkman Method relate to how you see most people. The reason for this is that, from the beginning, Roger Birkman realised there was great value in asking people questions about how they saw other people in their world. In short, how did they expect others to think and behave? He was convinced that understanding how people described most people had as much power as understanding how they described themselves. By asking questions about both self and others, as well as asking them to rank their preferred jobs, the resulting information is multi-dimensional and provides a more accurate assessment of the person's social style and motivating needs.

Sherrie Douglas, a Birkman-certified professional, provided an example of how asking how people describe other people provided valuable insights in considering new car design decisions at Ford back in the 1960s. When Ford decided to design a new family automobile in the early 1950s – which was ultimately named the Ford Edsel – it carried out comprehensive market research. It asked families what they wanted in a new car. With this information, Ford proceeded to design the Edsel. As you may know, this new car was a flop. Its sales were very poor indeed – fewer than 160,000 in total. In the early 1960s, Ford again began researching what families said they wanted in a new car. But this time, according to Douglas, Ford also asked what these families thought their neighbours would like in a new car. This research led to the Mustang, which was launched in 1964. It was a huge success and sold one million vehicles in the first 18 months. It is still being sold today, nearly 60 years later.

Dan Perryman, from Birkman (the company), puts it this way:

The power of 'most people' is that it advances our understanding of ourselves by allowing us to talk about our own character, values and expectations without filtering our answers through the lens of social desirability. When we get out of our own way, we can learn a lot about ourselves.

It is this feature of the Birkman Method that I, and my clients, find extremely valuable.

In working with my clients, I always work though their Birkman profile with them. Often, they are aware of their 'usual' behaviour (their behaviour when they are happy and effective) but have not really considered their underlying needs (the environment they prefer to work in, in order to make them effective), or their resulting stress behaviour (if their needs are not fulfilled). I also compare my own personal characteristics with those of my clients. And when I was a board chair, I used to carry out the same comparison with my CEO. In both these situations, understanding our differences, and how they might affect our relationship going forward, is extremely helpful as we work together.

Your leadership behaviours

Management Research Group (MRG), based in Maine, USA, has developed the Leadership Effectiveness Analysis™, a tool that measures 22 independent behaviours that each play an important role in leadership. MRG groups these competencies under six broad headings, as shown in table 3.3.

In the view of MRG, no individual score in each of the 22 competencies defines a leader. What needs to be understood are the pros and cons of each score in any situation. For instance, if you have a high Control score, you will probably follow up with your team regularly to make sure that projects stay on track, to remind people of their commitments and to ensure that deadlines are met. According to MRG's research, a higher emphasis on Control predicts leadership effectiveness in the biotechnology and manufacturing industries, where projects are distributed across different teams, and teams often work on different aspects of a project sequentially. Control is not generally predictive of effectiveness in the higher education or healthcare industries, where teams work more independently of one another and individual missed deadlines are less likely to affect the organisation broadly.

Table 3.3: MRG leadership behaviours

1. Creating a vision	• **Traditional:** Cautious decision-maker, respects lessons of the past • **Innovative:** Thinks innovatively, values new ideas. • **Technical:** High level of technical expertise, expert in field. • **Self:** Independent thinker, looks to self as prime decision-maker. • **Strategic:** Plans for the future, sees big picture.
2. Developing followership	• **Persuasive:** Strong advocate, convincing and can sell ideas. • **Outgoing:** Friendly, establishes strong interpersonal relationships. • **Excitement:** Expressive, enthusiastic and dynamic. • **Restraint:** Even disposition, restrains behaviour, stays calm.
3. Implementing the vision	• **Structuring:** Thinks in a structured way, methodical. • **Tactical:** Seizes opportunities and adapts quickly. • **Communication:** Communicates clearly and effectively. • **Delegation:** Delegates effectively, gives others freedom.
4. Following through	• **Control:** Monitors progress effectively, follows up. • **Feedback:** Frank and direct, provides straightforward feedback.
5. Achieving results	• **Management focus:** Willing to take charge and provide guidance. • **Dominant:** Competitiveness, will to win. • **Production:** Sets high personal goals, works hard to achieve them.
6. Team playing	• **Co-operation:** Works well with others, willing to compromise. • **Consensual:** Values ideas of others, encourages democracy. • **Authority:** Loyal to the organisation, accepts ideas of senior colleagues. • **Empathy:** Exhibits concern for others, builds strong personal bonds.

Your competencies and talents

You need to be able to highlight your competencies to fill the requirements of the role, but also to highlight them in the right way to the right people to win their votes. The following example illustrates this. Peter was in charge of logistics in a major paper products company. He won national awards from his supermarket customers for delivering to the exact order with over 99 per cent on time performance. He applied for a logistics role in a rapidly growing electronics retailer. The recruiter involved rejected his application without seeking an interview, arguing that Peter's experience in delivering paper products was not relevant to the needs of his electronics client. When key members of Peter's network heard he had been rejected, they contacted the CEO of the electronics retailer and convinced him to instruct the recruiter to interview Peter. Peter was interviewed but then rejected again. Peter's network went back to the CEO and, this time, convinced him to arrange for his CFO to interview Peter. The CFO interviewed Peter on a Thursday and then asked him to come back the next day to meet the CEO. The CEO met with Peter on the Friday and, at the end of their meeting, offered him the logistics role. The hiring documentation was completed and signed during the following Monday, just three working days after Peter had been rejected twice by the recruiter. The management could see that Peter would actually bring important new skills in warehouse management to the electronics business. The recruiter failed to recognise this and, in his view, Peter had the wrong skills and did not have relevant industry experience. A question for Peter was why he failed to convince the recruiter that, even though he came from a different industry, he had signature strengths that would benefit the electronics retailer?

In *StrengthsFinder 2.0*®, Tom Rath points out that Donald Clifton, who he calls the 'Father of Strengths Psychology', and his team discovered that:

> *People have several times more potential for growth when they invest energy in developing their strengths instead of correcting*

their deficiencies … The key to human development is building on who you really are … a strengths-based approach improves your confidence, direction, hope, and kindness towards others … we've discovered that the most successful people start with a dominant talent – and then add skills, knowledge, and practice to the mix.

Rath points out that strengths are built on talent and investment – practising, developing your skills and building your knowledge base. Using the *StrengthsFinder 2.0*® approach, the key first step is to determine your top five strengths. Rath reminds us that '*StrengthsFinder 2.0*® is not intended to anoint you with strengths – it simply helps you find the areas where you have the greatest potential to develop strengths.' The 34 strengths that are evaluated in *StrengthsFinder 2.0*® are shown in table 3.4.

Table 3.4: The 34 StrengthsFinder 2.0® *themes*

Achiever	Deliberative	Learner
Activator	Developer	Maximiser
Adaptability	Discipline	Positivity
Analytical	Empathy	Relator
Arranger	Focus	Responsibility
Belief	Futuristic	Restorative
Command	Harmony	Self-assurance
Communication	Ideation	Significance
Competition	Includer	Strategic
Connectedness	Individualisation	Winning Others Over
Consistency	Input	
Context	Intellection	

If you would like to take the *StrengthsFinder 2.0*® assessment to discover your top five strengths, you can do this online. The idea is to develop your strengths and work with others whose strengths complement yours. I once worked with a CFO who, unusually, was more interested in people than numbers. To be effective and to protect himself from disaster, he needed to have people on his team who loved numbers and detail so that nothing was overlooked in the accounts.

Your experience

In this regard, it amazes me how often industry experience trumps competency in the hiring process. The candidate with more industry experience is selected over another candidate who is technically more capable and has greater potential for growth. At the simplest level, deciding that experience is more important than competency relates to the desire of the hiring executive to avoid the risk involved in hiring a candidate unproven in their industry. Hiring someone who knows the industry, its people, and its language is more comfortable.

A similar decision that you or I might face is whether to select an experienced senior surgeon rather than a high-performing young surgeon. The senior surgeon might have successfully completed the specialist operation we require 1000 times, while the junior surgeon, although he or she has the latest training, has completed only 20 similar operations. Most people are likely to select the surgeon with more experience, on the basis that they believe he or she will know what they are doing and are likely to be better at managing complications. But the danger also exists that they are out of date or losing their mental or physical agility.

In one large beer brewing business, the CEO asked the CPO to find some new managers with 'fresh thinking' from outside the industry. When the CPO submitted a list of possible high-performing new hires, the CEO rejected the individuals because they were 'too extreme'. The CEO said he needed people who actually understood the industry. The CPO came up with a new list of less extreme individuals, with fast-moving consumer goods (FMCG) experience. Despite his desire for 'fresh thinking', the CEO also rejected this next list 'because they did not understand the beer business'. Once again, experience in the industry trumped competency and fresh thinking – even when this was the expressed desire. If you do not have relevant industry experience for the role, you will need to show you will bring special skills to help, in a positive way, to transform the organisation where you wish to work. You need to convince the hiring team that you will bring important new thinking that will outweigh the perceived risk of hiring someone with low industry experience.

Your energy and drive

President Calvin Coolidge believed,

> *Nothing in the world can take the place of persistence. Talent will not do it; nothing is more common in unsuccessful men than talent. Genius will not – unrewarded genius is almost a proverb. Education will not – the world is full of educated derelicts. Persistence and determination alone are omnipotent. The two slogans, 'Press On' and 'Deliver the goods' have solved, and always will solve, the problems of the human race.*

You might think this is over the top, but it is amazing what can be achieved if you are energetic and persistent. Not unrelated to this is whether you have a 'growth mindset'. Professor Carol Dweck coined this term in her book *Mindset*, where she differentiates those with 'growth mindsets', who see setbacks as important learning experiences to build on, from those with 'fixed mindsets', who see setbacks as confirmation that they have reached their limits and must stop aiming higher. The characteristics of these two mindsets are shown in table 3.5. Those with a combination of persistence and a growth mindset are more likely to grow and succeed.

Table 3.5: Fixed versus growth mindset

Fixed mindset	Growth mindset
Intelligence is static	Intelligence can be developed
Leads to a **desire to look smart** and, therefore, a tendency to: • avoid challenges • give up easily due to obstacles • see effort as fruitless • ignore useful feedback • be threatened by others' success.	Leads to a **desire to learn** and, therefore, a tendency to: • embrace challenges • persist despite obstacles • see effort as path to mastery • learn from criticism • be inspired by others' success.

Calibrating your attributes and strengths

To calibrate your strengths, various approaches are possible and, often, a combination of approaches is used by recruiting teams. Many assessment tools are available. CPOs and recruiters frequently use 'behavioural interviewing' – asking you how you handled a particular situation in the past. People using this technique believe past behaviour is the best predictor of future behaviour.

Another approach was used by Angela Ahrendts, former SVP of Retail at Apple. As she says, 'Building a brilliant team is your job. Nothing you do is more important or adds more value.' Ahrendts explains in 'How I hire', that she used four 'guiding principles' at Apple to see how interviewees approach their work. These principles were:

1. *Me versus we:* How do you see yourself in the world?
2. *IQ versus EQ:* How do you naturally navigate in the world?
3. *Left brain versus right brain:* How do you look at the world?
4. *Yesterday, today or tomorrow:* What guides you in the world?

Others will have different approaches in trying to understand what is important to you, what you know, how you think, how you handle stress and what you might contribute in a future role. The challenge for you, as a senior jobseeker, is knowing which of these areas is likely to be most important in any particular situation, and how to show your particular strengths and what makes you special to best advantage. I suggest one way to think about the question of what makes you special in the following section.

FINDING OUT WHAT OTHERS THINK MAKES YOU SPECIAL

How do you solve the difficult problem of defining what makes you special? I have developed a simple and quick approach that works well. You can get results in a few days if you wish, and can quickly identify what others see as your strengths. Most senior jobseekers tend to guess what makes them special without any validation from others. The fact that you have a good fix on what others think makes you special will immediately differentiate you – in terms of both content and clarity, and your gravitas and authenticity. You will be speaking from the heart – using actual evidence – as you deliver this information.

My approach is to send a simple email to 10 individuals who have seen you at your best at work over the past few years. I call this a 'Strengths Feedback Request' (SFR). This request is not provided to a random sample of colleagues – quite the opposite. It goes to people who have seen you when you are happy and productive. Usually, they have worked with you close up, day to day, and have seen your strengths firsthand. The best examples are direct reports, bosses, consultants, customers or board directors. Peers can provide feedback too, but they tend to see you in administrative situations rather than when you are leading your people and delivering results. Individuals who have reported to you and your previous bosses are usually best for feedback because you have often changed their lives for the better in some way. The idea is to understand how other people see you when you are happy and effective at work – when you are at your very best. Your email can end with a request for a response within one week.

Your request should ask for bullet point summaries of what makes you special in four areas. You might think this approach is too simplistic but, in my experience, it is unwise to add significant complexity to the email template I provide here. The only times this email has not worked for my clients have been when they have added more questions or complicated the message. Asking for feedback on what your colleagues believe you should improve might be tempting. Do not do this. It complicates the message.

I recommend the template shown in figure 3.2 for your email.

Figure 3.2: Example Strengths Feedback Request

Dear [name of colleague],

As you may know, I am working with a career coach to think through my future career options. I am currently seeking to identify my special strengths as an executive, as seen by my colleagues.

Since you have worked with me and seen me in action while I was at [insert a previous employer], I would be very grateful if you could take a few minutes to provide some feedback for me and my coach.

If it helps you could use the following headings to indicate my strengths:

1.   The way I think;

2.   The way I work with people, particularly teams;

3.   The way I communicate;

4.   Any other strengths not yet included.

I am looking for a series of bullet points and am hoping that this will not take you too much time. Please be frank.

If you could get me your thoughts by [date], I would be grateful.

Many thanks,

[Your name]

The feedback you receive from your colleagues tends to fall into one of three classes:

1. *Individuals who do exactly as you have requested:* These individuals often provide half a dozen thoughts under each heading, often with surprisingly expansive warm and supportive comments.

2. *Individuals who cannot resist providing you with some coaching:* They identify your strengths, but they also cannot resist pointing out some areas where they feel you could make improvements. This is fine, but you should concentrate on the positive feedback.

3. *Individuals who couple positive feedback with qualifications:* Instead of writing you are a gifted strategist, they write you are a

gifted strategist 'most of the time' or 'some of the time'. This is not helpful, and you cannot use this feedback. Fortunately, this kind of feedback is rare.

If you approach 10 people for feedback, you will typically receive 150 to 200 comments that describe your strengths. My guess is you won't have been offered positive feedback like this before. You will be both surprised and delighted. This feedback not only helps you to understand your strengths, but also provides you with a massive morale booster. And, as I discuss in the next chapter, it helps to identify those individuals who might give you strong recommendations for your LinkedIn Profile.

By the way, you may be tempted to take the feedback you received on your goodbye card or recent 360-degree feedback and use this to avoid sending out this email. This is rarely a good idea. Most goodbye cards tell you how much each person enjoyed working with you, and provide their best wishes to you for the future. And formal 360-degree feedback tends to be more administrative. Usually, the positive comments on these cards and in your 360-degree feedback, although generous, are too general and too bland. They do not go into specifics about what makes you really special in the way you think, work with others, and communicate.

STRUCTURING YOUR THINKING ABOUT WHAT MAKES YOU SPECIAL

Once you have completed your own analysis and asked others for feedback on what makes you special, you need to start structuring your findings. I suggest you analyse and group what makes you special under four headings:

1. *Your track record of achievement:* Include here your pattern of achievements over time.
2. *Your leadership strengths:* How others describe you when you are at your best as a leader.

3. *What you are known and respected for:* Skills and traits that differentiate you.

4. *Your education/professional development:* This does not always need to be formal.

As I have mentioned earlier, you need to be able to show you are a leader with a track record of achievement, with energy and with excellent judgement. I discuss the four topics from the preceding list in the following sections.

Your track record of achievement

What helps to define you is your pattern of achievement. As Daniel Kahneman points out, one achievement might show you are special, but you could just have been lucky. For most of us, achieving a low golf score one day does not guarantee we will obtain a low golf score next time we play. Far from it! Professional golfers, on the other hand, tend to achieve low golf scores consistently. If you have a consistent series of achievements, this goes a long way to supporting the idea that you are effective and you deliver impact in your job.

A particular seniority or role in an organisation is not the kind of achievement I have in mind – that is merely your job title. The impact and positive change you can point to in that role are the achievements I am seeking. The best examples of your achievements are areas where you have a track record of consistently delivering improvements and successful change, ideally in a way that outperforms others in similar situations. To communicate with maximum impact, all your achievements must be quantified. The statement that you led a company for three years during a growth phase is not compelling. A better statement is that you delivered 15 per cent per annum compound growth in earnings in three different companies during the past 10 years.

The acid test is always the positive impact you had in a particular role – and how long it took to make this difference and how significant the difference was. Growing a business may or may not be an achievement. A rising tide will lift all boats. However, being able to show you outperformed your competitors is usually a very significant achievement. At least one of your achievements must reinforce that you have made a difference as a leader of people. Effective leaders develop positive cultures and grow people. Therefore, you should show how you improved an organisational culture, or developed individuals or teams who went on to be significant contributors.

Your leadership strengths

You need to stand out clearly as a leader who makes a positive difference. Your leadership strengths relate to the ways you make a difference as part of a team, and how you deliver change and positive impact. For instance, you could be visionary, dynamic, focused on results, collaborative or persuasive. Professor Michael Shinagel, Dean of the Extension School at Harvard University, makes the point in his article 'The paradox of leadership' that, according to a recent survey, more than 15,000 books are available on leadership. Articles on leadership number in the thousands each year. An internet search for 'leadership' brings up over three billion results.

Shinagel says:

> *Leadership clearly is a crucial and abiding topic of interest to countless women and men in society. Despite the popularity of the topic, leadership remains a paradox. People who seek to understand it by reading a primer on the topic will inevitably be frustrated and disappointed. Leadership, after all, is an art, not a science. And leadership is not limited to a professional field or industry, be it corporate, governmental, military, academic, religious, or service. Leaders come in all shapes and sizes and transcend the confines of a defining box. Leaders are not born, but evolve into that role.*

Leaders emerge to replace previous leaders who have stepped down or failed. A great leader in one situation can be a failure in a different situation. People at all levels can be leaders. Warren Bennis, a noted authority on leadership, makes the point that,

The manager asks how and when; the leader asks what and why
... The most dangerous leadership myth is that leaders are born —
that there is a genetic factor to leadership. That's nonsense; in fact,
the opposite is true.

A leader usually has different qualities from a manager. As shown in table 3.6, based on the model developed by Genevieve Capowski outlined in 'Anatomy of a leader', leaders focus more on initiating change while managers focus more on stabilisation. Everyone can be a leader if they wish to be. But for anyone building stand-out skills, practice and being 'forged by fire' will also be important. The world needs both leaders and managers, and you should aim to be both an effective manager and a leader with transformational impact.

Table 3.6: Qualities of a leader versus a manager

Leader	Manager
Visionary	Rational
Creative	Persistent
Inspiring	Tough-minded
Innovative	Analytical
Courageous	Structured
Imaginative	Deliberate
Experimental	Authoritative
Initiates change	Stabilising
Personal power	Position power

In fact, many great leaders have gifts as both leaders and managers. They can see the big picture but they also have extraordinary attention to detail. Like eagles they can fly high and see the whole landscape, but at the same time they have no trouble identifying and swooping down to grab the tiny mouse in the field below.

If leaders are made rather than born, how can you show that you are a leader, or a leader in-the-making? One way is to use the feedback you received from the SFR email to your colleagues, explained above. The approach I use is to prepare a list of no more than five of the qualities your colleagues are likely to use when they describe you as a leader. I discuss how to highlight your leadership qualities in more detail in the next chapter.

What you are known and respected for

The characteristics you are known and respected for will go far beyond the usual competencies listed in CVs. They will be underlying traits, skills and attributes that others believe help you make a significant difference in a role. This includes not only your specialised functional skills such as accounting or marketing, but also traits such as effective leadership, integrity, talent acquisition, and strong negotiation skills. The feedback gained via your email will help you understand what people who have worked with you actually respect you for. This will be better than a long list of competencies developed based on your own ideas – which tends to look rather similar to the lists provided by other applicants. How do others describe what they know and respect about you? And have they done this with some kind of emotional connection?

If you have built an outstanding, widely held reputation in your business, industry or community for, say, exemplary leadership or great commercial judgement, that is a real achievement. We all know that it is difficult to build an outstanding reputation – it takes time to build, and even a seemingly small setback can damage what seems to be a fine reputation. Being widely esteemed for your skills or traits is something you can be proud of. This can and should be recognised as a special achievement.

External validation can also be important – awards can consolidate or highlight your achievements and your reputation. A word of warning, though: your photograph on the front cover of a national magazine can lead to problems rather than respect. It may be that key people question whether you are more focused on achieving personal publicity than doing your job well. Be careful about this!

Your education and professional development

Your education and professional development can be important markers of what makes you special. This is especially true if you have excelled, with academic honours or awards. If you do not have formal tertiary education, this is not necessarily a knockout. Some of the most successful people in business have never been to university or have dropped out before they completed their qualifications. But they have been well trained in the school of life. It is amazing what you learn about people if you start out collecting trollies in the supermarket carpark! Realistically, though, many recruiters and senior executives focus on your academic history and credentials as being important markers. This is especially true when you are starting out, attempting to secure your first job. These days, having educational credentials is usually essential to progress at all levels.

An important attribute in most roles is how you think about and work to serve your customers. Nigella took on the CEO role in a multibillion-dollar mobile phone company. In her first meeting with her team, she asked each member of her team an almost bewilderingly simple question: How would a tradesman decide whether to buy a mobile phone from us or our competition? Interestingly, not one of her direct reports could provide a clear answer to this simple question. This was even though they were responsible for planning and running a multibillion-dollar mobile phone business! What you know about your customers and how you think about serving them may be more important than your formal education.

It is difficult to decide what makes you special in any convincing way by yourself. Many of my clients struggle with this, particularly if they do not have the advantage of feedback from instruments such as the Birkman Method or MRG's Leadership Effectiveness Analysis. A common problem, if you work alone, is that you develop a long list of functional attributes but fail to sharpen and refine this list down to a few compelling, succinct and strategic ideas. It is tempting to write at length. Unfortunately, lengthy explanations of your attributes will usually go unread – and, if they are read, the content usually involves too much work by the reader to figure out exactly what it means. The recruiting team may also question the way you think and work because you have not taken the trouble to simplify your list. Look at your own CV to see what I mean.

I talk about the challenge of characterising your brand in the next section of this chapter. How you actually prepare to communicate this brand, in writing and verbally (intriguingly, the way you actually do this also helps to define your brand) is discussed in the next two chapters.

CREATING A STRONG PERSONAL BRAND

Whenever someone is describing you, they are describing their view of your brand. Often their description is not particularly helpful. It could be that you are 'a great person', or that you 'work in marketing'. When you are asked about yourself, you are likely to say something like, 'I work for a leading retailer.' Alf, who headed up 6000 staff in a bank that spanned the country, used to say, 'I work in a bank'. The response that he usually received was along the lines of, 'That's interesting. Which branch?' People can totally misunderstand your capability if you are too general, understated or vague. In this section, I take you through how to describe your brand in a way that is more profound and is more likely to help you obtain a senior role.

When considering how you want to position your brand, think of the following advice from Harry Beckwith:

> *In service marketing, almost nothing beats a brand, and your brand depends on integrity. Create the evidence of your service quality, then communicate it. Don't use adjectives, use stories.*

It is compelling and memorable when you talk about a time when you coached a poor performer who then went on to excel. Simply pointing out you are a good coach, without a story to illustrate this, is not as compelling.

In the following sections, I explain how you might expand your thinking about what your brand truly is. Then, in the next two chapters, I delve deeper into how you can communicate your brand.

What are your strengths and distinctive qualities?

In his article 'The brand called You', Tom Peters (co-author of *In Search of Excellence*) suggests that these days we all tend to be managing a continuous stream of projects. He argues that, as a result, we must be extremely aware of developing our personal brand so we can position ourselves to move successfully from one project to the next. He argues,

> *Regardless of age, regardless of position, regardless of the business we happen to be in, all of us must understand the importance of branding. We are CEOs of our own companies: Me Inc. To be in business today, our most important job is to be head marketer for the brand called You.*

Peters suggests that you should ask yourself the following questions when developing your personal brand:

- What is my greatest and clearest strength?
- What is my most noteworthy trait?
- What makes me different and special?
- What do I do to add remarkable, measurable, distinguished, distinctive value?
- What do I do that I am most proud of?
- What have I accomplished that I can unabashedly brag about?
- What do I want to be respected for?
- What is my personal mission statement?

This approach is valuable as a starting point. It forces you to be clear about your strengths, your noteworthy traits, and what makes you different and special. You then need to test your thinking with people who know you and respect you.

What do you stand for?

Peters' approach is tactical and focuses on your impact at work. A different and more strategic approach, which could supplement and enhance Peters' approach, is suggested by Dan Burrier, who was the Chief Innovation Officer of Ogilvy & Mather North America. In his article 'Create a Nelson Mandela brand', Burrier makes the point that a brand is not a list of attributes but a statement of your true values and what you stand for. He explains this using the example of Nelson Mandela. He explains an exercise where he asked the group to shout out attributes to sum up Mandela. Attributes such as brave, courageous, altruistic, wise, thoughtful and giving quickly filled the whiteboard. Burrier then explained the problem with this list:

> I pointed to a colleague in the room, let's call him Frank, and mused, 'The problem with the list is that it describes Nelson Mandela, and it also describes Frank, a caring, wise, thoughtful, loving, giving and peaceful father and husband. But Frank is not Nelson Mandela. Sorry, Frank.'

Burrier then asked the group what Mandela stood for. The cry of 'freedom' was unanimous. For Burrier, this highlighted the difference not only between Frank and Mandela, but also between an easy list of attributes and a true brand stance. In the forceful pursuit of this true stance in the world, the attributes you desire to be known for will follow.

Burrier makes an important point. What you stand for can be a powerful way of branding yourself. Deciding what you stand for – and pursuing this – can be challenging but taking the time to think deeply about this is worthwhile. Test your thinking with those who you respect.

What is your purpose?

In his *Harvard Business Review* article 'How will you measure your life', Clayton Christensen (former professor at Harvard Business School) talks about knowing your purpose. This question is different from 'What do I stand for?' and is, for Christensen, the most important thing anyone can discover:

> *If they don't figure it out, they will just sail off without a rudder and get buffeted in the very rough seas of life. Clarity about their purpose will trump knowledge of activity-based costing, balanced scorecards, core competence, disruptive innovation, the four Ps, and the five forces.*

He goes on to say that he decided that the purpose of his life was to teach, and he believes his life won't be assessed based on the amount of money he has earned but by the number of individual lives he has touched and those he has helped make better people. He argues this is how it works for everyone. His final recommendation?

> *Think about the metric by which your life will be judged and make a resolution to live every day so that, in the end, your life will be judged a success.*

If you know your purpose, you might find it relatively easy to articulate your brand. If you have not thought about what your purpose is, however, spend time giving this question real thought. Few of us would do what Christensen did – which was to set aside one hour a day to consider his purpose throughout high school and university. Both this article from Christensen and also Drucker's 'Managing oneself' are worth reading to help you think about this. Being between jobs might be the only period in your life when you have the luxury of real time to give these issues deep consideration.

The question also arises as to how you can turn your purpose into action and deliver impact. In their *Harvard Business Review* article 'From purpose to impact – figure out your passion and put it to work', Nick Craig and Scott Snook suggest a process for developing a concise purpose statement and a purpose-to-impact plan. Their approach is to 'mine your life for major themes that reveal your lifelong passions and values'. They then suggest an approach to developing three- to five-year goals, and a pathway to achieving these.

Structuring your thinking about your brand

If you consider the factors in the preceding sections, how can you display your situation simply and clearly? One way of doing this is to use the structure shown in figure 3.3. This differentiates the factors you can control, like the content of your LinkedIn profile, on the right side of the figure, from the factors that others may perceive when they see you physically or in the media while doing an internet search, on the left side. The idea here is that it is desirable for each segment of the circle to be consistent with the other segments, and that, as a whole, they project the brand you desire.

Figure 3.3: Building a consistent personal brand

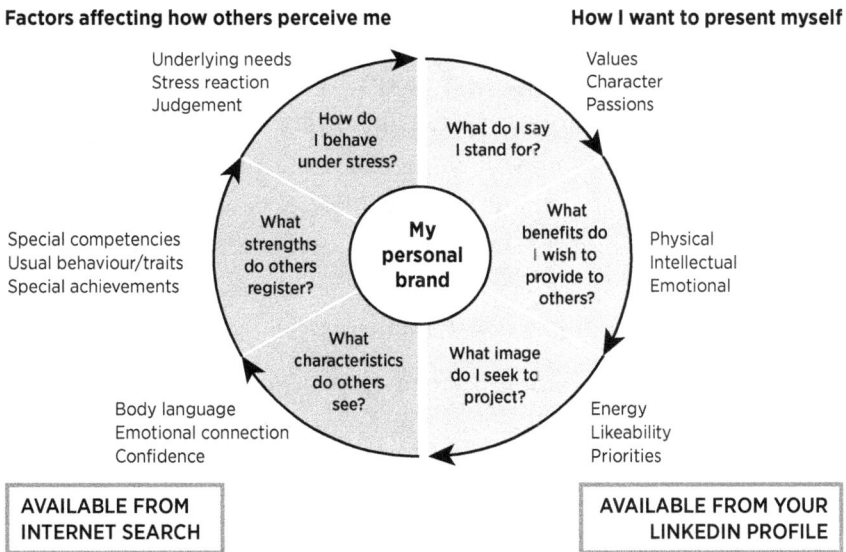

Factors affecting how others perceive me   **How I want to present myself**

Underlying needs
Stress reaction
Judgement

Values
Character
Passions

How do I behave under stress?

What do I say I stand for?

Special competencies
Usual behaviour/traits
Special achievements

What strengths do others register?

My personal brand

What benefits do I wish to provide to others?

Physical
Intellectual
Emotional

What characteristics do others see?

What image do I seek to project?

Body language
Emotional connection
Confidence

Energy
Likeability
Priorities

AVAILABLE FROM INTERNET SEARCH

AVAILABLE FROM YOUR LINKEDIN PROFILE

What makes you special is far more than a list of attributes or a combination of key competences. Can you speak from your heart about what makes you special, particularly what you stand for and your purpose? If you can do this, your description will be much more profound than the usual list of basic competencies set out on a typical CV.

THE IMPORTANCE OF BEING VISIBLE TO KEY DECISION MAKERS

If you wish to progress, performing well and having a distinctive brand are fundamental. But it will also be vital that you are visible in a positive way to the key decision makers who might influence your progress. That is the people who must "vote" for you if you are to progress. Your annual assessment may well be based on your work performance during the preceding year. But your career progression is likely to depend on your perceived potential to add value in the future. To progress, you must not only ensure that others appreciate and value what makes you special and your brand, but also that you are visible in a positive way to the relevant decision makers.

Harvey Coleman, the author of *Empowering Yourself, The Organizational Game Revealed*, discusses the relative importance of **Performance**, **Image** and **Exposure** (the **PIE** model) in influencing your progress. Coleman argues that having positive exposure to those who will influence your progress will be the key factor dictating your ultimate career success. Even if you are an extraordinary performer with huge potential, you are unlikely to progress unless you are visible to those who can influence your career. As shown in figure 3.4, Coleman says:

- Even if you are a strong performer, your job performance will account for only 10% of your future success.

- Much more important will be the brand you present to others, and how other people perceive you, at 30%.

- But, most important of all will be having positive exposure to relevant decision makers, with 60% of your career success depending on this.

This, according to Coleman, will be true whether you are seeking to progress within an organisation or elsewhere. Of course, this is why I argue, in chapter 7, that building warm relationships and expanding your network are both vital if you are seeking a new role. Remember, if you are not visible, you are invisible!

*Figure 3.4: Make sure that key decision makers know about you
and your potential*

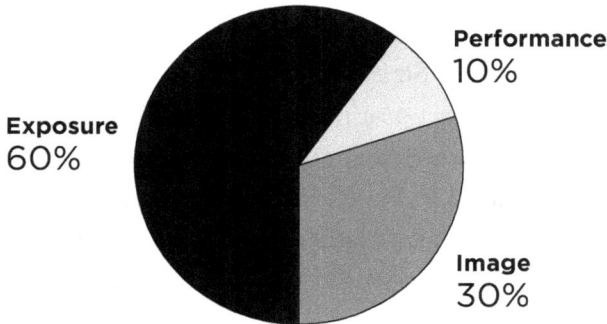

PERFORMANCE (10%)
- Enhancing the breadth and depth of your skills and experience.
- Ensuring consistent high quality in your work.
- Delivering what you promise and having measurable impact.

IMAGE (30%)
- Projecting a positive, authentic personal brand.
- Maintaining calm behaviour under stress.
- Displaying a growth mindset and resilience.

EXPOSURE (60%)
- Building positive relationships and conveying your possible future value.
- Making your contributions and growth potential visible.
- Building trust with key decision-makers and identifying sponsors.

A story related to the extraordinary international *bel canto* soprano, Nellie Melba, presents an excellent way of describing the power of Coleman's PIE model. According to Ann Blainey, Melba's biographer, in the early 1900s Melba was the most famous woman in the world. She was lauded – almost worshipped – throughout Europe, the US and Australia. In 1894, when she was in her early thirties, she sang in New York to astonishing acclaim: "Women wept hysterically and men shouted themselves hoarse". Oscar Hammerstein said of her: "Nobody sings like Melba, and nobody ever will".

Ten years earlier, she had been recognised by her teachers in Australia as having the potential to be a world-class soprano. She was urged to audition in the UK and in Europe. She went with her father to London. There she auditioned with various leading impresarios, including Sir Arthur Sullivan of Gilbert and Sullivan fame. But she made no progress in London. Her father agreed to pay to send her for one final audition. An audition was arranged with Madame Mathilde Marchesi, a highly regarded *bel canto* singing teacher in Paris. Melba's father made it clear that, if this audition was not successful, Nellie would have to return to Australia.

Half way though Melba's audition in Paris, Marchesi stopped playing the piano and shouted: "*At last, I have found a star*" (in French, of course!). This single event transformed Melba's life. Marchesi not only refined Melba's singing and performance technique (her **Performance**), but also the way she dressed and presented herself socially and on stage (her **Image**). This included changing her name from Mrs Helen Armstrong to Melba (after her home town, Melbourne), "so that Europeans can remember and pronounce your name". In addition, Marchesi was able to introduce Melba to all the key influencers in opera in Europe, the UK, and the US (her **Exposure**).

It has been said that a coach talks "to you", a mentor talks "with you", and a sponsor talks "about you". In the case of Melba, Marchesi was all three of these. And as Melba developed, each element of her PIE became self-reinforcing. This led to Melba becoming pre-eminent worldwide as an opera singer. Without Marchesi, it is likely that Melba would have returned to live in Australia as Mrs Helen Armstrong, without becoming world-famous. What did Marchesi see (and hear) that Sullivan missed? How different would Melba's life have been if she had given in too early, before she met someone who could recognise her true potential? Make sure you work to enhance your exposure to people who might not only vote for you but also go on to mentor and sponsor you! I discuss this further in chapter 8.

★★★

To be effective in a senior role, play to your strengths. Your strengths are the most important part of what makes you special. We all like to think we are special but most of us struggle to explain how we are special in a clear and succinct way. When put to the test, we cannot describe our strengths precisely, and then group these strengths in a powerful way. If we cannot describe our strengths clearly and objectively, we are underselling ourselves. If we don't know what makes us special, we may not be able to differentiate ourselves sufficiently from the others whom we are competing with on the shortlist for a senior role.

As a senior jobseeker, you must think about what makes you special and what differentiates you in a totally different way from more junior people. You cannot just use a long list of attributes or competencies. The better approach is to describe your ideas under five strategic headings – first, your experience and senior roles; second, your track record of achievement; third, your leadership strengths; fourth, what you are known and respected for; and fifth, your education and professional development. If, in addition to describing your strengths, you can describe your purpose and what you stand for in a compelling way, you will immediately stand out from the crowd.

Remember, what you intuitively believe makes you special may be wrong. So understanding what other people think makes you special is vital. The best way to achieve this is to seek feedback from people you have worked with and who have seen you at your best. You will be surprised how strong and supportive your colleagues will be. You are likely to find they praise you in ways that are totally unexpected. You can use this as evidence of what other people who have worked with you believe, rather than trying to guess your strengths. As a result, you will be authentic and will be able to speak about your strengths from your heart.

Finally, of course, it is no good if you are talented and have a great brand but key decision makers have never heard of you. You cannot allow yourself to be invisible, working diligently in some back room. Despite what many people believe, it is rare for results to speak for themselves. If your contributions are not visible you are unlikely to progress further or to be offered new opportunities to contribute. Being a good performer but being invisible is not a recipe for success. Are others aware of the value you are adding? And do they recognise your potential to contribute more in the future? By the way, being visible does not mean that you need to be a self-promoter. Rather you must consider how you can contribute to activities and groups, inside and outside your organisation, where the people who might support you can see you in action and learn more about you. Having supportive mentors and sponsors can be a huge asset in this regard.

In the next chapter, I discuss how you can frame your career goals and use your strengths and brand to write compelling materials to support your job-seeking process. I also show you how you can explain to others in writing, clearly and succinctly, what you want to achieve in your career. Then, in the following chapter, I suggest several ways to communicate your strengths verbally as you seek a job.

SOME QUESTIONS FOR YOU TO CONSIDER

- What are the attributes that make you special?
- Can you explain your 'signature strengths'?
- Can you frame these into the following five main areas?
  1. Values
  2. Behaviours
  3. Competencies
  4. Experience
  5. Energy and drive
- Are you willing to find out what others think makes you special?
- Who are the 10 people who have seen you at your best, and who could describe what makes you special?
- Can you structure what makes you special into five groups?
  1. Your experience and roles
  2. Your track record of achievements
  3. Your leadership strengths
  4. What you are known and respected for
  5. Your education and qualifications
- Is your personal brand clear and easy to communicate?
- Can you articulate what you stand for and your purpose?
- Is this consistent with how other people see you?
- How can you project the brand you desire?
- Are you and your work visible enough the key decision makers?

4

Writing about your strengths

We want to make our points more clearly, more elegantly; we want our writing to be appreciated, to be more effective.

Benjamin Dreyer, Copy Chief at Random House
and author of *Dreyer's English*

WORKING OUT WHAT makes you special is one thing. Being able to communicate your message in writing in an appealing way — and with impact — is quite a different challenge. If you can present what makes you special simply and clearly in writing, this will, in itself, make you special. Too many people overcomplicate their communications. Effective communication involves both strong substance and compelling style. As I noted in the previous chapter, the most important aspect of your communication is how it makes your audience feel. Many in the job-seeking process do not understand this. They think the information aspect of the content is all that matters. But this is wrong. A robot can play a piano concerto perfectly, but most of us are not going to buy tickets to hear a robot play a piano concerto. Great pianists connect with their audiences through their heart. Preparing yourself and your message is important so that you too connect through your heart. If you can do this, your reader is likely to feel good. If not, they may have no emotional connection at all. In fact, they may feel totally unconnected. As noted by best-selling author Harry Beckwith in

Selling the Invisible, 'Make your service [that's you!] vivid in words and pictures: you cannot bore someone into buying a service.'

People often believe that the main service provided by career transition coaches is to help you to write your CV. For senior jobseekers, this could not be further from the truth. CVs are administrative risk-management documents designed for recruiters and human resource executives. They are chronological lists to help these people understand what jobs you have had, and what you achieved in each job. CVs by themselves can be satisfactory for junior roles but, for senior jobseekers, they are a poor way to communicate your strengths. In many cases, if you wish to put someone to sleep, read your CV aloud to them. They will soon be nodding off.

Brevity and clarity and impact are crucial. They are the keys to getting your written message through and reinforcing that you are special. To be brief and clear and have impact, think deeply in advance. If your writing has these attributes it will immediately differentiate you from your competition. This is because many people preparing CVs and presentations do not understand the power of brevity and clarity. They try to cram as much information on to the page as possible, narrowing the margins and reducing the size of the print. Doing so is an immediate sign you have not given your document enough thought.

I work on the principle that virtually no-one wants to read your CV. In addition, if you can actually get anyone to read it, they will not want to have to think about what you are trying to say. I don't blame them. Why must they be forced to read long, poorly constructed documents that are unclear and full of incomprehensible jargon? Why must they have to try to work out what a particular job title means? Why must they have to track how your career evolved and why two jobs seem to be overlapping? Why must they have to try to make sense of material that is disjointed and poorly formatted? Why must they have to try to work out what information is important and what is peripheral? Why must they have to try to work out what impact you actually had in your various jobs? You need to minimise the work required of the reader, not push more work on to them.

In this chapter, I outline some approaches to preparing clear and brief written communications. Your goal is to present yourself well and with maximum impact. The approaches I cover have worked for me and my clients, but they are more difficult to master than you might assume. Once you have prepared a draft document, ask someone else to critique it. This could be your coach or an editor. An independent review will help you simplify your work and improve its clarity and impact. If you fail to put enough work into what and how you will communicate, and into polishing it, you risk being knocked out of a recruitment process before you get to first base.

I discuss in this chapter how to write four different documents well, providing examples. These documents are:

- *Professional Profile:* A two-page marketing document for use in networking.
- *LinkedIn Profile:* Crucial in delivering your career message to the world.
- *CV:* Important for recruiters and HR directors, but virtually no-one else.
- *Cover Letter:* Sometimes, but not always, important for recruiters.

Each of these documents has a different role to play in presenting you, and each deserves real effort. But the most important of the four is your Professional Profile. If you get this right, the others follow easily. It requires deep thought and several rewrites. The discipline of putting your story on to two pages is an important part of the challenge you will face. Before I get to the four documents, however, I explain why it is important to write the documents you will use in this process as well as you possibly can.

WRITING WELL

The work involved in writing about yourself must not be under-estimated. As William Zinsser argues in *On Writing Well*, his classic guide to writing non-fiction that has sold over one million copies:

> *Writing is hard work. A clear sentence is no accident. Very few sentences come out right the first time, or even the third time. Remember this in moments of despair. If you find that writing is hard, it's because it is hard … The newly hatched sentence almost always has something wrong with it. It's not clear. It's not logical. It's verbose. It's clunky. It's pretentious. It's boring. It's full of clutter. It's full of clichés. It lacks rhythm. It can be read in several different ways … The point is that clever writing is the result of a lot of tinkering.*

If good writing is this difficult for a writer who makes his living out of writing, where do you – as a senior jobseeker who does not make a living out of writing – start? First of all, remember the old, but extremely powerful, dictum: *'Don't get it right, get it written'*. Decide who you are writing for, and then get something down on paper. After that, work to make it simple and clear. This will take thought, time and several revisions. 'Give me one day and I will give you 10 pages. Give me 10 days and I will give you one page,' wrote Stephen King, the American author who has sold over 350 million books. Stephen King is a professional writer who knows how difficult it is to write something brief.

For most of us, our documents are unlikely to communicate effectively unless we obtain help. Paradoxically, so-called professional CV writers are often not the answer. They are good at presenting attractive layouts and graphic designs, but they do not always go through the hard yards with you to ensure the content is clear, accurate and compelling. Having said this, you will benefit immensely by having someone independent, if they help structure your thinking, help you prepare the documents you need, and also critique your work. Ideally, this should be your career transition coach because he or she will know more about you, your background and your goals than anyone else. Next best would be an editor or professional writer. You need someone who will give you frank feedback. If you are not working with a coach or a professional, ask a friend who can think critically and write well to be brutally honest about your efforts. You are likely to learn a great deal.

In the following section, I outline how I suggest you prepare your Professional Profile. This profile is a document that describes you in two pages.

CREATING YOUR PROFESSIONAL PROFILE

How do you market and sell yourself as you go through the process of building your network? Through what I call a Professional Profile. Think of this as a two-page marketing document for networking.

The power of your Professional Profile

Your Professional Profile is designed to be used when you are networking, and is a strong way of describing what makes you special to people who may be able to assist you in one way or another. These people do not want to read a long document loaded with information about your whole career to date. They want something simple where interesting information jumps off the page. They are trying to help you, but they don't want to have to figure out what all the writing means. They just want to know what makes you special. When they introduce you to someone they know, they want to be able to do this in a sentence or two. The Professional Profile is designed to clearly showcase what makes you special and make this introduction easy.

Remember – most people won't read your CV, so it shouldn't be used for networking. Even a reasonably good CV for a senior jobseeker generally tends to be a rather boring administrative document. One reason for this is that many people focus on writing down their job titles and roles rather than their achievements. And, even if they describe their achievements, they do not quantify them. CVs are also likely to be unbalanced because they describe the early part of your career – which is of least importance if you are a senior jobseeker – and this takes up disproportionate space. A CV is rarely a good way to show that you are a leader with a track record of achievement, with great commercial judgement and with positive energy. Again, you are in the marketing business, and to market yourself well, you need something better than a 5- to 10-page historical CV.

Be aware, though, that many recruiters will not like or accept your two-page Professional Profile because it does not show your complete job history. You will need your chronological CV for them. I take you through how to prepare a CV for recruiters towards the end of this chapter.

Preparing your Professional Profile

Your Professional Profile is designed to achieve 10 things as simply, clearly and efficiently as possible. If it is well prepared, your Professional Profile, in two pages, will:

- assist you to think clearly about your career and your special strengths

- summarise your story in a tight and compelling way

- provide the highlights of the last 10 years of your career

- set out and define your senior roles and responsibilities

- illustrate your history of achievement and of delivering positive impact

- show you are a leader with good commercial judgement and positive energy

- highlight you have important traits that are respected by your colleagues

- show you have other interests beyond your work and career

- provide a strong way of presenting yourself to people in your network

- provide most of the information you need to prepare a strong LinkedIn Profile.

Writing a quality Professional Profile is much tougher than writing a CV. It will, as Stephen King suggests, take 10 times as long. I recommend a strict standard format for your Professional Profile. Of course, you can design it any way you believe makes sense for you, but the format I suggest here is a proven approach.

My suggested format rules are:

- Use Arial (no smaller than 10 point) or Calibri (no smaller than 11 point) as the typeface for the body of the document.
- Highlight each section with a heading in bold type.
- Use a different but understated colour (such as dark blue) for section headings to help give the document more life and make it easier to read.
- Ensure spacing between lines is 1.15, and between sections is 12 point.
- Keep margins standard (narrow margins make the document look cramped).
- For the headers, ensure the front page shows 'Professional Profile' in the top right corner, and your name is in bold and is in the same position on the back page.

Note that some of these format rules have been adjusted in the sample Professional Profile shown here, to fit the profile to the page size of this book.

Suggested layout for the front page of your Professional Profile

The front page of your Professional Profile usually has four sections, as shown in figure 4.1.

I cover these four areas below.

Figure 4.1: The front page of your Professional Profile

Professional Profile

ROBERTO MORATTA

M: +6567 147 486   **E:** robertomoratta@gmail.com   **L:** www.linkedin.com/in/robertomoratta

Creative & digitally-savvy senior executive. Strong values. Highly collaborative.
Drives sustainable results. Strategic leader who builds high-performing teams.

SENIOR EXECUTIVE ROLES

United International Banking Corporation, Singapore (Rev. $25B)   **2003–2020**

Series of senior leadership roles. Responsible for leading complex business digital transformation & growth.

SVP Roles: *To build a culture of innovation, collaboration, and value creation – teams of 100, annual budgets up to $20M*

- ***Customer Experience & Service Innovation, Consumer Div. (2016–2020).*** 'Agile' ways of working.
- ***Business Development, Strategy & M&A (2015–2016).*** Think and operate like an entrepreneur.

VP Roles: *To transform and deliver sustainable value through digital – teams of 50, annual budgets up to $10M*

- ***Digital, United Group Business Bank (2010–2015).*** Accelerate growth of sales and self-servicing.
- ***Business Transformation, Retail & Business Bank*** (2010–2011). Online Transformation Prog.
- ***Business Online, Retail & Business Bank*** (2006–2009). Grow sales and service capability.
- ***Online Banking, IT*** (2005–2006). Oversee IT development of Online Banking platform.

Prior roles: Program Ajax CRM (2001–2005) United Bank; GM IT – Telecom Group (1994–2001)

KEY BUSINESS ACHIEVEMENTS

Directed design & change of digital platform, attaining global ranking of #1 in mobile banking: Award by Forrester. Project involved >$600M multi-year, highly complex digital change. Digital NPS increase 38 -> 44 in Business, 46 -> 54 in Consumer. Increased mobile "on-the-go" features for business customers. Introduced next generation digital authentication and security.

Devised and executed strategies to accelerate digital sales and service for Business: Generated 30+% increase in customers adopting self-service for transactional banking, 40% YOY growth of online sales, & 11% of bank-wide sales to SME. Simplified account opening & credit card acquisition. Delivered one-stop-shop STP of accounts for new SMEs. Short-listed for Good Design Award 2016.

Built and cultivated high performing diverse teams: Restructured teams & developed talent. Transformed skills from "IT order-takers" to initiators. Delivered rapid results. Without investment, increased Online availability by 20%. Increased payment limits for customers. Engagement scores (av. 80s). Nurtured customer focus. Delivered ambitious business goals and sustainable value creation.

Successfully piloted agile ways of working: Baselined service design for Everyday Banking & Consumer Finance. Operationalised two cross-functional agile squads to uplift customer/staff experience and business performance. Developed customer & data-led strategy to regain service leadership. Led to internal MFI measurement change. Justified continuation of investment.

Name and contact details

This information can be kept simple and clear. You don't need to provide your address or a photograph. You also don't follow your name with degrees, honours or membership details of professional organisations. Use a professional email address. Keep everything as simple as possible.

Your branding statement

This should be directly after your name and contact details, and stand out. The key test of a good branding statement is this: does the reader see clearly that you are a successful leader with positive energy and excellent commercial judgement? My rules are that it must be no more, and no less, than two lines, with a total of 20 to 24 words. The two-line statement is composed of three to five phrases – not one single sentence. It is in blue bold italics, and is a slightly larger font size than the body of the document. The final phrase on the top line should not run into the second line. This branding statement is usually finalised as the last step before completing the document. It takes time to work out how to make this branding statement brutally succinct. Every word is important.

An outline of your senior management career

Again, the goal is to be strong and simple. Highlight your leadership roles over the past 10 years or so. Give your employers prominence and then set out your specific roles – if you had more than one – at each employer. I like to abbreviate titles. For instance, I prefer CEO to Chief Executive Officer. Sometimes your roles must be explained, particularly if your title is not self-explanatory. Provide some information about the scale of your role, and the city in which you were based. Ideally, the information related to each role should be kept to one line, and the information provided in this section should be structured so that it is symmetrical. Your jobs will be shown in reverse chronological order. The one exception to listing jobs this way could be if you have been responsible for important roles in different, unconnected parts of a large organisation. Then it might be necessary to group the types of roles, to reinforce your expertise in each specific area, rather than showing the roles in reverse chronological order. After the outline of the last 10 years of your senior career, you can add a line or two starting with 'Prior roles ...' to provide some information about your roles leading up to the ones set out in this section. If you have been self-employed between roles – say, doing some consulting – I recommend that you do not show this in your list of key senior roles. You can add some brief information about your consulting roles in the 'Prior roles' section, if these were important.

Your key business achievements

The overriding idea in this section is to summarise your ongoing pattern of achievements, highlighting particular classes of achievements. For instance, you might have built a series of businesses, or transformed the cultures in a series of roles. Highlight that you have been able to make a difference and have had a positive impact in your various roles over time. Showing that you have a series of similar achievements reinforces the idea that you have a history of success. This is more compelling than an individual achievement where you might just have been lucky. For example, building three businesses is better than building one business!

Only present four or five classes of achievement. The bold headline for each achievement should begin with a verb (for example, built, developed, delivered, improved, led, launched) and it should take up less than one line. Your achievements should be quantified if at all possible. Highlighting that you grew revenues or profits by 20 per cent compound for five years is much more compelling and memorable than a general message that you delivered growth. And at least one of your achievements should relate to building successful teams (remember, you are a leader!) or leading positive cultural change, or both. If you have built a strong reputation for something special, include this as an achievement.

I believe symmetry is important. My rules are:

- Each major class of achievement should take no more than five lines
- Your achievements should not run past the end of the front page
- Your achievements should clearly support your brand.

For example, if you state you are a business builder in your initial branding statement, your key business achievements should support this. A particular job title or job level is not an achievement in itself. The key question has to be: What impact did you have in this role and can this be quantified? Each group of achievements must be at roughly the same level of abstraction as the others that you have set out, and take the same number of lines. Don't, for instance, highlight one outstanding class of achievement with one headline that sits next to a series of much less impressive achievements.

Try to achieve balance and symmetry while keeping in mind the idea of making the reader feel you are impressive and effective. People remember how you make them feel. We want readers to feel that you are structured and professional and a strong thinker – and a leader. They will believe this if they can see that you have invested real effort in explaining yourself and what you have achieved!

Suggested layout for the back page of your Professional Profile

On the back page of your Professional Profile, I recommend five main sections, as shown in figure 4.2.

I cover these five areas below.

Your education and professional development

For this section, list your education and development in reverse chronological order. For your education, put your university at the start of the line, followed by your academic degree. If you received honours, distinctions or prizes, note these. Try to keep each entry on one line if possible. If you do not have a degree, this section can be omitted.

You can also list your professional development activities in this section. Put the name of the institution or organisation you attended first. If you have attended a multitude of training courses over your career, these could be summarised or even omitted – unless they help to differentiate you dramatically. If your professional development activities have been extensive, you may wish to put them into a separate section headed 'Professional Development'.

Leadership strengths

Here you are emphasising the strengths that make you a leader in your area. Do this by selecting some bold headings that emphasise that you take charge and make a difference. In the example provided, the words selected are:

> Strategic and analytical; Values-driven and open;
> Results oriented with grit; Grows and develops talent;
> Collaborative and creative.

Use selected quotes from the email responses you received from your ex-colleagues, as set out in the previous chapter. These words highlight what makes you special. Use italics rather than quotation marks to show the quotes you have used from responses to your SFR email. You do not need to attribute the individual quotes or phases. Which colleague provided which quote does not matter to the reader. Sometimes you may need to alter a quote slightly to abbreviate it or change the tense, but make sure that the quotes are completely faithful to the intention of the person providing the feedback.

To explain what you are doing, include the following in the title in italics: *'supported by selected quotes in italics from recent 360-degree feedback'*. The process involved in building this section probably needs multiple drafts to select and crystallise the preferred quotes. You may find that the original characteristics you selected are supported by only a few quotes, but another characteristic is

Figure 4.2: The back page of your Professional Profile

Roberto Moratta

EDUCATION

Company Directors Course: Graduate (Order of Merit) 2021

BIRMINGHAM UNIVERSITY, UK: BSC. (HONS) SCIENCE – 1987; MSC. INFO. TECHNOLOGY – 1988

LEADERSHIP STRENGTHS *– SUPPORTED BY SELECTED QUOTES FROM RECENT 360° FEEDBACK IN ITALICS*

Strategic and analytical *– True leader. Big picture. Sees horizon of 10 years. Focuses on innovation. Master of navigating ambiguity. Analyses and cuts through. Has intellect and expertise.*

Values-driven and open *– Open and honest style. Positive. Leads by example. An inspiration. Strong values and principles. Empathetic. Positive attitude. Puts team and organisation before self. Articulate.*

Results oriented with grit *– "Can do" approach. Meets deadlines. Sees things to completion. Takes out obstacles. Operationally savvy. Customer first mind-set. Actively listens and adapts. Has presence.*

Grows and develops talent *– Passionate and caring leader. Stretches people to reach their potential. Empowers people to own their work. Teaches whilst doing the work. Lines-up skill sets and career goals.*

Collaborative and creative *– Great team mindset. Creative approach to find solutions. Simplifies using drawing/diagrams. Drives business strategy and outcomes through Human Centred Design.*

KNOWN AND RESPECTED FOR:

Purpose driven leadership: Building high performing teams to deliver outstanding results.

Passion for customer: Customer obsession. Anchors problem-solving with customer benefit.

Lateral and strategic thinker: Distils insight and develops into actions. Logical and thoughtful.

Innovative & technically astute: Balances tech. investment with sustainable commercial outcomes.

Strong values: Treats people as equals. Inclusive, respectful of others. Will do what is right.

INVOLVEMENT IN ENTREPRENEURIAL PARTNERSHIPS

Biosystem Advances: Developed strategy. Took further equity in **Pattern Pay** (tri-party claim and payments provider) and explored **Redcoats:** (TripAdvisor for logistics providers).

Biometrics/Identity Verification: Sourced a contactless facial identity verification solution by KKL Labs to accurately and securely verify new customers in the digital account opening process.

PERSONAL BACKGROUND & INTERESTS

Background: Born in Italy. Brought up in UK. Citizen of Singapore. Married, with two teenage children.

Work locations: Lived and worked in NYC, Sydney, London, Singapore, and Leicester.

Activities: Travelling, painting, tennis, bush-walking and keeping fit. NED: Planck Global Foundation.

supported by many quotes. If you have just a few quotes to support your leadership strength, you may need to revisit this. Limit the quotes to two lines to support each leadership strength. As you network, many of those you meet will find these quotes very compelling. In fact, a number of my clients have told me that this feedback from their ex-colleagues swung the hiring decision in their favour.

The following provides one example of how you can summarise feedback received to fit the required format for this section.

Summarising the quotes received from the email

Original email feedback before editing:

'You create a passion for success and this passion is infectious. You build rapport, are smart, and razor sharp. You see the future, articulate a vision, and are optimistic. You are pragmatic and fun. You make people want to give their best. You inspire people with energy & aspiration. Everyone knows you have their back. You lead people to continually grow and achieve.'

Abbreviated version for use in Professional Profile:

Inspiring. Creates infectious passion for success. Builds rapport. Smart & razor sharp. Sees the future & articulates a vision. Optimistic & pragmatic. Leader with energy. Fun.

Although these quotes are important for networking, be aware that some recruiters may not be impressed by these leadership quotes, no matter how positive the feedback you receive. Recruiters are in the risk-management business. They want to know what makes you special, but may be more interested in understanding issues that may derail you in a new job. Some of you may also not be comfortable if the feedback you receive is too complimentary, but I urge you to use even the quotes that you feel are overly generous. As I mentioned earlier, no-one I have worked with has ever been accused of overselling themselves, even though they sometimes feel the quotes are embarrassingly complimentary! If you are asked about a particular quote, you can explain that you received the feedback from one of your colleagues in recent 360 feedback.

Known and respected for

This is much more than a list of your functional competencies. The test is whether your colleagues, if you asked them, would confirm that you are actually not only "known for" but also "respected for" these attributes. The obvious question for you is: Who knows about these competences and who respects you for them? You need to be able to answer this question! Limit your list to five or so traits. In the example provided, the traits selected are:

> Purpose-driven leadership; Passion for customer;
> Lateral and strategic thinker; Innovative & technically
> astute; Strong values.

Limiting your list can be difficult because you may be able to think of a long list of competencies for yourself. I suggest that you limit the list to five ideas. Do not repeat the same ideas that are already presented under your leadership strengths. Support the characteristics that you list with words on the remainder of the line that explain why you are respected for this characteristic.

Special skills

Re-emphasise certain attributes and experience that might help to differentiate you from other senior jobseekers. This section builds on the front page of your Professional Profile, and provides more detail. Include experiences or capabilities you wish to emphasise, such as transactions you have been involved in or your business agility. This agility might include your ability to work in different sized businesses across different countries and cultures. Another possibility is to emphasise your experience at merging businesses and capturing synergies. In the example provided the topic chosen for the special skills section was:

> Involvement in entrepreneurial partnerships.

Personal background and interests

Most people you meet while you are networking will be interested in you and your family. What do you do outside work? What do you care about? How do you contribute to your community? What are your hobbies and other interests? I know one recruiter who looks at this part of the profile first, to see whether you are at all interesting above and beyond your work!

Some final points

Preparing this Professional Profile document by yourself is difficult. The editing requires laser-like focus on each word to make the document tight and clear. If you do not have someone you trust to help you, use Grammarly or another powerful grammar and spelling app to review your document. This software will highlight areas where your grammar or words must be improved or clarified.

Should you prepare different Professional Profiles for different situations? I recommend against this. Too much work is involved. What I suggest is that you reposition your profile by using your cover letter to reinforce the strengths that are required in the particular situation you are exploring. I discuss how to prepare a cover letter later in this chapter. Should you be seeking assistance from ChatGPT or another similar AI service to prepare your Professional Profile? I am not convinced right now. It is possible that AI could improve your grammar or presentation but, if you have been careful, your Professional Profile will contain information that's so personal and so tightly framed that I am not convinced you will benefit much or at all by using AI. But this all could change given the rate of development in this area!

PREPARING YOUR LINKEDIN PROFILE

According to LinkedIn, its platform currently has over 1.2 billion registered users worldwide, with over 300 million of these users active on a monthly basis. Even more importantly, 90 million of these users are senior-level influencers, and 63 million are in decision-making positions. Increasingly, companies are implementing customer relationship management (CRM) solutions that directly access candidates on LinkedIn, rather than relying on their own in-house candidate databases. More and more companies are using LinkedIn to bypass recruiting firms and target candidates directly for hard-to-fill roles.

It is vital, therefore, to present yourself well on LinkedIn. It will be a key part of your marketing and your networking armament. Prepare a clear, simple and strong profile. If you have not given much attention to LinkedIn before now (probably because you did not need to do so), you need to invest some significant time to learn how to use the system to your advantage. It will prove to be a powerful tool for you. One important advantage of LinkedIn is that you have complete control over the contents of your personal site. It is a rare client who achieves a score of even five out of 10 from me for the quality of their LinkedIn Profile when I first meet them.

LinkedIn will be a vital aid as you start to build your network. If you do not have over 500 connections, try to build your connections to at least this number (after you have upgraded your profile as suggested in the next section). This should not be difficult. Look at adding work colleagues and ex-colleagues, school and university friends, and individuals you have met at conferences and meetings. Once you begin connecting with people you know, the system prompts you with new names of people you might know. Don't be tempted to connect to people you do not know, and don't accept invitations from strangers, unless in special circumstances. In my case, my one exception is that I do accept invitations from university students from my alma mater even if I do not know them. I do this because I want to assist them to expand their networks with senior people.

My straightforward method for setting up a LinkedIn Profile involves you preparing 10 individual elements. The best way to do this is to prepare a Word document (or similar) and, once you have completed this and had it checked by your career transition coach or other trusted expert, upload it to LinkedIn.

Preparing the header section of your LinkedIn Profile

The first section of your LinkedIn Profile involves four elements.

Your headshot

Use a coloured headshot that is good quality – and where you look happy rather than glum! The photo does not need to be studio quality. Ideally, the background behind you in the headshot should be plain white or dark brown. Avoid any distracting backgrounds or unusual colours. You need to project a simple, strong, and professional image. The lighting on your face should come from the side not directly from the front. Crop your head tight so that it fills at least 60 per cent of the picture. Can we see the colour of your eyes? Do not have yourself pictured somewhere far in the background so that it is almost impossible to see you!

Your profile background

LinkedIn provides a standard background behind the circle that contains your headshot. This background is designed by LinkedIn to be simple and warm. Many people personalise this background with a photograph or graphic that they believe is inspiring. The key is to avoid the background being distracting or overwhelming. If you have written a book or wish to promote an idea, you could present a suitable graphic here.

The message flag beneath your photograph

LinkedIn permits you to attach a 'flag' under your photograph to indicate that you are 'open to work'. Unless you are starting out in your career, do not use this feature because it can devalue your profile if you are a senior jobseeker. But you should definitely use the option provided by LinkedIn to circulate your profile to recruiters.

If you do choose to use this feature, do not trigger it until you have completed a high-quality LinkedIn Profile. Most recruiters have their own search engines to scan LinkedIn, and research indicates over 75 per cent of recruiters use LinkedIn to search for prospective candidates.

Your branding statement

Use about 14 words from the branding statement at the top of your Professional Profile for your LinkedIn branding statement. The profile headline and recent job title are weighted heavily in LinkedIn's search algorithms as well as recruiter behaviour. The idea is to keep your statement to no more than two lines on the screen. These words will indicate your level, such as CEO or SVP (Senior Vice President), and what makes you special. The following example of a branding statement is 14 words long:

> SVP. Creative & digitally-savvy. Strong values. Strategic leader. Collaborative. Builds high-performing teams.

Do not set out a list of totally unconnected roles (although some may recommend this as a way to attract more search exposure). For instance, don't use a sequence such as CEO | CFO | Director | Team Builder | Global Executive. This is confusing and difficult to interpret. Anyone reading this has to try to work out exactly what you are – and they're unlikely to bother. In the worst case, they may take the view that you do not know what you are, and treat you accordingly. Once you have a new role, you might decide to replace your branding statement with your new title. This is up to you.

Preparing the About section of your LinkedIn Profile

Figure 4.3 shows an example of the way to set up the second section of your profile.

About section

The second section of your LinkedIn Profile is the About section. This part of your LinkedIn Profile gives you the opportunity to describe yourself in more detail. Some people take this as an invitation to write at length about themselves and their philosophies. This is a mistake. Anything lengthy will be read only by you and two or three of your most ardent admirers. Keep your sentences short and use a maximum of one or two sentences in each paragraph.

Figure 4.3: The About section of your LinkedIn profile

About

Over 25 years of leadership experience in financial services. Strong digital transformation, customer experience and execution background.

Known for being strategic, results-oriented and developing talent. Is collaborative and has a 'can-do' approach.

Signature strength is building a strong culture of innovation, collaboration and value creation.

Passionate about building high-performing agile teams that deliver extraordinary customer experiences and sustainable business value.

KEY ACHIEVEMENTS

1. Directed design & change of digital platform, global ranking of #1 in mobile banking
2. Devised & executed strategies to accelerate digital sales & service for business bank
3. Built and cultivated a series of high-performing, diverse teams
4. Successfully piloted agile ways of working in a complex organisational environment

LEADERSHIP STRENGTHS

- Strategic and visionary
- Values-driven and open
- Results-oriented with grit
- Grows and develops talent
- Collaborative and creative

KNOWN AND RESPECTED FOR

- Purpose-driven leadership
- Passion for customer
- Lateral and strategic thinker
- Innovative and technically astute
- Strong values

OTHER INFORMATION

Currently assisting a fintech start-up with strategic planning.

Make sure this section includes the key words that you expect people might use to search for someone like you. Put yourself in the shoes of a recruiter who is reading this at the same time that they are speaking to you on the phone. Keep it very simple, especially with your introductory information. You can then go into a little more detail in the next three subsections in your About description.

Introductory overview

This can be a summary of your experience, your business experience and strengths, and your passion at the beginning of the About section. This can be based on your passion, experience and competence (PEC) statement, which I discuss in more detail in the next chapter. As you can see in the example provided, this information should take up six to 10 lines separated into three or four short paragraphs. Remember that LinkedIn only displays the first three lines of this section unless the reader opens the rest of the page. So, the first three lines are important in terms of positioning you. I like you to provide a very short summary of your experience in these three lines.

Key achievements

List the achievements already set out in bold in your Professional Profile. You do not need more than the bold headings, unless a little extra description is required. Number each achievement so that you can refer to it in the future. The key achievements heading needs to be in capitals since bold print is not available on LinkedIn.

Leadership strengths

Use the leadership strengths already set out in your Professional Profile. An important reason for including these attributes is to remind your LinkedIn readers not only that you are a leader, but also what kind of a leader you are. Once again, the heading needs to be in capitals since bold print is not available on LinkedIn.

Known and respected for

Finally, transfer the bold headings from this part of your Professional Profile. Again, these are prompts only, to tell the LinkedIn reader something about the attributes that your colleagues respect you for. Ideally, this list indicates something about your character and values. It is not a random list of your technical skills. Once again, use capitals for this heading.

Other information

If you have been involved in consulting or contracting, you can describe this here by adding a line or two. Do this rather than setting up a separate job in the Experience section of LinkedIn. If you use the Experience section to show that you have been doing some consulting or contracting, you may lead readers to believe that you have set up your own permanent business as a consultant.

Preparing the Experience section of your LinkedIn Profile

Figure 4.4 shows an example of the way to set up one role in the third section of your LinkedIn Profile.

Figure 4.4: Example of Experience section of your LinkedIn Profile

---

Experience

United International Banking Corporation – 17 years
Singapore

SVP, Customer Experience & Service Innovation, Consumer Division: 2016–2020

Responsible for transforming Consumer Division's way of working to be customer-journey led and 'agile' and to build a culture of innovation, collaboration and value creation.

Achievements included:

- Baselined service design for everyday banking & consumer finance.
- Operationalised two cross-functional agile squads to uplift customer/staff experience.
- Developed customer- & data-led strategy. Moved performance from #4 to #1.

This section of your LinkedIn Profile is where you can list your work experience. The idea here is to briefly set out, for each job, your experience and your key achievements.

The system asks you to name your employer for each part of your career, and prompts you with the corporate logo once you've supplied the name of the organisation you worked for. Enter each job and its start and finish dates, using only years, rather than months and years. If you have left a role and do not have a new position, close out the role no longer than three months after your departure. Many people believe finding a job is easier if you have a job, so some people do not want to close off a job even though they have left it many months previously. I have seen no evidence to support this idea that it is easier to find a job if you are in a job. In fact, for senior jobseekers, the reverse is more likely to be true because many recruiters prefer candidates who do not have to be convinced to leave a role. One of the problems of attempting to hire individuals who are established in a job is that they may receive an attractive counteroffer when they announce they are about to resign.

Keep the description of your role brief – just two or three lines. You do not need to explain at length what you did in your job, unless it is a job where readers might not understand the depth or breadth. Follow this description, using a line space, with 'Achievements included:' with two or three bullet points describing specific achievements accomplished by you in that role, including, if at all possible, some quantification of the impact delivered by you. Always focus on your impact!

Preparing the fourth section of your LinkedIn Profile

Skills and endorsements

Define about five high-level skills and enter them in this section – using headings such as Strategy, Leadership, and Change Agent. Although lower level and more detailed entries may seem irrelevant, they will also be useful if they contain words that might be picked up by the LinkedIn search algorithm. Some people believe that it is good to enter at least 30 skills to help elevate you in a LinkedIn search, but make sure they are relevant to you and your career. If you are looking to apply for a role displayed on LinkedIn, the Premium Service will indicate how well your skills fit with the skills desired for the role. If appropriate, once you have seen how well the system says you fit, you can add relevant skills to your profile to improve your fit. Do this before you apply for the role.

Recommendations

Recommendations also elevate you in the LinkedIn search algorithm. I believe you should limit your recommendations to a maximum of, say, six true supporters. Any additional recommendations are not likely to be read. Ask anyone giving you a recommendation to keep it to fewer than 40 words. The best recommendations tend to include something like:

> Mary is one of the most strategic executives I have ever met. She builds great teams with positive cultures. She delivers what she promises and is highly respected by everyone who works with her.

You can review the feedback received via your email request referred to in chapter 3. This could help you decide who to ask for a recommendation on LinkedIn. Before you accept a recommendation, make quite sure it makes sense, is clear, and does not contain any typos. You can always ask your recommender to make changes before you accept the final recommendation. Typos in a recommendation, or indeed any part of your profile, will reflect poorly on you!

Charities

Describe your charity and community work in the separate section of LinkedIn provided for this purpose.

Board directorships

LinkedIn does not have a separate section for board directorships. This could present a problem if you have a number of director-ships, especially if you hold these while you were involved in one or more full-time roles. Your profile can become very confusing if board roles and jobs overlap. If you have held multiple directorships over your career, group them under job headings such as 'Corporate Directorships' and/or 'Not-for-profit Directorships'. These lists of directorships will usually be shown as the first items on the job list if your position on at least one board is current.

I return to the topic of LinkedIn in chapter 7, where I discuss how to gain the most out of its networking potential.

PREPARING YOUR CV

The only individuals who are likely to read your CV in any detail are recruiters and HR directors. They are in the risk-management business and most will want to know all they can about your career (and, in some cases, your life). They may be interested in issues such as why you moved from one job to another, or any gaps between job dates. They also may be interested in the kinds of enterprises you've worked for, and your contribution to each. Is there a strong pattern of success in your career? Have you worked overseas? Did you start your career in a strong professional firm? What are your likely development needs? Your CV is only an entry ticket into a recruiting process and, in some ways, is a formality. If you have done your networking well, recruiters will likely already know about you and your career. If they are switched on, they almost certainly will have read your LinkedIn Profile before they meet you. They may still want a Word version of your CV, however, so that they can cut and paste information from it into their report to their client.

Different types of profile may be more appropriate in certain situations, and example CVs are shown in the appendices for three types of situations:

1. Preparing your CV if you are a senior executive.

2. Preparing a CV if you wish to be a non-executive director.

3. Preparing a new graduate CV, if you are starting out.

Different countries have developed different preferred ways of presenting your CV. In the United States, for instance, one-page CVs are common, while in other countries longer CVs are expected. Professions have their own preferred way of displaying credentials as well. For instance, academic CVs can be 20 pages long, describing all your research and your publications. So, what I suggest here should be regarded as a thought-starter for you.

Preparing your CV if you are a senior executive

Your CV can be a completely separate document from your Professional Profile, prepared from scratch, but this seems to me to be a waste of time and effort. I suggest that you prepare your updated CV by attaching a detailed chronological employment history to your two-page Professional Profile. This attachment must clearly show the organisations you have worked for (with some brief descriptive background on each) and the jobs you had in each organisation. You need to be careful only to provide publicly available information. The format should be consistent with the format you used in your Professional Profile. See Appendix A for an example of the description of one job in your updated CV, for a senior executive.

Under each senior role in your employment history, include three sections:

1. *Responsibilities:* Who you reported to, a brief description of your role and responsibilities, and the scale of your job in terms of the funds under management, or revenues, costs or headcount.

2. *Key Challenges:* The challenges you faced when you entered the role – no more than four or five. Use bullet points and

keep them brief. These challenges provide the context for your achievements.

3. *Selected Achievements:* List about five achievements using bullet points. Be brief and quantify the impact you delivered.

If you follow these guidelines, you will present a very clean, brief description of each role and the challenges facing you when you took the role, plus your achievements and impact in the role. I have not seen the Key Challenges section used in other CVs, but I recommend you use this because it provides context for your Selected Achievements. It is usually best to frame the problems as opportunities. Try to quantify your achievements if you possibly can, so that your impact while you were in the role is obvious. Keep each bullet point to one or two lines if at all possible. If you take longer than this, you risk losing the reader. Obviously, you need to avoid providing proprietary information in the Key Challenges section or your Selected Achievements section. You can provide abbreviated descriptions for jobs early in your career.

Preparing a CV if you wish to be a non-executive director

If you wish to become a non-executive director, you will need a different kind of CV. I take the view that a board CV should be no longer than one page. There will be a variety of views on this! The key is to show that you have the attributes required to join a board. These attributes are quite different from the ones you require as a successful senior executive. Many of the required skills for directors and board members are soft skills – for example, to be an outstanding director, you will probably need to be a person who is:

•   an excellent strategic thinker, with commercial judgement and integrity

•   a team player and 'peacemaker' with balance and great interpersonal skills

- a good listener and debater with perspective and relevant business knowledge

- a quiet authority with wisdom plus humility, and the ability to stand firm

- a flexible thinker with gravitas and wisdom, who admits when you are wrong

- perceptive, and someone who can ask questions that lead to deeper insight

- a hard worker, who maintains confidentiality and board cohesion.

An example of a one-page CV for someone wishing to become a non-executive director is provided in Appendix B. Put yourself in the shoes of the Chair of the board. What is she or he going to be interested in? The first question often asked is, 'What board experience have you had?' Even if you haven't been a non-executive director, you've likely attended a number of board meetings. If you have attended meetings as an observer or as a presenter, you have had the luxury of observing the board directors in action. You may have been able to observe which individuals were effective directors, and why. If so, this could be a factor that helps you to differentiate yourself.

If you have not been a member of a board, making the leap from an executive role on to a board can be difficult, and is likely to take time. You'll probably need assistance from an established board director to coach and support you. Remember that your first board is likely to define you to some degree, so think twice before you join an unknown board with an unknown Chair. A position on this kind of a board is unlikely to catapult you to a more prestigious board later. In fact, the reverse is likely to occur. You'll likely be branded as a director of this kind of company and may not be given bigger opportunities. The same goes for advisory committees and government boards. If you are an effective director, you may find advisory committees and government boards frustrating.

And you may be branded in a way that does not help you to progress, if you join them.

New graduate CV if you are starting out

If you are a new graduate or someone with limited job experience, it is best to prepare a one-page CV. If you do this, you still need to emphasise your achievements, starting at school. Your work experience will be important. Highlight any work experience you gained while you were at school or at university. Many senior executives want to hire young people who have played in teams at school, worked in teams in their jobs, and have had direct experience serving customers. Showing that you have people skills can be more important than having top grades. The more concise you can be, the better. See Appendix C for an example CV for a new graduate jobseeker.

TESTING A NEW BUSINESS CONCEPT

If you are proposing to start a new business, you will need a simple way of describing what it does and your own strengths to people you meet. Testing a new business concept and doing your market research is fundamental before you launch your business. Asking people for their advice is much easier than trying to sell them your service. Just as you would do if seeking a role, you need to emphasise the idea that you are seeking advice before you make any final decision. A one-page document, setting out your credentials and the benefits you expect to deliver, is probably all you need in these discussions. An example is shown in Appendix D.

YOUR COVER LETTER

Cover letters are nearly always desirable with your CV or Professional Profile, particularly when you are applying for a senior role. However, about 50 per cent of recruiters do not bother to read your cover letter. Some recruiters I know think cover letters do not add any value because they can be full of platitudes and clichés. The real information these recruiters want to see is where you have worked and what you achieved in each role – your career trajectory. This information can be derived from your CV.

Cover letters can be particularly useful, however, if you have spoken to the recruiter or the recruiting executive in advance. If you have done this, you will have identified how your special skills could be valuable in this particular role. As a result, you can now use your cover letter to re-emphasise that you meet the requirements of the role. Keep your cover letter short (less than one page) and concentrate on how you will add value in the role and the benefits you will deliver to the organisation. Use bullet points to make sure your arguments are easy to read and clear.

I recommend against rewriting your Professional Profile and CV to tailor it to each application. Your tailored one-page cover letter, which reinforces what you have learnt from the person doing the recruiting and what specific value you can add in the role, should achieve this. An example cover letter is shown in Appendix E.

★★★

As you can see from the examples in this chapter, preparing your written materials before you begin networking involves careful, demanding work. The process requires great attention to detail and great precision. Use your Professional Profile when networking, and your CV with recruiters and HR executives.

Unfortunately, most senior jobseekers invest too much time on their CV which, in terms of networking, is the least important document you will prepare. Instead, investing real effort in your two-page Professional Profile for networking is more productive and will give you a competitive advantage when you meet some-one new. The most important benefits will be that you will show you are special and you stand out from your competitors. You will, however, need a CV for recruiters and HR executives. If you set up your CV in the way I suggest, using your Professional Profile as the first two pages, adding your detailed employment history is relatively straightforward. This detailed information can be easily attached to your Professional Profile. Your LinkedIn Profile is important because it represents you to the world.

In the next chapter, I discuss how you should prepare for face-to-face meetings. Once you have developed strong written materials and mastered your approach to face-to-face communication, you can explore your career options, work out who you want to meet, and what you want to discuss with them. Then you can start to expand your network in the most productive way.

SOME QUESTIONS FOR YOU TO CONSIDER

- What information would you include in your Professional Profile?
- Can you articulate a clear and strong personal branding statement?
- How well can you group your key business achievements?
- Are your business achievements quantified?
- How do you describe and support your leadership strengths?
- What are you are known and respected for?
- Does your final two-page Professional Profile look professional and is it easy to read?
- Is your LinkedIn Profile strong, concise and clear?
- Is your CV clear and succinct, with challenges and achievements?
- Do your strengths jump out of your Cover Letter?
- Who can provide a rigorous critique of your written materials?

5

Preparing to speak about your strengths

Dealing with people is probably the
biggest problem you face.

Dale Carnegie, *How to Win Friends and Influence People*

You will be best prepared to talk about your strengths, if you:

- Build strong rapport
- Understand why you must rehearse
- Think through how to answer three key questions

TO STAND OUT during the networking and interview process, you need to initiate interesting conversations and be able to answer questions asked by others – clearly and simply. Just as with your written materials, clarity and brevity are key. To be clear and brief – using what I call, 'plain spoken barbeque language' – make sure you are well prepared. Interestingly, if you are clear and brief, you will immediately differentiate yourself from others you are being compared with. Their answers will generally take too long and will not be clear. The way you communicate will reinforce you are special.

When you answer a question, the way you present the response is often more important than the content of your answer. Skilful politicians demonstrate how to do this every day. Consider whether the structure of your answer makes sense, as well as the content of what you say. Experienced interviewers may ask you an open-ended question, such as, 'What is important to you?' These questions are challenging and potentially tricky for you, and interviewers use them to not only hear your answer but also see how you tackle them. The challenge for you is that the questioner has not indicated anything about what they are specifically interested in. As a result, you may be tempted to speak at length and cover all the bases. If you do this, what you say may not be relevant and is likely to take too long – and, as a result, you may knock yourself out of the recruiting process.

As I describe in chapter 1, the Pareto Principle, or 80/20 rule, postulates that roughly 80 per cent of consequences come from 20 per cent of the effort. Using this rule, for example, if you speak for five minutes when answering a question, four minutes (80 per cent) of your answer is likely to not be interesting or relevant to the listener. You will be boring and come across as insensitive and self-centred. An example of this is provided by Harry. He was a senior executive who had been Head of Risk at a major bank. Harry was asked a brilliantly simple question by an interviewer: 'How do you manage risk?' Instead of asking, 'What kind of risk do you have in mind?' (in order to narrow the question), Harry proceeded to take 20 minutes to describe all facets of risk management. This turned out to be a bad mistake. Although he may have been technically correct, Harry was boring. In addition, he showed that he was not able to frame an answer to an open-ended question succinctly! Harry was not asked back for any further interviews.

Good career consultants can assist you in developing a high-impact, comprehensive approach to communicating your strengths with your network and with recruiters. This involves working with you to prepare you for networking meetings, applying for roles, handling the subsequent interviews, and negotiating the final job arrangements when you receive an offer. When it comes to brevity, I have always been fascinated that President Abraham Lincoln's Gettysburg address was composed of just 271 words and took less than two minutes. Lincoln's address is learned by heart by most American school children. The speaker who preceded Lincoln was regarded as the most eminent orator of the time. He was Hon. Edward Everett, the former Secretary of State, and he spoke for nearly two hours. His speech contained 13,607 words. Despite this, neither Everett nor his speech is remembered today.

To be an effective verbal communicator, you need to think carefully and rigorously in advance about what you will say and how you will say it. Throughout this chapter, I provide examples of verbal communication to help you prepare for networking and the subsequent interview process. Once you have decided what you want to say, rehearsing is critical. Without rehearsing, you will find it difficult to communicate what is in your head in a coherent and compelling way. This is especially true if you are distracted or if your meeting is not going the way you expected. If you fail to put the work into rehearsing what and how you will communicate – and polishing it – you risk being knocked out of a recruitment process after your first meeting.

BUILD STRONG RAPPORT

The hiring process to select an individual to fill a senior role usually involves five or more steps. The first step is reviewing your application, including your CV and LinkedIn Profile. These are simply your tickets to the dance, and are relatively unimportant after you have been invited to the first meeting or interview. Progress from then on will depend on effective verbal communication. Although recruiters might argue that a lot of science is involved in what they do, in the end it is closer to the Oscar voting process I've already mentioned. Whether you receive the necessary votes to progress to the next stage is usually based on their judgement and your ability to build strong rapport. The key at each step is to do your best to progress to the following step – from selection for the long list, to then being selected for the short list, and to then moving through one or more interviews by the client, and on to reference checking, to finally receiving the offer. To do this, you need to maximise the probability that you will obtain the most votes at each step in the process.

Many individuals who do not have a coach believe that they will be fine if they are spontaneous, making it up as they go along. But preparing in advance – not only what you will say, but also how you will say it – is a much better strategy for success. Being spontaneous and unprepared is likely to be a strategy for failure – especially if you are being compared head-to-head with someone who has made the effort to prepare. What and how you communicate will be a key differentiator between you and other candidates for a role. Your goal at each stage must be to stay in the game, impressing those involved in making decisions at each step and winning their vote to move you forward. This is rarely achieved by talking about yourself. Often you will do better, and differentiate yourself more effectively, by asking intelligent questions rather than trying too hard to sell yourself.

As mentioned earlier, Professor Amy Cuddy from Harvard Business School argues that people size you up super-quick when they first meet you. In *Presence*, she argues people have two questions in their minds at this first meeting:

- *'Can I trust you?'*: This relates *to* your perceived personal warmth.

- *'Can I respect you?'*: This relates to your perceived competence.

Ideally you want to be perceived as having both warmth and competence. But you may be surprised to learn that, as Cuddy highlights, warmth is more important than competence:

> *Most people, especially in a professional context, believe that competence is the more important factor. In selling themselves, people want to prove that they are smart and talented. In fact, warmth, or trustworthiness, is the most important factor in how people evaluate you.*

Quite often, I see a person with industry experience being offered a role over a second candidate who, in my view, is far more competent and has far greater potential to add value in the role. As Cuddy indicates, this is likely to be because the first candidate – possibly with greater industry knowledge and ability to refer to industry issues and relationships – tends to be able to build greater trust. As a result, these candidates build a stronger emotional connection with their potential employer, even though they may be less competent.

I saw the power of building an emotional connection firsthand when I was on a selection committee for a scholarship to Harvard Business School. Each member of the committee was sent the applications. All 30 applications were amazing. I read the first one and said to myself, 'This person has to be the winner.' She had almost perfect academic results, helped build a school in Cambodia, was a real contributor in her community, and had won a national debating competition. Then I read the next application. It was even more impressive. I had to select 10 of the applicants for an interview and I did this by coming up with my own version of a logical ranking system. Who knows whether I made the best selections? I used my best judgement but one of the individuals that I knocked out may have been just as good as, or even better than, the final winner. My selections were very much driven by my own personal decision framework. Very often the same problem is faced by recruiters who are asked to select the long list of candidates for a job. When it comes to selecting between several very capable people, the process is an art not a science. Someone's personal judgement will be key in the final choices made.

A major revelation for me in this scholarship process was that, as soon as we conducted our interviews, 80 per cent of the candidates we interviewed were easy to eliminate. They may have had a strong intelligence quotient (IQ), but something was missing in their emotional quotient (EQ). The final winner differentiated himself by telling an emotional story of his life as a refugee from Vietnam. He had arrived in the country with his parents when he was six years old, after sailing at sea in a leaky boat for over two weeks. His parents had then worked three jobs to put him through school and university. He told us he owed everything to his parents and to his new homeland. He explained how important each of these was to him. In doing so, he built an emotional connection with the selection committee that won him the scholarship. How can you build this kind of compelling emotional connection? One thing is clear: not by asking people to read your CV!

I mention Dale Carnegie's definitive *How to Win Friends and Influence People* in chapter 1. The book is one of the best-selling books of all time, and still sells over 250,000 copies each year. In a survey by the Library of Congress in 2013, it was ranked the seventh most influential book in American history. Warren Buffett, the billionaire and iconic investment banker, attended Carnegie's lectures and credits Carnegie for his success. 'In my office, you will not see the degree I have from the University of Nebraska, or the master's degree I have from Columbia University, but you'll see the certificate I got from the Dale Carnegie course,' Buffett told a documentary film crew. Many of the things Carnegie writes about are what you probably learned from your primary school teacher, but they are easy to forget in times of stress. Carnegie asks, *'How do you make the other person feel important? How, when and where?'* His answer to this question is, *'All the time, everywhere.'* What makes Carnegie's book so interesting, even 80 years after it was written, is his ability to tell human stories of how his approach works in a wide range of situations. These are the kinds of connections you should also be doing your best to make.

UNDERSTAND WHY YOU MUST REHEARSE

To be at your best, rehearse. Even Sir Laurence Olivier, one of the greatest dramatic stage actors of last century, needed to rehearse. In 1939, he played Heathcliff in the film version of *Wuthering Heights*, directed by William Wyler. Wyler was renowned as a master perfectionist. The story goes that, on one occasion, Olivier complained that he had been repeating one scene for 72 takes, exclaiming, 'I did it sitting down. I did it with a smile. I did it with a smirk. I did it scratching my ear. I did it with my back to the camera. How do you want me to do it?' 'Better,' responded Wyler. What a punchline – both brief and clear. And Olivier later said these multiple takes helped him learn how to succeed as a movie actor. If you rehearse, you also will be better than if you try to make it up as you go along.

You might be concerned that rehearsing your answers to simple questions will destroy your authenticity and spontaneity, making you seem stilted. After all, why not just prepare some general answers, write down the answers, and then use these when the relevant question is asked? Three things are important, and may go wrong if you have not rehearsed out loud:

1. *Remembering what you want to say:* When you are trying desperately to remember what you are meant to say, you can sound confused and hesitant. You are thinking aloud and, in some ways, doing worse than if you had not prepared at all. You will not be natural and you will not have a compelling framework for answering tricky open-ended questions.

2. *Being sharp and to the point:* The danger is that you will over-complicate your story and take too long. I have never, with the more than 1000 people I have worked with, found anyone who provides a good spontaneous answer, in two minutes or less, to the question, 'Tell me about yourself'. You need to have prepared carefully and rehearsed the answer many times. Otherwise, once you start, you tend to think of new ideas and lose track of time.

3. *Making sure you are passionate enough:* You are unlikely to be convincing if you have not worked out how to express your energy and passion. If your message does not come from the heart, it is likely to be wooden. A long description of your career may be interesting to you but is unlikely to be energising for your listener. Be passionate and energetic – otherwise, you will not be convincing!

Similar to Sir Lawrence Olivier, to be good you will need to rehearse many times. Rehearse to get the words right. Then rehearse to make sure your answer does not sound rehearsed! I once worked with a very competent accountant who started by saying he was passionate about delivering accurate accounts to his board each month. I told him this answer was not inspiring and totally failed to help him to sell himself. He came across as highly administrative. If he was a leader, he needed to be passionate about leading people in some special way. A better approach was to suggest that he was passionate about making sure *his team* delivered the best possible information to his board. As a result of this, he could then explain, his board would be in a good position to make the best possible decisions in relation to their role in running the company. He needed to focus on the benefits delivered, not the accounting process.

How much should you rehearse? Chances are you, like most of us, totally underestimate the amount of rehearsal that you need to be outstanding. If you are giving a presentation, Justin Aquino, Founder and Head Coach of Cool Communicator, indicates you need to rehearse much more than you might expect. Aquino argues, 'You need to practice until you know the entire presentation by heart, and you feel genuinely comfortable and confident with it.' He points out the typical rehearsal times for individuals involved in various types of performance are as follows:

- *Theatre:* From 30 to 90 hours before opening night.
- *Broadway:* Possibly 200 to 300 hours before opening night.
- *TED Talks:* Between 50 and 100 hours for a 20-minute talk.

Most of my clients assume a few run throughs will be fine. They are thinking of, maybe, 15 minutes of rehearsal! You may not be putting on a TED Talk but you will do better if you rehearse more. Aquino argues an inexperienced speaker needs at least 30 hours of rehearsal before speaking to an important audience. A successful opera singer who I know says she rehearses a part at least 200 times before a public performance. You need to decide how much rehearsal time you need, but it will be a miracle if 15-minutes of rehearsal is enough to show you at your best!

You might think I am overemphasising that you need to keep your answer brief and then rehearse so you can be spontaneous. To see how important this is for yourself, provide your own answer, off the top of your head, to the following simple request: 'Please tell me about yourself.' Record yourself on your phone. I can almost guarantee that you will take longer than two minutes. Also, because you are conscious of answering the question briefly, you will sound too rushed and too flat. In addition, you may not look particularly comfortable and will fail to come across with gravitas. Only practice, preferably with someone to critique you, makes your communication more perfect!

THINK THROUGH HOW TO ANSWER THREE KEY QUESTIONS

Before you begin networking or interviews, you should be prepared to answer three simple questions in a compelling way, quickly and with impact. These questions are:

1. 'What do you do?'
2. 'Can you tell me about yourself?'
3. 'What do you want to do?'

Answering these three simple questions requires thought and practice. In particular, make sure you know the basic structure of your answer by heart. If you are clear about the structure of your answer, you can modify each specific answer to suit the particular situation you face. As mentioned, also try to be very clear and brief when answering each of these questions. Work to limit any answer to any question you receive from a hiring team to two minutes or less. At the end of your answer, you should always ask the questioner whether he or she would like you to expand on anything you have said. This gives you the opportunity to expand on your answer if the person you are meeting is interested in exploring the topic. By the way, make sure you use the name of the other person when you provide your answers, to help build a warm connection with them.

Question 1: 'What do you do?'

Rebecca Okamoto, principal and founder of Evoke Strategy Group in San Francisco, helps people communicate more effectively. She has developed some simple approaches, and five specific ways to answer the question, 'What do you do?' She believes that today's attention span is about eight seconds, so you need to be able to answer this question in 20 words at the most.

How to construct your answer

To answer the simple question 'What do you do?' successfully, Okamoto's advice is to approach your answers in the following ways:

- *Always explain how you add value:* Grab people's attention by clarifying how you can help them.

- *Speak the way your listener does when they brag, complain or troubleshoot:* Use the language they use when describing themselves or their situation.

- *Practice, practice, practice:* Another believer in the power of rehearsing, Okamoto practises her introduction 5 to10 times a day for two to three days before attending a function or giving a workshop, and 10 to 20 times on the day of the event.

What words to use in your answer

Okamoto suggests five ways to respond to the question 'What do you do' in 20 words or fewer:

1. I help *[target audience]* do *[statement of need or opportunity]* through *[differentiator]*.

2. I help *[target audience]* to do *[statement of need]* + *[statement of benefit]*.

3. I help *[target audience]* *[fix their problem]*.

4. I connect *[target audience]* to *[something they want]* + *[differentiator]*.

5. I *[transform/translate/convert a problem]* into *[something aspirational]*.

For instance, in my case, I help senior executives to find outstanding jobs and build winning careers. For more of Okamoto's tips, and some examples of how to use the preceding five answer templates, see her article '5 ways to introduce yourself perfectly in 20 words or less', available online.

Most people who do not have a job answer the question 'What do you do?' by saying something like, 'I have just left a senior management role at a bank.' This provides almost no useful information. Perhaps you've heard the story about the information provided by the accountant to the balloonist who came down through the fog and hovered his balloon just off the ground. The pilot asked, 'Where am I?' to which the accountant answered, 'In the fog, three feet above the ground'. Perfectly accurate, but in no way useful. You want to trigger interest and enthusiasm in the person looking for your response. If you are a retail banker, describing your job as negotiating mortgages or lending money isn't the best answer. A much better response is that you help young families live better lives by assisting them to finance their new homes. By answering in this way, you focus on the benefits you deliver in your job – not some vague description of who you worked for and what your job title was.

Question 2: 'Can you tell me about yourself?'

This question is commonly used as an 'ice breaker' while networking or in an interview, and is often the first question you will be asked when meeting someone new. In answering this question, you will want to be articulate and confident and interesting. This question is much more difficult to answer well than you might think. Many people waffle. I have heard recruiters describing how to answer this question and, in my view, they too have waffled. You are probably thinking, *Where do I start? How much detail do you want me to go into? Do you want me to talk about my whole life, my family, my business life, or what? Do you want me to be serious or light-hearted? How long have I got?* Rather than exploring these questions, I suggest you provide a simple, punchy response to get the conversation rolling. I call this your PEC Statement. PEC stands for:

Passion >>> Experience >>> Competence

As you might guess – since I am a believer in the 80/20 rule – I like to keep the answer to this question brief and structured. Aim for a two-minute answer.

Using this approach provides five advantages:

1. The model is easy to remember and it fits together well.
2. You project energy and enthusiasm.
3. You deliver memorable personal information quickly.
4. It shows you structure your thinking, which questioners may be testing.
5. It should trigger specific questions about what you have done and why.

In constructing the substance of your answer to cover the three PEC areas, consider seven distinct elements, all closely linked, within the two minutes.

Introduction (15 seconds)

Start with something like, 'Thanks so much for asking. This is a big question, but let me simplify and give you a two-minute overview. First, I'll describe what I'm passionate about. Next, I'll touch on my business experience at a very high level. And, finally, I'll explain three things that my colleagues say make me special.' With this, you're signalling you'll be concise, structured and high level.

Passion (20 seconds)

Explain what you are passionate about first. This allows your genuine commitment and energy to come through. Individuals starting with their job experience tend to provide a long list of jobs, often starting from their first job. This derails the clarity of the answer and makes it boring. Instead, reinforce that you are a leader in your sphere and passionate about building teams that deliver impact. For example, you could say, 'I have always been passionate about working to build world-class teams. I want these teams to have strong, positive cultures that help to build successful businesses. I am happiest when it's clear my teams are delivering real value for all stakeholders, particularly for our customers.' Use terms such as 'world-class' or 'high-performance' or 'best-of-breed' when you talk about teams to highlight you are not happy with second- or third-rate performance. You may not have always been able to build world-class teams, of course, but, I hope, you aspire to do this.

Segue (10 seconds)

To move from your passion to your experience, use a transition sentence such as, 'I've been extremely fortunate that, in the last 10 years, I've been able to build a series of successful teams that were highly motivated and delivered real value.'

Experience (30 seconds)

With only 30 seconds to talk about 20 or 30 years of experience, your comment is going to be high level. This can be difficult for you to master because you have so much you could talk about! Touch on your most senior roles and, maybe, include one or two notable successes. You could say something like, 'During this time, I held two senior CFO roles, one with Company A and the other with Company B. In each business, I was highly respected by the board. I led the refinancing of each business. The total money raised was over $100 million. I am proud to say that each business went on to grow at more than 20 per cent compound per annum.'

Segue (10 seconds)

You then move to what your *ex-colleagues* think makes you special – for example, 'If you ask my colleagues in these businesses what they think makes me special, they'd talk about three things.'

Competence (30 seconds)

Next, describe the three most important things your colleagues would say make you special. Because of the feedback you received from your email (described in chapter 3), you already know what others think makes you special. Using what they say – even quoting it – is more credible, comfortable and compelling than trying to guess possible things you believe make you special. You can select three big ideas from the feedback you received, and can be authentic and accurate as you speak on this topic.

Make sure that you select three big ideas that do not overlap and are of similar strength and importance. It is no good saying that your colleagues think you are, first, an extraordinary strategic visionary, second, good at analysing the monthly accounts and, third, good at day-to-day management of small teams. Instead, sequence the ideas with 'first', 'second' and 'third' and make sure they are of similar strength. For example, say something like, 'First, they see me as a leader who sets a clear vision for the organisation and who energises my people to deliver outstanding results. Second, they would point to my commercial skills. They see me as a highly commercial executive – someone who really cares about customers and is an excellent negotiator. And, third, they'd suggest that I'm a strong, effective communicator – someone who is able to simplify complex messages in discussions with everyone from the shop floor up to the board.'

Note that you can vary the three competencies you discuss to suit the situation you face. For instance, if you are meeting with a CEO, you may choose to emphasise your capacity to develop and lead transformational teams. If you are with a CPO, you may talk more about your ability to build strong cultures where individuals flourish. Or if you are talking to a future peer in the organisation, you could describe your ability to work across silos and collaborate with others.

Conclusion (5 seconds)

Conclude your two-minute answer with something like, 'That's a very quick overview. I'd be happy to expand on any of this if you wish.' The idea is to encourage your questioner to ask for more information, so that you can build on what you have said in your two-minute response. When they do this, you will be on very firm ground since you know they are asking about something that interests them. They are also asking about something where you are the only person in the world who knows the correct answer. Do not get too carried away, however. Try to also limit your next response to two minutes. You can always ask them, at the end of the two minutes, 'Does that answer your question?' or 'Would you like any more detail?'

If you read the example sentences I've provided, without hurrying and with proper pauses, you will see that the answer takes approximately two minutes. Many people are surprised that such a limited amount of information takes two minutes to communicate. This presents the real challenge, of course. How can you communicate important content quickly and clearly? Once you get started, unless you have rehearsed, you may end up speaking for four or five minutes. Time flies when you are talking about yourself! Detailed and thorough rehearsal is vital. Every word counts. Often my clients answer this question rather proudly on their first try, and are amazed when I tell them their answer has taken five minutes. Without rehearsing, you are unlikely to be crisp enough or disciplined enough, and you will speak far too long.

The power of the PEC Approach was reinforced for me recently. Janette, one of my clients, was about to be interviewed by a top executive recruiter for a CEO role. We decided that she would offer to introduce herself using PEC. Janette had a great story to tell and we rehearsed it several times. At the end of her interview, Janette asked the recruiter how well she fitted the CEO role she was being interviewed for. The recruiter repeated her PEC back to her – almost word for word – saying that the person they were looking for to fill the CEO role would have the qualities Janette had described. It was immediately clear that Janette had made an excellent impression!

Question 3: 'What do you want to do?'

Your answer to this question, which nearly everyone without exception will ask you, will evolve as you expand your network. It seems simple enough. People are, of course, asking what kind of job you are looking for. But early on in the process, immediately after leaving a role, is too early for you to be definitive about possible future jobs. While you are preparing to network, before you have started to meet people to test your thinking, you should be emphasising that your initial goal is simply to expand your network. You can respond along the lines of, 'I am keen to prepare myself to expand my network, with the goal of meeting at least 50 new senior people.' Talking about possible future jobs is usually premature at this stage, since you have not had time to structure your thinking and test it with your A-List.

When you are at the beginning of your preparation for launching your job-search process, the probability of identifying your exact next job is close to zero. This is because you have only a vague idea of the type and range of opportunities out there. In addition, you don't know what jobs you are likely to be offered, or what you are likely to accept. More detailed and relevant knowledge of what jobs might make sense for you as a senior jobseeker only comes as you expand your network and your thinking develops.

At this early stage, you have the distinct luxury, which you have probably never had before, of taking significant time – at least a month – to look after yourself by getting fitter, thinking more about the future and preparing a strategy to move forward. It is important that you explain this to people who ask what you want to do. As you meet more people and build your network, new opportunities for you will become clearer. Then your answer to this question – of what you want to do – will evolve to frame the areas that interest you most. I discuss this in the next chapter.

In formulating your answer to the question of what you want to do – if asked this while you are doing your initial preparation before you begin to network – consider incorporating some or all of the following five elements in your answer, depending on the situation you face.

Element 1: 'I want to take at least a month to prepare thoroughly.'

I recommend to my clients that they do not meet anyone for at least a month after they leave their job. During this month, many good things happen. They start to look and feel better as a result of more sleep, more exercise, better eating, and the elimination of work pressure. You want people who meet you to see you at your best, not the version of you that is worn out and run down! After a month away from your job, you will be simply amazed at how many of your friends will comment spontaneously on how well you look.

Do not explain this first month of preparation by saying you are exhausted and must take time off to rest, even if you believe this is true. You don't want others to think you are complacent or have lost your drive. Instead, be clear that you are using this valuable time to prepare. In the early days, just after you have left a role, your answer should be something like, 'My main goal right now is to take a month to prepare myself for networking and test my thinking about possible future roles. I want to be able to explain clearly what makes me special, and to frame how I want to conduct my job search. Then, I want to test my thinking with my colleagues and advisors.'

Element 2: 'After that, I want to invest the following three to six months in growing my network.'

As a senior jobseeker, you need to clarify you will not be rushing to find a role once you have completed your initial preparation. Your immediate goal, after preparing yourself, is to generate and explore opportunities. To do this, you will need to build your network with a goal of meeting at least 50 new senior people. Your ultimate goal is to be offered two or three roles, but this is well down the track. This positive outcome – more than one job offer – occurs with surprising regularity for people who go through this process and who do the work involved. As I have already noted, receiving more than one offer puts you in a far superior position in any subsequent negotiations. You can compare and contrast roles and think deeply about the pros and cons of each. And you are in a much stronger negotiating position in terms of the compensation offered and other arrangements, including the precise nature and definition of the future role.

So, add some words to your answer along these lines, 'Once I have concluded my initial preparation, I will be thinking about the people I would like to meet and what I could discuss with them. I am keen to meet at least 50 new people who can help me understand my options and who might turn out to be mentors and guides.' If the individual you are talking to is an interesting person, you could add, 'I would be grateful to catch up with you in a month or two, to seek your advice and to test my thinking with you.'

Element 3: 'I do not expect to be making any job decisions for three to six months.'

It is understandable that you might be reluctant to say out loud you're delaying making any job decisions for three to six months. The strong advantage, however, is that it indicates you are not desperate and you will not accept any offer presented to you, unless it is very attractive. You are likely to benefit in two ways as a result of taking this position:

1. You will have time to generate and consider job options without being distracted by early offers that are difficult to evaluate given you do not know what else is out there.
2. People who are interested in you know they will have some time to negotiate with you and that they will not lose you if they do not present you with a role immediately.

If this approach makes sense for you, add some additional words to your answer along these lines, 'I want to make sure I do my networking and have thought through my options carefully. I intend to hold off on accepting any role during the next three to six months. This will give me time to understand what is out there and to think through my next career steps.'

Of course, if your dream job is presented to you early on, you can still accept it. In this case, as I have already mentioned, if needed you can explain why you have moved so fast by stating, 'Amazingly, an offer came up that I just could not refuse.' In this situation, others will understand why you changed your intentions. This test – *Have*

I been given an offer I just could not refuse? – is actually a very good test whenever you come to making your final job decision.

Element 4: 'I will not be accepting any board positions until I know what I will be doing next.'

Because you are accomplished, your friends and your network might come up with ideas where you can join a not-for-profit board, or get involved on the committee of some sort of charity or community activity. Hold off on accepting anything like this until after you know what you will be doing in your next role. Otherwise, there is a danger you will be distracted by this activity when you should be focusing on your own future. Say something like, 'I am honoured that you would consider me for a role like this. But I have made a commitment to myself, and to my family, not to accept any positions until I understand what I will be doing next. In the meantime, I would be happy to learn more about your organisation and how I might contribute if I were to join your board.'

I realise that some coaches advise accepting a board position if it is offered. They argue that it permits you to meet, and work with, other senior people. I think it is too early to do this, before you know your next role. The exception might be if you are invited to join a prestigious board with a highly regarded Chair. Always ask yourself: *If I join this board or committee, will this assist me in building my career, or will it be a distraction?* The British rowing eight, which for the first time since 1912 won the gold medal in the 2000 Sydney Olympics, had a basic question they asked before each and every activity leading up to the Games: 'Will this make our boat go faster?' Going to the local pub did not make the boat go faster. So, they avoided this. You need to ask yourself: *Will this activity help me get a better job and position me to build a winning career?* If not, don't do it.

Element 5: '*I will not accept any consulting work until I am well into my networking.*'

You may be approached to help an organisation you know with some consulting or contracting work. Taking on consulting before you are well established in your networking is likely to be a mistake. The danger is that you become so committed to your consulting assignment that you slow down or stop your networking. I have seen this loss of networking momentum happen several times, and it is damaging because you may need to restart from scratch. Once you are well established in your networking, doing some limited consulting will be possible – and perhaps even desirable. As a general rule, this would be after you have met all your A-List and have started meeting your B-List (see chapter 7 for more on this).

As already mentioned, even when your network is established, try to avoid consulting assignments that involve working more than three days a week. You need at least two days a week to continue your networking. If you are approached for consulting early on, you could say something like, 'Thanks for this suggestion. I am very interested but I must focus on preparing for my job search right now. Once I have some momentum in my networking – in a month or two – I would be happy to talk about consulting with you some more. Even then, I must maintain my networking momentum so I would only be available three days a week. If this is okay, I would be happy to keep talking about this possible assignment so that I can understand it better.'

By the way, if you do accept a consulting assignment, make sure you prepare a formal proposal. This should set out your approach and who will be involved in the assignment, explain what will be delivered by when, and make your billing terms crystal clear. It is important that the end products to be delivered, and precise arrangements involved, are agreed by all stakeholders! Also, do not forget other aspects, such as professional indemnity insurance. If necessary, obtain professional advice as to whether you should consult as an individual or a company. Again, ask yourself: *Will this help me build a better career, or will it slow down my networking and delay my job search?*

Keep these five elements in mind when you are asked what you want to do. If you answer along the lines I suggest, you will communicate that you have thought clearly about your next steps. You should also have sparked interest about your job-search process. This will enable you, if you wish, to co-opt the person who is asking the question and allow you to seek their help and advice in growing your network. This is much better than providing them with a vague answer that indicates you are not sure exactly what you will be doing.

★★★

In this chapter, I have discussed how important it is to be an effective verbal communicator and how to prepare to communicate clearly and concisely. If you follow the advice provided, you will be able to answer three common, and deceptively simple, questions quickly and with impact. Thinking deeply about what you will communicate, and then rehearsing thoroughly, are both vital. If you do this well, you will dramatically improve the quality and power of your communication. And you will also improve the likelihood that you will build a strong emotional connection in any meeting. This, in turn, will help you develop trusting relationships that will allow you to expand your network. Finally, the very fact that you are clear and brief will reinforce that you are different and special compared with most of those you are competing with.

You might think that all this preparation is overkill. You might argue that anyone who is accomplished will find all this comes naturally. This is not my experience – rather, the reverse is the case. The smarter and more accomplished you are, the less likely you will get this right without putting in significant effort – possibly because you have more to talk about! In addition to focusing on how and what you communicate, you need to make it clear that you wish to avoid distractions when you begin your networking.

This will mean not joining activities that could be interesting but will take your eye off the ball. Two examples of distracting activities are joining not-for-profit boards and agreeing to intense consulting. You must not forget that you are undertaking an important project that involves preparing yourself for the rest of your life. You need to focus on this to the best of your ability.

In the next chapter, I discuss what else you need to do before you begin networking. This involves working through the career ideas you wish to test while you are networking. It is important to be able to articulate your work goals for the next three or four years, and the various pathways that might assist you to reach these goals. This will help set you up with a framework for seeking advice that will help you move forward to achieve excellent results.

SOME QUESTIONS FOR YOU TO CONSIDER

- What should you do to set the right expectations in early meetings?
- How can you inspire trust and respect in the people you meet?
- How can you ensure you're displaying warmth *and* competence?
- Will your answers be concise and clear, and have impact?
- Can you answer 'What do you do?' in about eight seconds?
- Can you tell people about yourself in two minutes or less?
- How will you answer 'What do you want to do?' before you start your networking?
- Have you thought through how to maintain your momentum and avoid distractions?

PART III

GROWING THE POWER OF YOUR NETWORK

6

Exploring your career options based on your strengths

We delight in the beauty of the butterfly, but rarely admit the changes it has gone through to achieve that beauty.

Maya Angelou

Prepare to explore your career options, based on your strengths, by:

- Formulating your preferred career direction
- Creating a Framework for Seeking Advice from your network
- Validating your ideas with referees before you begin networking

SO FAR YOU have worked out how to describe what makes you special, and you have practised how you will communicate this. Your next challenge is use your knowledge of your strengths to identify and explain the pathways you wish to explore as you begin to search for a job. If you can explain this well, those close to you will provide you with useful critique and helpful advice. As I already mentioned, being successful in a job does not automatically mean you will be successful in the process of finding a job. The trick in finding a job is to build a team of supporters who will help you. Before you start meeting people, having clear ideas to test and explore is vital. To begin with, your task will be to formulate a series of reasonable hypotheses about where you should be exploring, and then to test these with some of your referees. To use the pond analogy again, you need to decide which ponds to fish in.

When you meet someone – whether you know them or not – it is not helpful to start your conversation with, 'I have just left my job and I am thinking about what I should do next. Do you have any ideas?' If you do this, it will be obvious that you are not pre-pared. The person you are questioning is likely to have very few – if any – useful ideas. They probably have little or no understanding of where you might add the most value, what would be most inter-esting for you, or your personal priorities. So, expecting them to provide you with good advice is not at all reasonable. The advice that will help you most will depend on what makes you special and where you wish to go from here. If you were in a taxi, you would tell the driver where you wanted to go. The idea here is similar. Even though you may not know the exact destination, you need to be able to explain in broad terms where you are heading. Once you are on your way, your thinking will evolve as you meet more people, and you will be able to be more specific as you get closer to your destination.

In this chapter, I show you a framework for thinking about your career goals and considering the issues you will face in various pathways forward. Although you may consider many possible options, with multiple permutations and combinations, I discuss here your four main potential pathways going forward:

1. evolving your current career
2. changing to a new career
3. transitioning to a portfolio career
4. starting your own business.

As you may know, a portfolio career is where you take on a number of activities rather than a full-time role. For example, you may decide that you would like to be a corporate director, help a new business in its start-up phase, provide some consulting and contribute to society with charity work. I personally strongly believe that, if you are considering retirement, you would do well to investigate some kind of a portfolio career to keep yourself active and productive.

In this chapter, I show you how to frame your career goals in a way that will help other people to help you. You should avoid being too broad or too narrow – either will mean you're unlikely to attract the best advice. Something to be aware of is that your close colleagues and friends will want to be supportive and will not want to hurt your feelings by being critical of your ideas. In fact, they are likely to want to err strongly on the supportive side. It will not be helpful to you if they are not frank, even though they may help you feel good in the short term.

What you really need is objective input. When you give your colleagues and friends specific hypotheses to consider, they are more likely to provide you with frank and honest advice. To present yourself in this way might be challenging. But it will pay off because you will receive specific and clear advice. You may say something like, 'I think I could be the CEO of a $1 billion business in three years. Do you think I should be aspiring to this kind of role?' Your colleagues may agree that this aspiration makes good sense. Or they may say something like, 'You are an excellent person but, personally, I think it would make much more sense for you to aspire to a great role as a number two.' If you receive negative or diffident responses to the choices you are suggesting, you may decide to go back and rethink them. Alternatively, you may, of course, stick to your guns and test them more widely.

This chapter will help you to think through how to launch your networking effectively. Being properly prepared will help you generate the best results when you meet other people. What you are seeking is the widest variety of relevant opportunities to give you the best prospects for success. The people you are introduced to, as you expand your network, can help you best if they know:

- the types of individuals you would like to meet
- what you would like to discuss with these people.

You want your network to provide you with warm introductions to relevant people they know. To achieve this, you will need to have clear hypotheses to discuss and to test with your A-List before you begin to expand your network.

FORMULATING YOUR PREFERRED CAREER DIRECTION

Your first step is to sharpen your thinking on your career options. As just outlined, you probably have four main career directions that you might explore. Each of these directions will involve different opportunities and risks, and different conversations. People on your

A-List (people you already know) should provide considerable help to you in thinking about your various career options.

It is best if you settle on one future career path to explore by the time you're ready to meet your B-List and C-List people (see chapter 7 for more on this). People who do not know you well will find it difficult to assist you if you take multiple career directions to them to consider. They have not seen you in action, so they will not know you well enough to add real value or help you with this kind of a deep question. Even some on your A-List might struggle to help you with this question. Therefore, your first challenge is to take a view on which of the four pathways you wish to explore in depth. Working this out and being able to explain your rationale well will help others to help you!

Option 1: Evolving your current career

You might well expect to continue with your current career. This usually makes good sense. The rationale is that you can build on your accumulated knowledge, experience, intellectual property and relationships. You can carry these forward to add real value quickly in a different organisation. Recruiters and future employers tend to favour continuity too. If this is the direction you wish to explore, you should consider the various issues related to how to position yourself strategically, and how to maximise your opportunities and minimise the risks you will face in a new role. The following outlines some of the questions you should be asking yourself.

What strategic positioning do I want?

If you have worked in a major business, you would do well to address this question directly: 'Do I want to be a whale or a tiger shark?' In other words, do you want to find your next role in a well-established business? Or do you wish to explore other businesses in the same or a similar industry that are smaller and more agile and, maybe, more aggressive? In the current business environment, where radical change is occurring every day – in regulations, laws, technologies, global pressures and so on – do you want to join a large established, legacy business (a whale), which is fending off the predators, or do you want to join the predators (the tiger sharks)? You may have a non-compete agreement that constrains you in various ways – and this may mean you won't find the right next job for yourself until after it has expired – but this should not restrict you from investigating all options.

These days, many senior executives from established businesses are joining smaller businesses financed by private equity. They are opting to become tiger sharks, bringing their broad management experience to smaller, less mature and more agile businesses with high growth potential. They are willing to take a lower salary with equity. They are expecting that the equity will be valuable in three to five years. Some have even ended up buying the businesses they have joined. See more discussion on this in the section 'Option 4: Start your own business'. This latter option, of joining (and perhaps buying) a smaller business, has many similarities to starting your own business.

How can I maximise my opportunities?

As I mentioned in chapter 2, it is useful to think of the job-search process as a farmer sowing seeds. The more seeds you sow in the best soil, the better your opportunities of a successful crop. The same goes for a job search. The bigger the network you can build, the more likely is a successful next role and, after that, a successful career. Also, switching to the fishing analogy I used earlier, you need to decide where to fish. This will depend on the equipment you have and your particular skills but, most importantly, you need to fish where and when you are likely to catch the best fish. You will need to be disciplined. I recommend that you decide on three ponds to fish in and then ask your network to help you identify and explore these.

The farming and fishing analogies only take you part of the way. The final element in maximising your opportunities relates to building strong emotional connections with those you meet. This will not always be possible. Some of those you meet will not know how, or will not want, to help you. You will have some setbacks, but remember that you only need one success to change your life. Revisiting the 80/20 rule, remember that about 20 per cent of those you meet while networking will probably provide you with 80 per cent of the opportunities likely to be relevant to you.

Albert went much further than most of my clients in terms of taking steps to maintain warm connections with his network. Every six months, he sent everyone he had met during his networking a brief status report. He continued to do this even after he obtained a new job. This paid off for him in an extraordinary way. In one of these emails, he indicated that his new job was excellent but involved too much time away from his family. He needed to find another job so that he could spend less time travelling. As a result of this email, his name was recommended for a special role in a large public company by one of its board directors. The CEO met Albert and he was hired without going through a competitive process. So, this simple email update to his trusted network resulted in Albert achieving his goal of finding the excellent job he was seeking, with much less time away from home!

How can I minimise the risks I face in a new role?

The more career variables a new role contains, the more risk you are taking on and the higher the likelihood of challenges and possible failure. This is why recruiters tend to target individuals who have been successful already in a similar job in a similar organisation. For example, a recruiter would almost never suggest that a CEO from a private company take on the role of CEO of a public company. The public company role involves a series of challenges that have not been faced by the private company CEO. These additional challenges include reporting to a board of professional directors, communicating with public shareholders, dealing with company analysts and interfacing with the stock exchange.

All new situations you face will have various risks associated with them. Some examples are:

- *Lowest risk – same location/same organisation:* The possible risks you will face in this situation might involve changing your boss, changing the scope of your role, or changing the nature of your role. If you have a new boss, you will face increased risk even if you continue in your established job. This new boss might be much more controlling than the boss who hired you, or they may not be as committed to your future success. However, on the plus side, you do know how things work in your current role and in your current organisation. And you will also have the advantage of established relationships with individuals you trust and who can provide you with advice and help.

- *Moderate risk – new location/same organisation:* Changing to a new city or country affects not only you but also your family. You will need new housing. You might move away from your established family support systems. If you're in a relationship, your partner likely has their own job. So, moving could involve two people having to make a job transition. In addition, if you have school-age children, they face the challenges of building new friendships in a new teaching environment. All these incremental changes can add more stress and risk.

- *Higher risk – same location/new organisation:* Here you may face all the changes from the first point in this list, plus working in a new, unfamiliar culture. You will not have the familiar network of your colleagues to support you. Sometimes you are moving to a new role because you have colleagues there who have also worked with your previous organisation. This reduces your risk. One important saving grace when joining a new organisation is that the person hiring you will do their utmost to make you successful.

If you are not successful, this will reflect poorly on them and their judgement in hiring you.

- *Highest risk — new location/new organisation:* Here you have all the risks from the preceding points, plus the additional challenges facing you and your family of building new relationships and finding your way around. If you have a partner, quite often they face the greatest challenges, particularly if he or she does not have a job, or is not permitted to work. CPOs have told me that family unhappiness, rather than failure in a new job, is the issue that causes most geographic moves to fail. This is because of factors such as the loneliness of the non-working partner and/or their children not fitting into the new environment.

As you can see, when you take a new job, in a new company, in a new location, with a new boss, within a different culture, the risks you face usually increase markedly. Experienced recruiters, who are aware of these compounding risks, try to manage them during the hiring process. Despite this, they find that a certain number of people they place with their clients do not work out. If you have a family, start your job search close to home. If suitable opportunities cannot be found where you live, then the search can be expanded to other cities and states — and then, if necessary, other countries. In chapter 10, I discuss, in more depth, how to minimise the risk of failure in a new role.

Option 2: Changing to a new career

From time to time, a client tells me they do not want to continue in their current career. They are bored and would like to try something completely new. Or they have had a successful professional career and want to use their skills in, say, a corporate or not-for-profit. While you are in a career transition process, you have the luxury of testing whether changing to a new career makes sense for you and your family. But be careful. The grass may look greener on the other side of the fence, but greener grass is rarely available. You might find the grass is actually greener where you care for it and water it, rather than on the other side of the fence! So, don't automatically look for new pastures. Unless you can transfer your current skills and these skills clearly differentiate you in the new environment, you will not be special there. Your current network will be sceptical about such a move too. They will ask why you want to do this when you have been so successful in your old career. Finally, if you take a significant cut in income to start a new career where you find it difficult to differentiate yourself or add significant value in the new environment, your family may be unhappy.

Changing careers is possible, as long as you carefully think through how you will add value in your new role. Three examples of individuals who have made successful career moves follow:

1. Nigel had been a high-performing senior executive in three industrial companies. He came across an opportunity to manage a mid-sized disability organisation that presented him with totally new challenges. These issues related to clients, staffing, board directors, government regulation, fundraising, multiple stakeholders, and difficult-to-manage service levels. I was concerned that he might find the new culture difficult to adjust to. Five years later, the skills Nigel brought from his industrial background had helped him lead a total transformation of the organisation he joined. Nigel not only changed the original organisation for the better, but also grew it to become a preeminent national organisation though a series of mergers and acquisitions.

2. Adina was a highly regarded management consultant who made a successful transition into academia. She had worked her way up to a senior level in a global consulting firm and was a partner. She took a big step from there into an academic role, running a junior college. After a successful transition, she accepted the role of heading up a well-regarded university. An issue for management consultants is usually whether they

can make a successful transition from a role which involves analysis and advice to a role managing people. I always remember that, when I moved from consulting to a CEO position, I was amazed at the amount of time I needed to spend on people and legal/regulatory issues. As a result of my experience in consulting, I was concerned whether Adina would be able to thrive in the new environment. In fact, she was able to manage this transition brilliantly.

3. Anna was a successful professional commercial lawyer who joined a global IT consulting firm as head of its internal legal services. The usual issue for people joining a consulting firm is that they find the pressure for precision and results is far beyond anything they have experienced before in a 'normal' commercial role. Fortunately, Anna excelled in her role. From there, she moved to a project management role in a bank, and from there to a COO role in an emerging business with clients worldwide.

To summarise, while you are in a career transition, you can think through whether a change of career makes sense for you, before you make the change. Having time to do this is a luxury. It is an opportunity that is unlikely to be available to you while you are flat out working in your job. Changing careers tends to be more challenging as you go further into your career. Although some have managed to successfully change careers after they are, say, 50, this is relatively rare. You are most likely to be successful if you move from a commercial role into the not-for-profit sector, like Nigel in the preceding example. If you do this, your strong management skills may be a real asset. But Steve Clifford, who has made a successful transition from senior lawyer to not-for-profit CEO, points out just how complicated these organisations are, and how you need to 'listen, and then listen some more'.

Be careful not to be seduced by the idea of starting in a new field and being immediately successful. The best way to be successful in a new field is through using your special skills from your previous role effectively in your new job. The least likely situation for success in moving to a new, entirely different role is when you have been a true specialist – in, say, medicine, the law, or astrophysics. In this case, you have built a successful career based on deep knowledge in your field. You are a 'knowledge specialist'. If you are not able to leverage this deep knowledge in your new field, you may find your new situation very challenging because you have no competitive advantage.

Option 3: Transitioning to a portfolio career

Many executives and other senior managers are attracted to a portfolio career at some stage. A portfolio career allows you to leave the corporate treadmill and permits you to balance your life around various activities of interest to you, including helping others with coaching or mentoring, or assisting not-for-profit activities to help your community. A portfolio career allows you more flexibility and control over your work life. You can manage your priorities, and you can modify these as your thinking evolves and new opportunities arise. As mentioned earlier, I see a portfolio career as far preferable to retirement.

If you wish to explore the possibility of launching a portfolio career, keep the following four aspects in mind.

Be clear with your network about your goals

Don't split your focus and try to research, at the same time, the possibility of continuing in a corporate career and launching a portfolio career. You need to research one clear career option at a time. Attempting to explore both options in parallel will rarely work. You will confuse the people you are asking to help you. They will not be clear about whether you want a full-time job or a portfolio career. As a result, they will struggle to help you. Worse, they may believe you do not know what you are doing. So, if you are keen to test whether a portfolio career is right for you, focus on exploring this from the start and make this your priority.

You may be attracted to the idea of a portfolio career but uncertain whether this makes sense now or whether you should wait. In this case, start your networking by concentrating on ways of continuing your established career. Make this your priority when you are seeking advice. As an aside, at the end of a networking conversation, you can mention that a portfolio career seems to have attractions. After you have built your network out to the third circle (your C-List – see chapter 7), and met more than the target minimum of 50 new people, you may well see various portfolio opportunities beginning to emerge. Your thinking will evolve. You may then see specific opportunities that make it clear that a portfolio career is preferable to the idea of continuing your corporate career.

Do your homework and test your thinking

When you have a portfolio career you are, in effect, going into business for yourself. You need as much validation as possible that you are on the right track before you commit. Detailed research is difficult at any time, but particularly while you are in a full-time job. In a career transition process, you have the unusual luxury of having real time to do thorough research. The other good thing about being in transition is that you can test your thinking before you commit to a particular idea.

For instance, if you are thinking about starting your own consulting or advisory business as part of your portfolio career, you can carry out detailed market research and testing before you commit. You can formulate your consulting business concept, prepare a business plan, and test the various services you will offer. You will need to work out what your services will cost to produce, your overhead structure and your proposed pricing schedule. You will be able to prepare some mock-up marketing materials.

Once you have identified your target markets and your potential clients, you can approach people you trust and test your thinking with them. Let's look at an example. Naira wanted to launch a business where she provided branding advice to individuals and corporates. She produced a beautiful glossy brochure that set out the four main areas where she would provide advice and the benefits she could deliver. The people in Naira's network were very impressed with the quality of the document she had produced, but they were worried the content was too broad ranging and not focused enough. They thought the material was too complicated and that Naira was offering to solve too many types of problems. They believed her prospective clients might be confused by the scope of the brochure and be reticent to retain her. As a result, she dramatically simplified her service offering and reduced the size of her brochure by two-thirds.

Once you have a strong service concept, your next step should be to visit key prospects to test your ideas with them. Approaching potential prospects is much easier when you are testing, rather than selling, your ideas. You can explain that you are keen to obtain their advice before you commit to any particular way forward. When you are actually in business and committed, you will need to sell your service to stay in business. If you need to make a sale, rather than seeking advice, you will feel (and may transmit) much greater stress. If, during this market testing phase, you meet 20 people and they all say they like your idea and would buy your service, you will be much more confident that your idea will work. If many of them say no, you will probably have to go back to the drawing board. The key to most successful businesses is repeat purchases, and warm recommendations to other prospects by your established clients, so this must be an important part of your conversation with your prospects.

When my clients become anxious that 'everything is taking so long', I like to remind them of the Disney story I used to read to my daughter when she was young, about Mulan. In the story, Mulan's visit to the matchmaker was disastrous but, when she returned, her father observed how beautiful the flowers were that year. He then pointed out one nearby that hadn't bloomed yet, saying, 'My, my, what beautiful blossoms we have this year. But look, this one's late. I bet when it blooms, it will be the most beautiful of all.' Take comfort that the best results are not always the fastest, and don't rush.

Do not commit too early – be patient

Portfolio careers tend to evolve. For example, even the most attractive and highest potential board directors might take a year or more before they obtain their first major board position. This is because many boards know, at least one year ahead, who will fill their next director position. If this is the case, the best you can hope for is a position in two years. In my experience, the least attractive or smaller boards tend to present themselves first. It will be tempting to accept a board position when it is presented. However, think carefully about this. Accepting something too small or which might involve high risk, because of an immature board or management team or poor systems, is likely to be a mistake. Before accepting a board position in an unproven public company, you should take steps to protect your assets. The risk of class actions against directors is increasing daily.

Another issue is that you are likely to be pigeonholed and branded by the boards that you accept early on. For example, if you initially accept government boards, you are likely to define yourself, maybe unintentionally, as someone who belongs on government boards. This could pre-empt other more attractive opportunities, which might take longer to mature. One further possible downside of accepting boards too quickly is the potential to spread yourself too thin. If you accept lesser opportunities early on, you may not have enough capacity when additional better opportunities emerge. Some coaches will argue that any board could be a good experience for you, allowing you to expand your knowledge and your network. I disagree. I recommend that you wait until you can see how your career is likely to evolve before you accept any board positions.

One thing you should be aware of when it comes to seeking a board position is that you are unlikely to be successful if you are too assertive about wanting to be a director. Chairs do not respond well to people they believe are too pushy. It makes sense to test, in a very low-key way, the idea that you would like to be a director. Do this with established board directors. Do they think you would make a good director? If they say yes, ask them how they suggest you progress this. This is a subtle process: like dropping a pebble into a pond, and then letting the ripples move out and then return. Having a successful director as a sponsor will provide you with a major advantage.

Do not downplay your strengths

Finally, if you have been a corporate leader, be yourself during a board interview process. Some senior executives are tempted to be too deferential in order to convince a board Chair they will be a good team player and won't rock the boat. You may think this makes sense in order to be offered the board position. But this is unlikely to be a good strategy. Instead, I recommend you show your true colours. If you are feisty, show this during the interviews. You are unlikely to be invited to join boards where the Chair wants you to be a rubber stamp – but who wants to be a member of a board like this anyway? Aim to join a board with a respected Chair who appreciates your strengths and is keen to help you develop into an effective director and a future board leader. In this regard, you should think through, from the beginning, how you could continue to develop as a director. A reasonable goal might be to become a board Chair within, say, five years.

A portfolio career can be exceedingly attractive and desirable if you want to be in charge of your own life. Many high-performance managers and leaders find it is attractive option after they reach their mid- to late-fifties, rather than looking at another full-time role or early retirement. The earlier you can begin planning and exploring the better. If you can, you should begin this planning process three to five years in advance. Using this time for advance planning and testing, before you launch into a portfolio career, will be beneficial. The key is to identify and then minimise, or at least to be in a position to manage, any future risks you will face.

Option 4: Starting your own business

At some stage, you may be attracted to the idea of starting your own business. This is more feasible these days, with venture capitalists and private equity investors willing to finance start-ups and acquisitions. Many of my clients investigate these opportunities. They find the idea of heading up their own business and calling the shots attractive. As digital technology penetrates more and more industries, many 'whales' are vulnerable. And thanks to the cloud you can take a good idea global very quickly. Julian, for example, developed a way of tailoring PowerPoint presentations to personalise the formatting quickly and easily. His service is particularly appealing to management consultants. Julian now has clients around the world, largely as a result of word-of-mouth recommendations from individuals who have used his software in their consulting firms and then moved on to other roles. His clients are set up on a monthly fee schedule, paid automatically by credit card, and he has one employee – himself. Julian's income is much greater than any salary he might command in the IT market. And he loves being his own boss!

If you are thinking about starting your own business, you must understand your total financial exposure. Be certain you have the financial capacity to avoid running out of money, especially in the first 12 to 18 months. Set some checkpoints to measure your progress against plan. In some ways, the worst situation for you could be to become an owner of a 'living dead' business. These businesses are just surviving. You are tempted to continue because you have put tremendous effort in to the business and, even though it is not going anywhere, it is not doing so badly that it needs to be closed down. And a slight possibility exists that it might take off. In this situation, you may be trapped. At some point you will need to face the difficult decision of whether or not to continue. Finally, it is important that any investment you make is a decision made with your family or those most important to you. Your family might have a different risk profile to yours, and might not want you to mortgage everything you own on your new business bet. In Silicon Valley, it is common for one partner in a couple to have a steady job to support the family while the other takes the entrepreneurial risk.

Hockey stick projections, where the financial projections of a business are projected to suddenly turn around, take off and grow strongly in the near future, are common when planning new businesses. In *Thinking, Fast and Slow*, however, psychologist and economist Daniel Kahneman points out that projects very often fail to meet their financial and implementation targets – because planners do not carefully consider everything that might go wrong. Indeed, they tend to assume things will go right rather than wrong. Even sophisticated venture capital investors, who are skilled in selecting where they will place their investments, assume that 9 out of 10 of their investments will not succeed. If the odds are so poor for professional investors in start-ups, be careful not to bet everything you have on your new business. You need to understand exactly what you are doing, and be sure you can manage the downside.

In his article 'How to write a great business plan', published in the *Harvard Business Review*, Professor William Sahlman argues,

> *Most business plans waste too much ink on numbers and devote too little to the information that really matters to intelligent investors. An entrepreneurial venture faces far too many unknowns to predict revenues, let alone profits.*

He argues there are four key factors that must be evaluated:

1. *The calibre and experience of the people involved:* This is the most important determinant of success.

2. *The nature and scale of the opportunity being addressed:* What will be sold to whom, and what stands in the way of success?

3. *The context:* This includes factors which cannot be controlled by investors, such as new government rules and regulations.

4. *The risk and reward:* An assessment of everything that can go right and wrong.

Professor Sahlman also suggests that three questions are key when assessing an investment. These are: What total cash investment is required to finance the business? When does cash flow turn positive? What is the expected magnitude of the future payoff and what is the likelihood of achieving this? Sahlman highlights that business plans are very often full of jargon and terms that conceal the inadequate planning behind the business. Sahlman's full article is available online, and is valuable reading if you are thinking of launching your own business.

CREATING A FRAMEWORK FOR SEEKING ADVICE FROM YOUR NETWORK

Once you have decided your broad career direction, you need to frame the career and job hypotheses you would like to test with your network. As explained later in this section, I call this your Framework for Seeking Advice (FSA). To prepare your FSA, you need to answer three questions, as covered in the following sections.

Question 1: What role do I aspire to in, say, three to five years?

As already discussed, clarifying what position you would like to achieve in three to five years helps others you meet for advice to understand your near-term goals. My advice is to be strategic and to aim high. Be courageous. Remember – this near-term goal is aspirational. If you cannot find any support for your thinking when you begin networking, you can always lower your sights – but, even so, you will have thought through where you wish to go. You will at least understand why it makes sense for you to aim lower.

As already mentioned, I initially came across this issue when I worked with some senior CFOs. I first asked them whether they wished to remain as financial experts for the rest of their careers, or to become CEOs. The nature of their preferred next roles would be heavily influenced by the answer to this question, so raising this issue during the recruiting process was important. An organisation may be looking for someone who wishes to remain in the CFO role for the rest of their career. If so, they are looking for someone quite different from an individual who aspires to be the CEO within the next few years.

Many of my clients are tempted to identify multiple possible near-term goals, rather than one single goal. They say they could be a CEO or a CFO, or a business unit head, or head of a specific function. My advice is to concentrate on defining one mid-term goal. You will benefit by forcing yourself to select one aspirational goal that, in the best of all possible worlds, you would like to attain. You cannot predict the future and you may not achieve your aspirational goal. But at least you will be clear about what you are aiming to achieve and what you are seeking to test with your network. Many of my clients struggle with this. They think it is too hard to see where their career might lead. But I want you to make the effort to think about this as deeply as you can, even if deciding on one goal is a struggle. Aim for the stars and you might hit the moon. Aim low and you will probably hit your target, but you may be functioning way below your potential.

Your friends and colleagues will want to avoid hurting your feelings. They might feel obliged to encourage you, even though they may not truly believe in your aspiration. Ask them to be clear and honest about their view of your potential. By suggesting a singular goal to them, you encourage them to give you their honest view, rather than some vaguely supportive answer. In my late-thirties, I set myself the goal of becoming a CEO by the time I reached 40. This was somewhat arbitrary but seemed possible. When I tested this with my network, they also believed that this was possible. As a result, I was introduced to a series of individuals who helped me achieve this. Several members of my network agreed to become investors in a new business that I set up. This business then bought an established business. Had I not made my aspirational goal – to become a CEO by the age of 40 – clear to my network I most likely would have accepted a much more routine job. And my subsequent career would have been totally different.

It is important to indicate the likely size and scope of the role you would like, and the scale and nature of your ideal organisation. Otherwise, your network is likely to underestimate the role you might be aspiring to. Most of us have no idea what it takes to manage a large number of people. We think in terms of something we can understand, such as running a small business. If you say you would like to be a CEO in three to four years, it is important to be specific. Do you wish to head up a public company, a private company or a not-for-profit organisation? What size of organisation – in revenue, people, assets or profits? What geographic scale and complexity? Obviously, leading an organisation with 500 people is totally different from being responsible for 10,000 people. Being in charge of a local business is different from being responsible for a national or an international business. In a bank, being a local branch manager is quite different from having a broad role in the corporate office. Make the scope and scale of your aspirational goal clear.

Providing a real-life example of a business where you think you might fit will also help others understand your aspirations. When you discuss your medium-term goal with others, test your thinking this way:

> 'If I could wave a magic wand, I would like to think that, in three to five years, I could head up a national public company employing about 1000 people, such as company XYZ. You have seen me in action in my most recent role. Could you tell me frankly whether you think this kind of aspiration makes any sense for me?'

I have used heading up a business as an example here, but you can choose any position that makes sense to you as an aspirational goal.

If you are starting out in your career, your goal needs to be some kind of a step up in your organisation or elsewhere. If your A-List confirms that your aspirations are realistic, you will achieve three important things:

1. *You will have refined your aspirations* – as a result of having tested your hypotheses with people who you know and trust.

2. *You will be more confident going forward* – since you will have received feedback from your future referees and others you trust.

3. *You can explain that your key supporters endorse your aspirations* – when you meet new people, including recruiters, in the future.

If your colleagues tell you that you are a wonderful person but they do not believe you should be aiming for a role you aspire to, you can probe this and learn why they have this view. Then the question becomes what, if anything, you should change or develop to convince them to support the idea that such a goal would make sense for you.

Question 2: What roles are pathways to my aspirational role?

Having a clear goal is helpful, but how can you then achieve this goal? Similar to playing golf, you might score a hole in one, or it may take you one or two extra shots to achieve your goal. Work out three possible pathways to your goal. For the sake of argument, if you wish to become the CEO of national company with 10,000 employees, you might consider these three pathway roles to position yourself to achieve that position:

- *Head of a division for a global business:* In this role, you might be running a business of a similar size, but you would be reporting to the global CEO. This would prepare you for a standalone CEO role in three or four years.

- *Second-in-command in a larger business:* You would be benefiting from learning from a CEO who is running the larger business, while proving that you can manage and lead multiple activities effectively.

- *CEO of a smaller business – say, with 5000 employees:* This would permit you to learn and develop as a CEO, perhaps in a relatively straightforward business. This would prepare you for something bigger and more complex.

Identifying these pathways to your mid-term goal is important for three reasons. First, more of these intermediate roles are available and so are easier to find. Second, working in these intermediate roles is less risky for you than taking on a large CEO role in a new business. Being exposed to the more visible, more challenging role may put you under an intense spotlight too soon, before you are ready. The third reason is you're forced to be disciplined as you search for a role. I have seen situations where my client became interested in a particular role that would not have helped them meet their aspirational goal. You and your coach must be able to step back and ask, 'Is this role likely to lead me to where I ultimately want to go?' If not, consider stepping away from it. It is likely to be a waste of your energy and a distraction.

Only colleagues who have seen you in action are able to provide authentic advice to you on your aspirational goal and possible pathways towards this goal. These are likely to be people on your A-List. Even though these people will have a view on whether your aspirations make sense, do not expect them to identify a specific role for you. Job opportunities will begin to emerge once you have established a larger network, involving people in your B-List and C-List (see chapter 8). Do not expect people you do not know to validate your aspirations. They do not know you well enough to make a strong contribution to this topic.

Question 3: What specific sectors should I explore?

The next step for you is to identify three sectors you would like to explore. These sectors could be, for instance, financial services, telecommunications and infrastructure. Or they could be any other way of segmenting different types of organisations into three groups – for example:

- private equity firms, professional service firms and universities
- regulated, partially regulated and unregulated businesses
- government, semi-government and public–private partnerships.

The idea here is to help you determine which sectors – and then which organisations within these sectors – make sense for you to learn more about and explore. Once you have a list of possible organisations to explore, this will trigger ideas to discuss with your contacts while you are networking. You can ask the people you are meeting whether they can provide you with additional information, firsthand advice, or leads who might have more relevant information for you.

Once your network and your coach see the kinds of businesses that interest you, they will be much more helpful in identifying good people to provide you with advice. Most people – and particularly recruiters – will typecast you narrowly. Most people who know you will expect you to do more or less the same job that you have just left, but in a different organisation. With the process I explain here, you can highlight you are exploring a wider range of opportunities, and seeking advice in regard to these opportunities. You will also be making it easier for your network to suggest additional people for you to meet to help you. Without these prompts, it is much more difficult for your network to help you. With these prompts, they can suggest possible additions to your list, and also deletions.

Your choice of sector options needs to be guided by three considerations:

1. *Are they easy to explain and independent?* Try not to have sectors that overlap, even if they are related. As suggested already, you could have financial services, telecommunications and infrastructure. Another approach could be to have subsets

of financial services, such as retail banking, insurance and superannuation. Pick three sectors that interest you and are mutually exclusive and easy to explain to other people.

2. *Do they lead to balanced lists of multiple organisations to explore?* Ideally each option will lead to a similar number of target businesses or organisations in each sector. If your options are unbalanced – perhaps one sector leads to 20 target opportunities but another only leads to three – rethink or redefine the sectors you wish to explore to try to achieve a better balance in the number of specific target opportunities for you to learn more about and explore.

3. *Are they areas and organisations where you could add significant value?* You may not have deep experience in a particular industry, but you have to be able to add value in some obvious way. Walking away from all the intellectual property, relationships and knowledge of the industry you have built up during your career and then starting from scratch is risky. In some industries, such as telecommunications, it takes a year just to learn what all the acronyms refer to! If your skills and knowhow are advanced, you may be able to help transform a lagging industry. If this is your hypothesis, it should be tested and explored. Some skills such as financial accounting, logistics or being a company secretary may be fairly readily transferable. Others, such as running a smelter in a copper mine or specialised brain surgery, are not likely to be easily transferred to another industry or sector.

Pulling everything together

I have created the formal FSA, shown in figure 6.1, as a way to collate your thinking on your career options and outline your hypotheses. You can use this as a visual guide with your contacts when discussing your options and seeking advice.

Figure 6.1: Framework for Seeking Advice (FSA)

Your preferred mid-term target role – Select one aspirational role only
Indicate nature and size of enterprise

Example roles to explore as pathways to your preferred goal

Pathway 1	Pathway 2	Pathway 3

Target sectors and organisations for analysis

Type of business	First sector	Second sector	Third sector
Public companies			
International MNC			
Not-for-profit organisations			
Private equity			
Private companies			
Other organisations			

As you complete this framework, you will be obliged to consider a series of important activities and questions, including:

- identifying your aspirational mid-term target goal
- selecting possible pathways to this role
- deciding which industries or sectors are likely to present the best opportunities for you
- identifying the highest priority organisations for your research and investigation – and working out how to progress in this research
- considering who in your network will have useful information about the key businesses and which people are working or have worked in them
- identifying from LinkedIn who might introduce you to senior executives in relevant organisations.

You may wish to explore sectors that interest you, but where you do not have detailed knowledge. For example, you might be a sports fanatic and be attracted to the idea of working in sport. This might be a good opportunity, or it may be crazy. Do your research carefully. As Shakespeare notes in *The Merchant of Venice*, 'All that glitters is not gold'. As you conduct research through your network, you will work out where the true opportunities lie and whether they make sense for you to explore further. If you research a sector that turns out to be a dead end, you can replace this sector with one that seems to have better prospects.

When you show your framework to people in your network – and, in particular, the chart setting out the three sectors and the organisations you are interested in – they will immediately see the kinds of organisations that interest you. You will be amazed how often someone in your network will then think of someone who might provide you with good advice. By going through this process, opportunities that make sense for you will begin to be presented to you. It is helpful to be introduced to people who have taken a similar path to yourself, because they could become good role models for you.

The kinds of people most likely to be able to help you are:

- *Super-networkers:* These are people who know a lot of people and are comfortable making introductions, particularly those with contacts in your target sectors.
- *Experts:* These are people with detailed knowledge of businesses or industries you are interested in, particularly industry experts and leaders of industry organisations or associations.
- *Insiders:* These are people who can give you special insights not readily available to others, including those who are, or have been employed, in these sectors.

Use LinkedIn to find individuals who might be able to help you. Let's use the logistics industry as an example. If you search 'logistics in People', for instance, you will find over 11 million names presented to you. You can then filter these to search out various categories of people who have logistics in their profile. You may wish to meet some of these, and can do this by working through a mutual connection or, if they are an industry leader, by contacting them directly. You never know how or when someone in your expanded network will be able to assist you. It could be next week, next month or next year. I describe how to get the best out of LinkedIn in the next chapter.

VALIDATING YOUR THINKING WITH REFEREES BEFORE YOU BEGIN NETWORKING

Once you have developed your materials, test your thinking and materials with a few selected individuals who you know and trust from your A-List. To begin with, the most important people to help you validate your thinking will be two or three of your prospective referees (who I call '*panel members*' in the rest of this section). These panel members are likely to be your referees when you are offered a role, although there may be other referees as well, depending on the job that you are being offered. It is best if those helping you with your validation come from different organisations or different backgrounds, because they are then likely to have different individual networks. Ideally, those helping with validation need to be senior individuals who know you and your previous roles well enough to appreciate your strengths and what makes you special. They will likely have provided you with feedback on your strengths when you sent out your email requests (as described in chapter 3). Find energy givers, and avoid energy takers.

The best panel members are those who can be available to meet you face to face. They could live interstate or overseas but, if they do, you lose the advantage of more intimate conversations. They should be people who care about you and want to help you move into a better senior role. Finally, they need to be willing and able to invest time in helping you. In relation to this, make sure they understand that you would like to circle back to them every couple of months, as your networking activities progress. Hopefully, they will welcome this idea.

The benefits of involving your panel before you network

Your panel members should be very important and positive assets to you. Quite possibly, they could be your secret weapon! Too many jobseekers treat their future referees as a passive resource, calling them just before a job is confirmed. This is a mistake. You will miss a great opportunity to validate your thinking with people who are your supporters and who will be able to help you by introducing you to their own personal networks.

The three benefits of involving your panel members early and asking them to validate your thinking are:

1. *Validation of your thinking will be a valuable confidence booster:*
    Your confidence will be improved because you will know that key referees have signed off on your work. If any questions are raised during interviews, you will be able to say something

along the lines of, 'I am glad you asked about this. Please be assured that I checked this with two of my most senior referees and they have endorsed what I have written.'

2. *Your panel members will learn more about you and your achievements:* Most senior referees know only one part of your career– perhaps the five years or so when you last worked together. They do not necessarily know about other aspects of your work, your recent pattern of career achievement, or the things you do outside your work. You may have swum the English Channel. You may play 10 musical instruments. You may have won important scholarships or awards. By asking prospective referees to review your Professional Profile, you are helping them to learn more about you, your interests, and your accomplishments. As a result, they will become better and more enthusiastic referees.

3. *Your panel members should become active advocates for you:* Your networking goal is to grow your list of advocates and it is important that your panel members are strong advocates for you. You want them to help you to meet more people in the most effective and helpful way. You want them to help you generate more votes as you go forward with your networking. You want your panel members to excite others to become advocates for you.

You certainly don't want referees who say, 'Sure, I would be very happy to be a referee for you. Just get the people who are thinking of hiring you to give me a call.' What you do want them to say is, 'I really believe in you. I want to help you. I would like you to meet X, Y and Z. I will call them and arrange for them to meet you. Is there anything else I can do to help you?' Ideally, you want your panel members to become close confidants and positive advocates, and to always be available to test your thinking as your networking progresses.

The validation you need from your panel members

You should ask your panel members to review your written materials. Also, you should talk through your proposed positioning and networking approach with them. You are not asking for a detailed critique, but rather an overall assessment and endorsement. The following outlines the specific areas to focus on.

Your Professional Profile

Obtain broad validation of what you have written in your Professional Profile. Ask them whether they believe this is a useful document to leave with people as part of your networking, and whether it is a good representation of you. Focus on your profile, not your CV. One issue with these kinds of documents is that everyone thinks they are an expert. Some individuals will think they have better answers than you. They may attempt to line-edit your work or change the order of the sections. This is rarely helpful. A perfect document is impossible. What you need is broad validation from people who know and respect you.

Sometimes you do receive important new insights from your panel members. These should, of course, be incorporated. Bianca was a senior partner in a leading law firm. To her surprise, she was told by her panel members that she had left out a key attribute that made her rare and special. 'What could that be?' she asked. 'You are the only senior professional lawyer we know who is fun to work with', was the response. She incorporated this idea in her Professional Profile and it was a great talking point as she expanded her network.

Your answer to 'Tell me about yourself'

You might feel uncomfortable presenting your rehearsed answer to a friend or colleague and then asking them to critique it. But hardly anyone is better than your panel members to do this. Ask them whether they believe your answer to this question is credible and authentic. Since they know you well, they are in a good position to provide feedback. Again, you are asking for directional input, not wordsmithing.

Your answer to 'What do you want to do?'

It will boost your confidence immensely if the members of your panel endorse your mid-term career goal and the pathways you see for achieving this goal. In addition, knowing and agreeing with your aspirations will help them to be better referees. They should also be helpful in identifying the sectors you could explore and the organisations you should target. If they can supplement your ideas with good ideas of their own, this will make meeting with them particularly worthwhile.

Be wary of someone who feels they must send you red-lined corrections to your Professional Profile or a rewritten answer to the question about yourself. Be extra wary if the corrected version comes back with a message to send it back to them – 'your editor' – once you have redrafted it. Then, they say, they will be pleased to check your work to make sure it is correct! If this happens, respond by thanking the individual, and saying that you look forward to thinking about their input. It is not usually at all helpful if you feel you need to respond to other people's 'corrections'.

You might question whether seeking this validation and support is worth all the effort. My view is that, without this validation, you are flying blind and failing to benefit from the advice and advocacy of people who can and will help you most. You may find that your panel members will change your life.

★★★

Making the effort to think through your career options will help you immeasurably as you move from the preparation phase to launching your networking. You will be more confident and more thoughtful, and will present yourself with more gravitas and balance. Over the years, several recruiters have sent me new clients after spending just a few minutes with them. These executives had just left their jobs and had arrived on the doorsteps of these recruiters. They typically ask just only two questions, 'What's the market like?' and 'Do you have anything going that might suit me?' Senior recruiters are immediately aware that these individuals are not prepared. They can see that these people need help from someone who understands the issues related to career transition before they begin their job search.

Despite what you might think, if recruiters haven't met you before, they don't know enough about you to be able to judge whether any role they have is suitable for you. Most successful senior recruiters pride themselves on knowing in advance who the best candidates for a role will be, and most only work on about 12 assignments each year. The probability that any assignment they're working on would actually be a good match for someone they don't know, and who just happened to walk through the door at the right time, is close to zero. As a result, if you present yourself to a recruiter in this way, the recruiter is most likely to suggest that you need some help from an experienced career consultant to prepare yourself properly.

The ideas set out in this chapter provide you with a framework to help you prepare a good plan for yourself. If you do this well, you will be more confident and your communications will be clear and convincing. As Dale Carnegie once highlighted, 'A talk is a voyage with purpose, and it must be charted. The person who starts out going nowhere generally gets there.' If you want to go somewhere, identify your goal and work out the way to get there. The frameworks in this chapter will help you to achieve this.

In the next chapter, I suggest a number of ways to manage your face-to-face networking to achieve the best results. As with everything you have read in this book so far, you will see a structured approach. As you know, you are not networking to find a job; you are networking to seek advice. By seeking advice, you will find a job and build an extended network that can help you in various ways for the rest of your career. During your networking, your thinking will evolve, and new and unexpected job opportunities will begin to emerge. It might seem counterintuitive, but this is the way this process works!

SOME QUESTIONS FOR YOU TO CONSIDER

- Which of the four basic career directions should you investigate?
- Have you analysed the pros and cons of each career direction?
- What is your dream role in three to five years from now?
- If you are considering retirement, should you investigate a portfolio career?
- Have you prepared and tested your plans before launching your own business?
- What roles could act as pathways for you to get to your dream role?
- What sectors are most attractive to explore?
- What organisations do you wish to investigate?
- Have you prepared your formal Framework for Seeking Advice?
- Which referees can validate your thinking before networking?
- Are these the best people for you to invite to join your 'panel'?

7

Creating strong new connections for life

The power of networks is an exponential multiplier.

Professor Ram Charan, business advisor,
author and speaker

IN THIS CHAPTER:

Prepare to create strong, lifelong connections by focusing on the following *before* you begin networking:

- Decide who should be on your A-List
- Take your time before meeting recruiters
- Complete thorough, detailed research
- Prepare to launch your networking conversations
- Know what to cover in your meetings with your A-List
- Avoid distractions
- Maximise your positivity

AS I'VE MENTIONED, most career transition professionals believe about 80 per cent of job opportunities will originate from someone in your extended network. You may find this difficult to believe, but it proves to be true time and time again, especially for very senior jobseekers. Surprisingly, even though a recruiter is involved in your hiring process, a positive result often depends on help from your network. If you are looking for a great outcome in your career transition, do all you can to broaden and deepen your network. If you do this well, you will be creating strong new connections for life.

When you have an intense, full-time role, building your network outside your work is almost impossible. If you are between jobs, you will have a once-in-a-lifetime opportunity to build a much stronger network. This is a luxury you may not have again and you need to grasp this opportunity. Having this 'free' time is a gift that many senior jobseekers squander.

Once you have met with the 10 to 20 people you already know (your A-List, as described in chapter 1), you should set yourself the target of meeting 50 or more new people. Ideally, you should meet about five people a week. This weekly goal may seem too easy to you, or it may seem too challenging. On balance, most senior people find that it permits a good momentum to be maintained without excessive stress. You need momentum because stopping and starting is disrupting. If you lose momentum, you are likely to dramatically reduce your effectiveness and impact.

An essential step in preparing to network is to be well informed. This involves doing detailed research to understand as much as you can about the individuals you will be meeting and their business. What is their background and what issues do they face? Part of this research is to try to determine what 'emotional' connections you have with them. Are they in the same 'tribe' as you? If so, you are likely to have an immediate emotional connection with them! You are likely to be a member of a number of tribes: your school and university friends, your colleagues from various jobs, and people you know with common interests – for example, you support the same football team, play in the same basketball team, belong to the same club, sing in the same choir, or even that your parents came from the same island in Greece. An important question when meeting potential connections is, are you passionate about any of the same things? A superficial meeting without any real human connection is unlikely to lead anywhere productive. On the other hand, if you have good meetings with strong emotional connections, you will find your networking can be exciting, stimulating and fun.

You're aiming to build a broader, deeper network, not just for your next job but also for the remainder of your life. If you think of your networking challenge as building an asset for life, it is easier to see that all your networking effort will be worthwhile – and that it can and will change your life. When you are prepared and do your networking well, amazing things will happen. I have seen this time and time again. To achieve effective networking and to manage yourself well throughout the job search process, prepare in advance. Many elements are involved in successfully building and obtaining advice from your network, and I cover them in this chapter.

You may find some of the most senior executives you know recommend that you approach recruiters as your top priority. Usually, these individuals have been fortunate enough to have never had to look for a job in their career. They are trying to be helpful, but their advice is not correct. Do not try to meet recruiters until you are properly prepared. You need to present yourself at your best. Just like the butterfly, you must go through a transformation process before you present yourself to a recruiter. If you are not prepared, your meeting will be disappointing for you and for the people you are meeting (unless you are very lucky or particularly clever). You want all the new people you meet to see you with your wings fully developed, not as a chrysalis. To build your confidence and present yourself at your best, don't approach recruiters or new contacts until you have met and confirmed your thinking with your A-List.

Testing your hypotheses with your A-List is vital. If you do this well, you will become very proficient at explaining what you are trying to achieve in your networking. In addition, your credibility will be enhanced because you will be able to say that people who know you well have endorsed what you are trying to do. Most people you meet while networking will find it easiest to introduce you to someone they know in a particular sector. For instance, if you say you wish to meet more people involved in agribusiness, these individuals will, most likely, be able to make introductions. As you meet more people in your target areas, you will develop a stronger and stronger view of your best future career direction.

As I have mentioned already, networking is a numbers game. You cannot predict how any one individual meeting will turn out. But one of them may change your life. People who you thought would be very helpful sometimes turn out to be disappointing. What you thought might be a frog, could be a prince. In this chapter, I cover the topics that will help you be a better networker and achieve more productive networking meetings – for life!

DECIDE WHO SHOULD BE ON YOUR A-LIST

As discussed, you should meet about 10 to 20 people you know (these are the people who will be your A-List) and about 50 new people (who, once you have met them, will be your B- and C-Lists). Create your A-List with people you know well and who, you expect, will want to help you. You will only find out whether they will be able to help you once you approach them. When you meet them, you can test your hypotheses, and explain to them how you think you might move forward. Ideally, you should try to meet people who will test your thinking and come up with creative new ideas. Also they should be comfortable with helping you build your network.

The key criteria to use in your selection process for your A-List are discussed in the follow sections.

Who are the most accomplished networkers you know?

The value of super-networkers is that they do not have to be convinced that networking is a good idea. They already believe in networking and are comfortable introducing you to new people in their network. Because they have an extensive network themselves, they likely know several people who can help you. One of my clients met with a super-networker who introduced him to five senior people via text during their meeting.

People you meet who are less comfortable with networking may find making introductions difficult. Sometimes they want to call their suggested contacts and check with them first, to see whether they would like to meet with you. This often leads nowhere and becomes embarrassing for the person who said they would help you. It could also be embarrassing for you too, because it is tricky following up with your contact to check progress. Help these people by being as clear as possible about the kinds of people you would like to meet. Ask whether you can contact their suggested contacts directly. Alternatively, ask whether they would simply copy you into their email to their suggested contact so that you can then connect directly, without going through the introducer, going forward. If you have looked at the connections of your A-List contact in advance on LinkedIn, you might see individuals you would like to meet. As a result, you could then suggest these names to your contact when you meet them.

Who can help you most?

Work out who is likely to be able to help you most. Born in 1901, Willie Sutton robbed over 100 banks during his 'career'. According to legend, he was asked by a reporter in 1952 why he robbed banks. He did not complicate the answer: 'Because that's where the money is.' Go where you think you will receive the highest networking payoff. The people who are most likely to help you will be the ones who know you best and who have a view on where you will build the best relationships. Often these people will be about your age.

The best connections will be the people who:

- have contacts in the sectors you wish to explore and have industry knowledge
- used to work with you and now work in an organisation of interest
- make a living as a problem-solver and have access to a range of businesses, such as partners in accounting, law or consulting firms
- are involved in an industry body that represents a wide range of businesses or organisations
- have gone through a transition similar to the one you face, and could be a good sounding-board or role model for you.

Putting together a strong A-List of 10 to 20 people is vital to launching your networking properly. Ideally, these people will be willing to help you over an extended period.

Where do you have the most trusted relationships?

People who trust you the most are likely to go out of their way to help you the most. If they are also accomplished networkers *and* know how to help you, you have hit the jackpot. I have had clients who found great jobs because someone who trusted them took the initiative to speak up for them.

Sebastian, for example, had lost his job in a reorganisation. He had joined a local manufacturing business when he migrated from South Africa 15 years earlier. He went back to the owner of this business, who was also a South African, and asked him to be a referee. He agreed to assist Sebastian and, therefore, became a member of Sebastian's A-List. This referee then introduced Sebastian to the partner of a consulting firm, who was then a member of his B-List. This individual had worked on several assignments at the referee's firm. She liked Sebastian and introduced him to one of her clients who managed a business in Sebastian's area of expertise. This client was impressed with Sebastian too. At this stage, the consulting firm offered to put Sebastian on to one of its teams with this client, so that they could see him in action – a 'try before you buy' deal. Three months later, this client (who was by then on Sebastian's C-List) offered him a senior role. All this had been achieved without Sebastian having to prepare a CV! This example shows the power of transferring trust, step by step through the three networking circles.

TAKE YOUR TIME BEFORE MEETING RECRUITERS

As I have already mentioned, it is tempting to arrange meetings with as many recruiters as possible, as soon as possible. However, the best time to contact recruiters is when you have met the bulk of your A-List.

You may already know one or more recruiters. These recruiters could be helpful, particularly if they have placed you in a previous position, because they should know quite a lot about you. More importantly, they may have already invested time and energy in understanding what you have to offer. This means you are attractive to them because much of their basic due-diligence work has been done already. Contact these recruiters early to let them know you are in the process of preparing yourself to seek a role. If they suggest a meeting right away, however, say you would prefer to wait until you are fully prepared. Suggest a meeting in four to six weeks. By doing this, you achieve three positive things: first, you have let them know you have begun the process of seeking a new role; second, you have communicated that you are confident about your future and are not in any rush; and, third, you have signalled to them that you will be well prepared when you do finally meet them. If these recruiters worked with you several years ago, it is important that you bring them up to date with how you have developed in the meantime. You do not want them to evaluate you on the basis of their previous 'frozen-in-time' perceptions of you.

Recruiters who contact you, or who you contact, generally ask for a CV. If you are early in the preparation phase, and do not have a final CV, tell them this. Do not rush to send them something you put together quickly to please them. Suggest that you will send them your CV when it is ready, probably in four weeks or so. If they say they need something urgently, check with them why. (If they have a role that might suit you, you can, of course, prepare your CV without delay.) Suggesting that you take some time to prepare your CV sends a positive message if you position the conversation properly – that you wish to prepare an excellent document and do not want to be rushed. Most recruiters will respect you for this and, if anything, you are likely to go up in their estimation.

If you do not know any relevant recruiters, or feel you need to meet more, do not rush into making contact. Meet your A-List first to test your ideas and your hypotheses with them. In the process of meeting your A-List, you will achieve two things:

1. *You will be more confident and self-assured:* You will have validated your thinking and developed new ideas. As a result, you will be much clearer about your strengths and you will have generated new ideas about possible ways forward. You will have also determined who can help you by introducing new people who will become your B-List. Finally, you will have tested and firmed up your strategy for the future.

You will have a clearer idea of what makes sense for you, what you want to test, who is likely to help you and how to explain your search strategy.

2. *You will have identified target recruiters:* One of the questions you should ask each of your A-Listers is who they recommend as a recruiter – in other words, which recruiters do they believe can help you most? In reality, you are only likely to need to meet half a dozen recruiters during this process. Members of your network will, quite likely, already know who the most relevant and effective recruiters are likely to be for you. It is important that you are introduced personally to a recruiter by people in your network. Cold-calling recruiters will not work because recruiters try to avoid individuals who are looking for roles, as I explain in more detail in chapter 8.

By the way, I am always sceptical of career transition consultants who say one of their competitive advantages is that they will introduce you to key recruiters. This makes no sense for either the consultant or for you. You need to be introduced by an ex-colleague or a friend who can recommend you as a result of having actually worked with you in an organisation. Someone who has only just met you, and who is receiving a fee to assist you, is not likely to be credible with a recruiter in terms of making a warm introduction. If you are not introduced personally, you are likely to be told by reception at the recruiting firm that they will file your CV and call you if an opportunity arises. So, don't rush to meet recruiters. Wait until you are properly prepared and have validation of your ideas from your A-List. Then you can seek warm introductions and, once introduced, suggest to the recruiter that you should meet in four to six weeks, when you are fully prepared.

COMPLETE DETAILED RESEARCH BEFORE NETWORKING MEETINGS

Detailed research will be fundamental to your networking success. Your command of the relevant facts immediately differentiates you from others who are less well prepared. You will speak in specifics while they will speak in generalities. You will draw on hard facts, they will not. You will be unambiguous while they will tend to be vague and too broad in their comments. You will be able to probe particulars while they only ask broad general questions. You have the strength that comes from being in command of a subject. An example of how this works is when you hear a politician say something like, 'In my electorate, only a few people were hospitalised with measles last year.' Compare this with another politician who says, 'In my electorate, three children under the age of 10 were admitted to hospital with measles during the last year.' The first answer is vague and raises questions about their precise grasp of the facts, while the second answer builds their credibility because they are so clear and precise.

Research gives you a great starting point for your conversations. If you are in a networking meeting or an interview, you can raise specific issues and ask how their business is tracking. The fact that you have identified key issues is impressive in itself. Beyond that, you're able to have a much more intelligent and probing conversation. The more you can find out about the person you will be meeting and their organisation, in advance, the better! Time and time again, my clients have identified issues that raised questions that were not obvious from the formal public relations communications of an organisation. Sometimes these issues are good (the company is growing successfully, and hiring) and sometimes they are not so good (the company is struggling, and losing good people). Again, forewarned is forearmed!

The following sections outline your different potential avenues for research.

Using professional research

Good career transition firms have researchers on staff who can help you develop a fact base related to industries, specific organisations and even individuals. They can provide you with all sorts of information, including industry overviews, company reports, expert analyses, stock analyst reports, newspaper clippings, company announcements, individual biographies and YouTube presentations. If you are researching a public company, you should also study its share price movements over the past five years and try to understand any issues that have affected the company during this time. Also look for any unusual movements or changes on the board of directors and the management team. Assess the calibre, experience and diversity of the people on the board and in top management. Boards can be too inbred or they may include too many directors without relevant and deep industry experience.

If you do not have access to a researcher, you can do your own research thanks to the internet. You can, relatively easily, access and investigate publicly available information about organisations and people yourself. You may not have easy access to proprietary company and industry reports, but you may have friends who can help you obtain these through their contacts.

Using LinkedIn

LinkedIn is a very powerful tool for senior jobseekers, and one that can open up all sorts of opportunities for you. If you have not used LinkedIn before, you should invest time becoming familiar with the system. Once you become familiar with it, explore the opportunities presented to you. You are likely to be surprised by how much it can help you. The power of LinkedIn goes well beyond presenting your own profile and looking up the profiles of other people on the system.

You can use LinkedIn for three kinds of research:

1. finding people who can introduce you to current employees in a target organisation
2. finding connections to ex-employees of a target organisation who may be able to provide insights
3. learning more about the background of current or past employees in any organisation or industry that interests you.

Finding who can connect you to people in a target organisation

You may have a direct connection via LinkedIn to someone who is currently an employee or director of an organisation you are researching. Obtaining useful information and insights from them about the organisation may be possible. If you do not have a direct connection, you may be able to be introduced to someone in the organisation through someone you know. The people who can be connected by someone you know are called '2nd connections' on LinkedIn. Your ability to be introduced to 2nd connections can be a hugely powerful asset for you.

Here's how this works, researching an organisation that interests you, using the consulting firm Accenture as an example:

1. In LinkedIn, search for 'Accenture' and go to 'in People'. Nearly 1.4 million names will be presented to you. These are people who currently work at Accenture or have previously worked there, or who mention Accenture somewhere in their LinkedIn Profile.

2. Sort through this list using the various filters provided on the system. You can see these filters by clicking 'All filters' or by using the specific filters already provided at the top of your screen – you can filter using Connections, Locations or Current company. To find people who currently work at Accenture, use the 'Current company' filter and check the Accenture box. This gives you the list of individuals currently working at Accenture – in my case, 370,000 names come up.

3. You can then use 'Connections' and check the box for 1st connections. These are the people currently working at Accenture who are already connected to you. You might be surprised to learn how many people you know work at Accenture.

4. If you do not have any 1st connections, search using the '2nd connections' filter. Access to 2nd connections might well be your secret weapon. You likely have a large (and

perhaps surprising) number of 2nd connections at Accenture. These are people at Accenture who know someone who you know – meaning you can be introduced to this person at Accenture by someone you know. In my case, I have 11,000 2nd connections worldwide into Accenture.

5. You can now use the filters to refine this list further to select individuals of interest at Accenture. For instance, you can search for those based in the United States, or focus your search in further on those based in Denver. You can continue to further filter the list by their school, their area of expertise and so on. Limit your list as far as you can by using the filters so that you do not need to search through too many names.

6. Once the list of Accenture names is manageable, you can scroll through to see which of the current employees you have the most joint connections with. For instance, you might now have 20 people you know who also know someone you would like meet in Accenture. Select the people in Accenture who have the most contacts in common with you – chances are, they also have interests in common with you.

7. Look through your common connections to see who you think would be the best person to introduce you to the person you want to meet.

8. Approach your immediate contact to see whether they will help you with an introduction to their contact in Accenture. If they say they do not know your target person at Accenture very well, even though they are connected on LinkedIn, try another person on your list.

9. Do this until you find someone who is happy to connect you to the person you would like to meet in Accenture.

Thanks to LinkedIn, a friend or colleague you know well can introduce you to someone you would like to meet in an organisation of interest to you.

Finding connections to ex-employees who may be able to provide insights

You can use a similar process to identify ex-employees who may be able to help you. In this case, select the 'Past company' option in the filter section of LinkedIn. You will find that some of the names presented as ex-employees will actually still be at the organisation you are researching, but they have been promoted from a previous role. If you can find people who have left an organisation, they might be open to discussing the advantages and disadvantages of working there. So, they are definitely worth following up, whether they are 1st or 2nd connections. Of course, you should not expect these connections to provide proprietary information to you. However, even general comments might help you identify strengths and weaknesses that should be explored further. Recently, two of my clients decided not to continue in recruiting processes after learning about issues in organisations from ex-employees introduced to them by their friends.

Learning more about the people you will be meeting in an organisation

You can also use LinkedIn to understand more about specific people in the organisation before a meeting or an interview. Luiz, for example, was about to take part in series of interviews for a senior role in a major consulting company. He was able to use LinkedIn is three ways:

1. to understand the backgrounds – education, career history and mutual connections – of the partners and senior associates he would be meeting in the interviews

2. to work out what kinds of education, skills and experience seemed to be important in individuals who were recent hires at his level

3. to identify individuals who had left the organisation and had been re-employed, to assess whether their new jobs showed they had moved forward in their careers.

By having this background information, Luiz was able to prepare a series of questions that immediately made him stand out from the other candidates for the role. He showed he was thoughtful, creative, and willing to carry out detailed research. Also, that he could use data well to explore strategic questions. He was offered the role.

PREPARE TO LAUNCH YOUR NETWORKING CONVERSATIONS

In chapter 5, I emphasised the importance of rehearsing before you have a meeting or networking conversation. This involves thinking through the issues you would like to cover and how you wish to represent yourself. In her 2012 TED Talk 'Your body language may shape who you are', Professor Amy Cuddy from Harvard Business School points out the importance, first, of what you say and, second, how you present yourself. She talks about the importance of 'power posing', arguing that individuals who appear strong and confident do better in interviews and meetings than those who appear weak and withdrawn. Obviously, you are a lot more likely to appear confident and strong when you are properly prepared and rehearsed. This will put you in a better position to impress the individuals who you are meeting. The following sections cover three areas to consider when preparing for networking conversations.

Presenting yourself well

In 1960, the whole world learned a lesson about visual presentation from the televised (in black and white) presidential debate between Richard Nixon and John F Kennedy. This was the first time a presidential debate had been televised. The incumbent Vice President, Richard Nixon, was the Republican Party nominee. United States Senator John F. Kennedy was the Democratic Party nominee. The video showed Nixon, who was recovering from the flu, as tired, dishevelled and nervous. His make-up had been poorly applied and he had 'five o'clock shadow'. Kennedy, on the other hand, appeared polished, relaxed and calm. He moved with confidence and ease. He smiled. He was suntanned. It turned out that Kennedy had spent the previous two days with his aides, fielding practice questions and resting up. Americans who watched the debate on TV ranked Kennedy as the winner, taking the view that Nixon was not trustworthy compared to Kennedy. Those who listened on the radio, however, gave the win to Nixon. Even though Nixon may have had better content (as suggested by the radio rankings), Kennedy was perceived to be the better performer, and more trustworthy, by those viewing on TV. Kennedy, of course, went on to win the presidency.

Here are my presentation tips for meetings (and interviews):

- Do your homework in advance and rehearse out loud.
- In particular, rehearse your PEC and FSA.
- Find out in advance how you should dress in the meeting.
- Rest up before your meeting and walk around the block in advance.
- Do not over-engineer your preparation (otherwise you may sound wooden).
- Have the questions you wish to explore well thought through in advance.

Plan to arrive well before the meeting so that you will not be rushed. If the meeting is via video conferencing, check your setup carefully in advance, and keep the following tips in mind:

- Define and project your own personal image and brand.
- Make sure you check out everything you can control in advance.
- Become your own producer and do not leave anything to chance.
- Act as though you are a member of a meeting in person.
- Check everything with the office conducting the interview in advance.

Obviously, what can be seen on screen is vital to get right. Some potential issues here are the background (which should preferably be white, off-white or grey), the lighting (which could include an uplight and some lighting from either side of your face), and the audio quality (hard surfaces may cause too much echo).

All video tends to reduce your warmth and make you seem more transactional. To show yourself at your best, you may need to over-perform. But, if you do this, you may feel out of your comfort zone. The problem is if you do not do this, you are likely to appear flat and lacking in energy (unless you are an accomplished actor). It is best to rehearse in advance to minimise this potential problem. Remember the presidential debate and its important lesson: you will not be at your best if you are not properly prepared, rested, relaxed and energised.

Being confident about your strengths

People want to back winners! When you meet your A-List, you need to be confident about what you will say about your strengths and the way you explain them. As discussed in chapter 5, you need to have good answers to these three questions:

1. What do you do?
2. Can you tell me about yourself?
3. What do you want to do?

Without rehearsal, you can easily forget how to answer these questions simply, concisely, and clearly. Also, you need to present in a way is expected for the role you are seeking. If you are a CEO (or hope to be one, one day) you need to look and behave like a CEO.

Understanding differences

Although you may think you know them well, it is also helpful to understand, in general terms, what kind of values any person you are meeting might have, and whether their values are likely to be different from yours. For instance, are they monochronic or polychronic? Public speaking and executive communication specialist

Brett Rutledge has described the differences between these types of people and why these differences can be problematic:

- *Monochronic individuals:* These people value time and orderliness. They concentrate on the task at hand, take time commitments seriously, and adhere to plans and rules. They do not appreciate interruptions. Their heritage is often from countries away from the equator, where time can be at a premium with short winter days. The United States, Canada, Australia and Northern Europe are monochronic cultures. Monochronic executives cannot understand why the person they are meeting allows the meeting to be interrupted by phone calls and people stopping by. Is it meant to be insulting? When do they get down to business? They are perplexed when time does not seem important to others.

- *Polychronic individuals:* These people value relationships. People are their main concern, particularly their family, friends and colleagues. Time and being punctual is less of a concern. Their heritage is often from countries closer to the equator, where winter daylight time is not at a premium. They tend to build lifelong relationships. Southern Europe, Latin America and the Middle East are polychronic cultures. Polychronic executives cannot understand any separation between work and personal time. Why would you let something as silly as a schedule negatively affect the quality of your relationships? They are perplexed that warm relationships do not seem to be important to others.

You can see the possible problems if you do not understand the values of the other person. Recognising whether you are dealing with a polychronic or monochronic culture, and the attendant differences in how time and relationships are valued, is crucial to being able to communicate effectively across some cultures.

You also need to be aware of the kinds of topics the person you are meeting may be most interested in, and prepare in advance to address these topics. For instance:

- *A CEO (Chief Executive Officer):* May be interested in business growth and sustaining profitability, board relationships, and competitive threats.
- *A CFO (Chief Financial Officer):* May be interested in financial results, reporting to the audit committee, audit issues and regulatory issues.
- *A CPO (Chief People Officer):* May be interested in corporate culture, attracting talent, diversity, leadership development and engagement scores.
- *A CIO (Chief Information Officer):* May be interested in IT system problems, procurement, cloud functionality and security, and cybercrime.
- *A CMO (Chief Marketing Officer):* May be interested in branding, new products, corporate reputation, client relationships and net promoter scores.

The point here is that people in different cultures value time and relationships differently. Also, individuals in different roles are likely to be interested in different issues and topics. You need to be prepared in advance to respond appropriately to these differences.

Doing thorough research before each meeting

You need to be well prepared for each meeting, even for members of your A-List, across three levels:

1. *Industry level:* What can you find out about the industry that the person you are meeting is involved in? Is the industry thriving or under pressure? Who are the key players? What issues are important for the industry?
2. *Organisational level:* What can you learn about the organisation where the person works? What information is on its website?

Can you see any issues that might be confronting them? What about the board and the management? Using LinkedIn, do you know any other people who work in the organisation, or used to work there? Can they help you?

3. *Personal level:* What can you find out about the individual you will be meeting? Have they received recommendations on LinkedIn? If so, what do these recommendations say? Do they know people who you know? If so, can your contacts provide you with some helpful background about the person you will be meeting (in addition to what you can learn from LinkedIn), including what they are passionate about? Search their connections to see whether they are connected to people you would like to be introduced to.

If you prepare well for your meetings, you will find common interest areas, as well as common connections and people they know who you would like to meet. Armed with this information, you will likely be able to build an even stronger personal connection and have a more productive meeting. Being able to say that you are very impressed with their career and the recommendations they have received on LinkedIn could be a great start! Remember that asking good probing questions, based on what you have learnt during your preparation, makes you interesting and attractive.

KNOW WHAT TO COVER IN YOUR MEETINGS WITH YOUR A-LIST

Before you meet with people on your A-List, work out what advice you are seeking and what you want to achieve in the meeting. Being clear about your purpose and your goals makes it easier to evaluate, after your meeting, whether or not you have achieved what you set out to do and whether you have had a good meeting. Your goals will become more specific as you meet more people and as you learn more. In the early days of your networking, when you are meeting with your A-List, cover the following five issues.

Make sure your contacts know you are okay

You may not have seen your friends and colleagues since you left your previous role, and they will no doubt want to know that you and your family are okay. Make it clear that you, your family and those important to you are doing fine and looking forward to the future. Avoid spending time on questions about why you left your job (such as whether you jumped or were pushed). These kinds of question are a distraction. Simply respond with something along these lines:

> I am very proud of what I achieved in my role over the last five years and I will have some very strong references. But a number of changes at work, including a reorganisation, made it obvious that it was a good time for me to move on. I am very much looking forward to the future since I believe I can make a major contribution in another organisation. I want to spend the next three to six months meeting senior people, building my network and seeking advice. I am confident these senior people will help me identify where I can make the best contribution in the next stage of my career.

It is important that you communicate that you and your family are fine, you left on good terms (assuming this is true), you are taking some time to prepare, and you will be seeking to build your network of senior contacts. If you left because of an issue with your fit with someone in the organisation, talk about this in general terms. Explain that you found your values were not compatible with some people in your previous role, so it became obvious to you that it was best for you to move on. These fit issues occur every day and should not be a surprise to anyone.

Check how much time you have to meet

Confirm how long the person you are meeting has available. If their time is limited, do not get side-tracked with small talk. A meeting starting late and then needing to finish early is not uncommon, so make the most of your time. Start by saying something like:

> I am very grateful that you have agreed to meet with me. I realise that your time is valuable. I am keen to seek your advice on some issues related to my next career move. You could be very helpful indeed in clarifying my thinking. Your EA mentioned that you would have about half an hour to meet. Is that still okay?

The less time you have, the more important it is to focus on and address the issues that are important to you. I have had clients who became hopelessly side-tracked in meetings. Before they were able to seek the advice they were after, they ran out of time. Beware of spending too much time talking about the good old days, when you were both at school together!

Set realistic expectations on the length of your job search time

Many people, even senior executives, have no idea how long it takes a senior jobseeker to find an appropriate role. Make it clear that you do not expect quick results. State that you have made a decision with those important to you that you will not accept any role for three to six months at the earliest. This puts your networking contact at ease. They are happy that you are not in a rush (and that you are in a position to feed your family for an extended period).

The advantages of stating that you intend to take your time before you accept a role include:

- The people you meet will see you are not in a rush, and they will be relieved that you and your family are not stressed.
- You will have the time needed to generate and understand a variety of career options. You will not be distracted by early opportunities that may be somewhat tempting but are not the right answer for you.
- Taking your time before you make a decision takes the pressure off others who are interested in you, including recruiters. They will have more time to discuss opportunities with you.

- If a role you cannot refuse is presented to you early, and it is clear that it is a role you cannot refuse, you are still quite within your rights to accept it.

The kind of comment I suggest is:

> I have been very fortunate in my career to date. I have had great jobs and am proud to have made important and valuable contributions where I worked. My next role is important to me. I want to make sure that I can continue my track record of success. Therefore, I have agreed with my family that I will not accept another role for three to six months at the earliest. This discipline will allow me time to explore all my options and I will not be rushed into a decision that I may later regret.

Explain what you would like to achieve in your meeting

Explain what you would like to achieve in the meeting, in broad terms. Your thinking will evolve as your options and the issues related to them become clearer. In the early meetings, with your A-List, you will be focusing on testing your storyline and your hypotheses and generating ideas on how to build your network. In later meetings, with your B-List and C-List and in interviews, you will be investigating the pros and cons of specific roles. Indicating upfront your goals for the meeting will help you keep the meeting on track. You need to make it as easy as possible for the person you are meeting to help you. Often, the best way to achieve this is to raise specific, rather than general, questions.

Your comment could be something like:

> I know you have a lot of knowledge related to private equity. I am keen to seek your advice on whether it would make sense to focus my efforts on understanding start-ups. In this regard, I would very much like to be introduced to two or three others who have made a successful transition to start-ups from roles similar to the one I have been in.

Since you are meeting with someone from your A-List, you will know them quite well already. Even so, you should still take care to research their background to understand as much as you can about them, including their job history. You should also review who is on their list of connections, assuming they have made this available on LinkedIn. If you know their connections, you will be able to ask for specific introductions. As already mentioned, avoid being side-tracked by discussions of the 'good old days'. This trap is easy to fall into, especially when meeting with friends or ex-colleagues. Also beware of the individual who wants to talk about themselves or wants you to solve a problem they face. Before you get too far into the meeting, you must remind them that you are there to seek their advice. Get the meeting back on track!

Do not waste time talking about what you do not want to do

Many of my clients, initially at least, find it easiest to talk about what they do not want to do. This is a mistake. It does not help you to progress, wastes time and makes you appear negative. Also, it does not help the person you are meeting give you constructive advice. You need to focus on your hypotheses related to what you want to explore. A friend asked me to meet an individual from out of town, hoping I could help him with his thinking about finding a new job. I asked my visitor what he wanted to do, in order to see how he would answer this simple question. Unfortunately, he then told me about all the problems in his industry, which was suffering as a result of digital competition. I tried to put myself in the shoes of anyone else he was likely to visit, and let him continue to talk. Near the end of our meeting, he asked me whether I could introduce him to anyone who might help him with advice. I said that, as much as I would like to do this, he had not provided me with any information on what he wanted to do. Therefore, I was at a loss as to who to introduce him to. I asked him to come back in one month with a better answer to my question. I suggested he should prepare a series of hypotheses, based on the Framework for

Seeking Advice (FSA) set out in chapter 6, to help me to help him. I doubt whether anyone he met in ordinary networking would have bothered to invite him back. He wasted the whole meeting by talking about what he did not want to do.

Wrapping up your meeting

Wrap up your networking meeting with an A-Lister by thanking him or her for:

- the time they have spent with you
- their validation of your proposed approach
- any new ideas they have suggested
- their willingness to introduce you to two or three other people.

Also ask them whether it is okay to contact them again in a couple of months. Your comment could be something like:

> I am extremely grateful to you for giving me your time this morning. You have been really helpful. In particular, I am delighted with your idea that I should explore company X and company Y. They both sound as though they are attempting to build businesses that are in my sweet spot.

> And thank you for being willing to introduce me to A and B. I am wondering whether you would be agreeable to sending them an email or a text to introduce me. If you copy me into this, I will follow up with them directly to avoid troubling you further.

> I would very much like to keep you in the loop. Would you mind if I contacted you in a couple of months to let you know how I am progressing?

If the person you are meeting says he or she cannot think of anyone to introduce you to, or that they need time to think, this is not a good sign. See chapter 8 for my tips on overcoming roadblocks such as this when networking. Asking them whether they would be willing to meet you again for an update in six or eight weeks is wise, and makes arranging a follow-up meeting, if you need one, easier. Even if you do not think you will benefit from a follow-up meeting, you should ask for permission just in case.

After your meeting, make sure you send a thank you note. If you have an article that might interest them, send that too. Later, assuming you meet the people they offered to introduce you to, it is important that you send a note to your introducer to thank them for the introduction. Also you can tell them that the meetings went well. This will help you to cement your connections with your A-List contacts.

One way to think about these meetings with your A-List is that you are the pilot of an aircraft accelerating along a runway towards flying speed. Once you reach flying speed, you begin to climb using your B-List. Finally you reach cruising altitude, using your C-List.

AVOID DISTRACTIONS

You may have heard that looking for a job is a full-time job, and many of my clients say they have found this to be true. Some people I have coached say they have never worked so hard. But if you are well-organised, your job search is not likely to take more than 30 hours a week once you begin networking. You may have worked double this time in your previous role, so you likely will have some extra time on your hands. Involving yourself in contract work, or in executive interim management or in board directorships – either corporate or not-for-profit – while you conduct your search may be tempting. As I have explained already, these activities are likely to be distractions and may cause you to take your eye off the ball. My advice is to avoid them until you are well into your networking. This will probably be after you have met at least 10 or 20 new people, above and beyond your A-List.

Do not accept contracting or consulting roles too soon

It is tempting to seek out contract work, particularly if you need income. But remember, intense contract work can consume all your time, limit your flexibility and exhaust you – meaning you won't be able to manage your networking effectively. If you lose networking momentum, restarting can be difficult. If you do decide to take on some contracting or consulting work, consider the following questions.

When should I start a consulting assignment?

Hold off on taking up any contracting or consulting work until you are well into meeting your B-List (those people introduced to you by your A-List). Once you have met, say, 15 new people in addition to your A-List, you will have generated a rhythm and a good level of confidence. Starting some contracting or consulting work might then make sense.

How much consulting time should I offer?

Set aside two full days a week for meeting with and expanding your network, including preparation for meetings. This leaves you the rest of the week for consulting work. The danger is your consulting work will expand if you are not very disciplined. Always remember that your long-term goal should be to build your future career, so don't get distracted by short-term activity. Doing too much consulting or contracting work might limit your effectiveness in networking, just when your emphasis should be on generating future career options. You do not want the rest of your life to be derailed by committing to an intense contracting schedule that reduces your networking effectiveness.

It is possible, of course, that you believe your consulting assignment might evolve into a full-time role. Even in this situation, still try to limit the consulting assignment to three days a week, so you can keep networking. This way, you can make the final decision whether to convert your consulting into a full-time job, by comparing this option to the other choices you've generated. Your goal should always be to maximise your job choices at the point when you make your final job decision.

What fees should I charge?

Accepting a low consulting fee may be tempting on the basis that it is a short-term assignment. You might be concerned that, by trying to negotiate a higher fee, you will miss out on the work. I take the opposite view. Only accept work where you add a substantial amount of value and where, therefore, you can command a high fee. Otherwise, the fee is too low to justify the risk of derailing your job search. You are also putting your brand at risk if people see you accepting a low fee. They might think you are damaged goods or that you are a poor negotiator. Finally, a low price point may affect what you will be paid if your contract work turns in to a full-time role.

If you do take on contracting work, as I have already mentioned, always write a formal proposal so that your arrangements are clear and agreed on by all parties. Each party must be clear about who is responsible for what, what deliverables are due by when, and what your payment arrangements will be. Invoice your client fortnightly so that any payment problems become obvious quickly. It is not a good sign if your fee receipts slip to 60 or 90 days. Agreeing to fees that are contingent on results is usually a mistake and will almost certainly lead to arguments down the track, related to who delivered what and when.

Avoid searching for executive interim management roles

Executive interim management is also tempting to explore. This is where you fill in for a full-time executive in an established role for an extended period. Often, these positions come up quickly because of an unexpected change in an organisation – for instance, a company finds it needs a temporary CFO because the current CFO has resigned and a replacement is expected to take several months to find. Some search firms have professionals who specialise in filling these positions, which usually last for six months or even longer. They seek senior executives who can hit the ground running and take charge immediately. They tend to prefer experienced individuals who have seniority and gravitas, but who are also willing to roll up their sleeves to get things done. The most desirable interim executives are senior executives who want their future careers to involve a series of interim management assignments. In other words, they are individuals who are happy for their future career to involve working six months a year, and then to be on call at short notice during the rest of the year.

If you want your next role to be full-time, exploring interim executive opportunities will usually be a waste of your time. If, for some reason, you are offered such a role, think twice before you accept it. A clause in the agreement for an interim role may seek to restrict you from resigning early if a permanent role is offered to you. If you believe that you will be bound by such a clause, you could miss out on a plum role. Make sure you negotiate an arrangement that allows you to resign from the role with, say, two months' notice. If you cannot achieve this, do not take the assignment.

Avoid or delay non-executive directorships

You may be presented with an opportunity to join a board as a non-executive director. My advice is to hold off on accepting anything like this until you are re-established. As I have noted already, your first board tends to define you. Selecting a board position that causes others to question your judgement – because, for instance, the company faces more problems than you were aware of when you joined the board – is a bad idea. Instead, thank the Chair for his or her interest in you, and explain you have decided not to accept any board positions until the next steps in your career are clearer. In fact, this makes sense both for you and for the board.

In the case of a public company, you do not want to be in a position where you accept a board position but then must resign six months later. This may be necessary if your new employer will not permit you to serve on a board in parallel with your new job. This restriction is not uncommon these days, since most employers are very wary of problems and distractions arising from external public company board positions. If approached, you might say that you would like to continue the conversation until your future job is confirmed. This will permit you to learn more about the board in the time before your next career step is clarified.

The same thinking is relevant for positions on not-for-profit boards, but the exposure for you, if you accept a not-for-profit board role, is different. The danger of joining a not-for-profit board is that, because you do not have a job, the board is likely to be keen to load you up with work. This can be a special problem if they believe you will be an effective fundraiser. The credo of some not-for-profit boards is, 'Give, get, or get off'. The more effective you are, and the more committed you are to their cause, the more work you will be given. In my view, you need to concentrate all your efforts on your job search, and avoid being distracted by board work before you know what your next job will be.

An issue for many not-for-profits is 'mission creep'. Make sure you understand the purpose of the organisation, and take care that the organisation is not spread too thin. Recently, I was reading about a charity which described its 'specialties' as 'Humanity, Impartiality, Neutrality, Independence, Voluntary Service, Unity, Universality, Climate Change, Youth Engagement, Gender, and Cultural Diversity'. If I was being approached to assist this group, I would be very keen to understand precisely what it was trying to deliver and how.

If you are tempted to join a not-for-profit board, make sure you attend a board meeting before you make a final decision. One of my clients did this and, as a result, decided that the board was dysfunctional. Attending this board meeting made it easier to decide he did not want to accept the invitation to join that board. Another client did join a not-for-profit board and did not carry out enough due diligence. Because she had an accounting background, she found almost immediately that all the members of the board, although extremely kind, helpful and well-intentioned, were financially illiterate. As a result, the members of the board did not realise that the organisation was in danger of running out of money and that urgent action was required. In other words, there was a distinct danger that the organisation would be trading while insolvent (which is illegal) without the board realising this until it was too late.

MAXIMISE YOUR POSITIVITY

The job-search process at a senior level can be long and drawn out. Some people are fortunate to find a new role quickly, but the results typically follow a bell curve with its peak somewhere between nine and 12 months, even in good times. In difficult economic times, your job search may take even longer. There can be many ups and downs along the way. Just when you think the planets are aligned, everything falls apart. You need to be resilient and maintain your positivity. Even if you have the financial resources to keep going, you may be concerned that you will reach your 'use-by date' if you are unemployed for too long. I have never seen anyone reach their use-by date, unless the individual involved believes this has happened and starts to act accordingly. Then it becomes a self-fulfilling prophecy. Without exception, the people I work with have found roles that worked for them, even if some took longer than others.

My clients who are most successful in maintaining and building their positivity through the inevitable ups and downs of the job-seeking process have ten common elements in the way they tackle the process. These common elements are covered in the following sections and they should be a good guide for you.

Focus on the long game

Successful jobseekers understand from the beginning that they must remain focused for an extended period – as much as a year! They realise that there will rarely be any quick answers, and there will almost certainly be setbacks along the journey. They explain this to their friends and family, so the correct expectations are established and there are no surprises.

Set clear priorities

Successful jobseekers work out how to best allocate their time, and understand this will change as the networking evolves. To begin with – while you are meeting your A-List – most of your time will be spent networking. Later, as you meet your B- and C- Lists, you should probably spend 80 per cent of your time preparing for network meetings and networking. Another 10 per cent could be spent following up on job leads and 10 per cent on meeting recruiters. Once interviews begin, this time allocation will change again, with less time given to networking and more time spent preparing for interviews.

Display a positive mindset

Successful jobseekers see each setback as a learning experience rather than a failure. In fact, setbacks are inevitable, and they are generally important learning experiences. It is almost as though early opportunities are destined not to work out, but they teach you a lot. Don't forget the story of the young woman who found an old car covered in dust in her uncle's barn. She took in to a metal dealer and they offered her $50 for scrap. Then she took it to an auto dealer and they offered her $200 as a trade in. Finally, she took to a vintage car club and they told her it was worth $100,000. Your value may be very different in different roles. You need to explore options to find the role where you will be really valued. Although you may be bruised by the setbacks, they teach you how to handle certain situations better and, as a result, your learning accumulates. When you look back you may say the setbacks were the experiences that made you more effective and led, in the end, to a great job where your true worth was finally recognised. Remember (from chapter 3) that Nellie Melba, who became a world-famous opera singer, was rejected by several leaders in opera in London and was only recognised as having huge potential in Paris in her final audition. Don't dwell on your setbacks, always look forwards. The one question I would like you not to have to ask yourself is: 'What if I had not given up?'

Stick with the process

Successful jobseekers build a routine to maintain their networking momentum. As part of their networking, they focus on continuing to build the seniority and quality of their network. This quality improvement is likely to be noticeable over time. If you are not meeting more and more senior people as time goes by, you need to re-evaluate your approach.

Do not hesitate to follow up

Successful jobseekers continue to make follow-up contact with the members of their network and with recruiters. Some of my clients are concerned that, if they do this, they will be regarded as too pushy. I believe failing to maintain contact is a missed opportunity. I always remember the successful salesperson who told me 'the best salespeople make seven calls'. Follow-up calls reinforce that you are enthusiastic and eager to understand more. Also that you respect the person's judgement and are keen to obtain their advice. In the case of a recruiter who told you they would call you, and who does not, it is quite proper to make contact to seek clarification. Uncertainty is a great cause of stress and you should be trying to minimise uncertainty. The key question to ask yourself is, 'What is the downside if I call?' Despite your concerns, it is likely that the downside is minimal, whereas the upside could be substantial.

Meet with others who have been through the process

Successful jobseekers seek advice and counsel from others who have come through the job-search process successfully. These people will be able to reassure you that the process does work. Also, they will undoubtedly have some constructive advice to help you manage your own process and maintain your resilience.

Maintain a good life balance

Successful jobseekers have a routine and pattern in their non-job-seeking activities. They look after themselves physically and mentally.

They pursue other interests in addition to networking. A great tip is to have something else – a special project – that you wish to achieve in parallel to seeking a job. This could be renovating part of the house, learning a language, learning to play the guitar, or writing your autobiography. Aim to have something you can look back on in six to 12 months and say to yourself, and to your friends and family, that you are proud to have achieved it. One of my clients attended a detective novel writing program at Oxford University. She later said it was one of the best things she had ever done!

Obtain support from a trusted confidant

Successful jobseekers usually have someone they trust who they can turn to. If you have a career transition coach, this person should be your confidant. They will help you address setbacks and provide perspective, and will offer new ideas on how to progress. They will tell stories about others they have worked with to show you how the process works. If you do not have a professional coach, try to find a mentor who can give you some of this support. The ideal person is someone who has made a successful transition themselves, and has worked with a competent career coach, so they know how to manage the transition process and feel confident providing you with guidance.

Build long-term relationships

Successful jobseekers do not treat meetings as individual activities, but instead see them as the beginning of longer-term relationships. They realise they are building a team to support them. This team will, as in the Oscar analogy I used in chapter 1, vote for them when needed. The bigger and better your team, and the more closely it is connected and interconnected, the more likely you will be successful! You can tell you're making good progress when you find that various members of your network are starting to talk about you with other members of your network. By the way, joining 'common interest groups' can be a great way to build long-term relationships.

Remain flexible and innovative

Finally, these jobseekers have the ability to roll with the punches and innovate. The Duke of Wellington credited his success at the Battle of Waterloo to his army's flexibility. He used the following analogy to compare the French army's love of precision to the British army's greater flexibility and agility:

> *They planned their campaigns just as you might make a splendid piece of harness. It looks very well, and answers very well, until it gets broken; and then you are done for. Now I made my campaigns of ropes. If anything went wrong, I tied a knot, and went on.*

Be like the Duke of Wellington! Remember, negative energy is wasted energy!

★★★

This chapter has covered many of the issues you will face in planning and preparing for your networking activities. The key message is that you need to be organised and thorough. Do not let others rush you. It is better to be well-prepared than to go off half-cocked. A measured approach is best, time and time again. If you get distracted or do sloppy work, you are less likely to build the momentum needed to deliver success.

Do not forget the power of seeking advice – it increases the probability that members of your network will go out of their way to help you. Very few people know how to help you find a job, but nearly everyone will help you with advice. Frame your goals and strategy – using your FSA to develop your hypotheses – in a way that gives those you meet clear guideposts about the options you wish to explore. If you prepare and test these hypotheses, so they are clear and easy to understand, you will position yourself best to obtain sound advice.

Seeking a new role takes time. In most situations, you do not have multiple opportunities waiting for you when you initiate your job-seeking efforts. In fact, if you are senior, you may face a situation where only two or three suitable opportunities come up in the next six to 12 months. You need to be resilient. You will experience setbacks and not everything will work as planned. If you understand this, the process becomes more manageable. You can do little to accelerate this process unless you take the first job that comes along. I usually recommend that you resist doing this unless it is vital that you generate income without delay.

The best results depend on good preparation and on harnessing the power of your network. Some luck is involved. Things click when your preparation finally meets an opportunity. Once I had a client who found a new role in a very specialised field in three months. If this particular opening had not arisen then, it might have taken him 18 months to obtain a similar role. You can never tell when a desirable opportunity will be presented to you. You need to be prepared when this happens.

In the next chapter, I discuss how to generate attractive job offers. This starts with building your network to identify opportunities, and then moves through the multiple steps in an interview process until you are offered a role. This can be a complex process with many pitfalls, so understanding how it works and how to maximise your chances of success is worthwhile. The next chapter shows you how best to stay in the race and position yourself to win.

SOME QUESTIONS FOR YOU TO CONSIDER

- Who will you invite to join your A-List?
- Do you know how to use LinkedIn to explore your connections?
- Do you understand the power of your 2nd connections?
- How well prepared are you for networking conversations?
- Are you sure that you have rehearsed enough?
- Are you focusing your efforts and avoiding distractions that might derail your search process?
- Are you giving sufficient attention to the activities that will help you maintain your positivity while you seek a role?

8

Putting your networking to work

Sail away from the safe harbour.
Catch the trade winds in your sails.
Explore. Dream. Discover.

Mark Twain

How to manage your networking to identify job opportunities, by:

- Understanding the power of asking probing questions
- Maximising networking opportunities
- Understanding recruiters
- Meeting with recruiters while networking
- Applying for a role that emerges while networking

IF YOU HAVE followed the steps set out so far in this book, you are now prepared to launch your networking activities. This is the next step towards generating attractive job opportunities. The key is to maximise your job options. This chapter reinforces the idea that you need to take an active role in generating leads and then job offers. If you can generate more than one job offer, you will change the dynamics of the recruiting process in your favour. You will have more negotiating power if two or more organisations want to hire you. You can also evaluate job options more effectively and size up the opportunities and risks in more detail. Finally, you are better positioned to identify which role is likely to lead you to the best long-term career outcome.

What often happens, of course, is that not all your opportunities emerge at the same time. A less attractive role will commonly be presented to you early in your search. In this case, working to slow down this offer and accelerate others is desirable. You may decide to reject an early offer and keep searching. This is all part of the process of generating and synchronising job offers. It is also why seeking a job is not usually an easy process.

So, what do you need to consider as you work to create attractive job offers? It all starts with networking, and building your relationships and knowledge base.

UNDERSTANDING THE POWER OF ASKING PROBING QUESTIONS

As in any marketing process, your job while you are networking is to generate new leads. You may be familiar with the 'sales funnel' taught in marketing courses and shown in figure 8.1.

Figure 8.1: The sales funnel stages

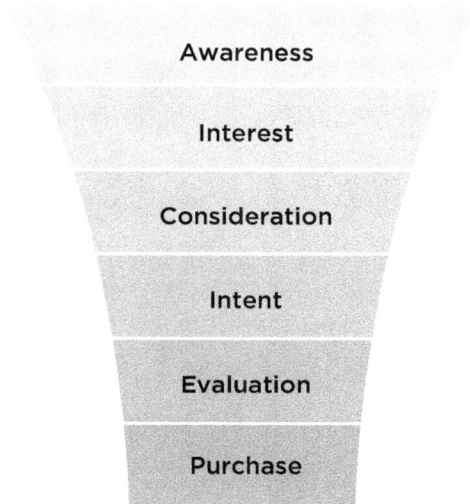

Awareness

Interest

Consideration

Intent

Evaluation

Purchase

Salespeople understand this funnel. They are aware that they must be discussing their product or service with a number of people – for example, 10 prospects – to ultimately generate one sale. You need to do the same. To achieve the best results, you need to expand your network and generate as much awareness as possible. But your challenge is more subtle than for a regular salesperson. You will generate more leads by actively seeking advice, rather than attempting to sell yourself.

In fact, the most effective salespeople do the same thing. They seek to understand the needs of a prospective customer before suggesting a solution. Neil Rackham, who developed the selling framework described in his book, *SPIN Selling*, emphasises that you must identify and clarify the 'implicit needs' of a prospective customer by using probing questions. If you do this well, you will help your customer to identify their real needs, which are often hidden or not well understood, even by the customer themselves. For instance, a customer may initially say they want the lowest price solution, when what they actually want, if they think about it, may be a high-quality solution that lasts. (As Aldo Gucci said, 'Quality is remembered long after price is forgotten'.) Assuming your product or service meets the needs identified by your customer, they are highly likely to convince themselves that it presents the most appropriate solution for them. This often happens if you use a questioning technique to work through the SPIN selling process with them.

As Rackham outlines in his book, his research showed that the quality of questions asked by a salesperson were key to whether or not a sale was closed. The right questions can speed up the process, whereas the wrong questions can stall it or even halt it completely. Rackham suggests four types of questions:

1. *Situation questions:* By asking situation-type questions, you can develop an understanding of context. In turn, this background information can be used to guide the conversation in an appropriate way. By doing research in advance, you can often limit the time you spend on situation questions.

2. *Problem questions:* If you can get a customer to acknowledge the problem that needs to be fixed, they're far more likely to give you the attention you need to move forward to a sale. Problem questions can be effective at encouraging a prospect to identify issues that are causing pain, or which have been overlooked.

3. *Implication questions:* Smart implication questions will help your prospect identify for themselves the continuing effect and consequences of their problem. In order to encourage your prospect to properly consider your solution to their problem, they need to have a firm grasp on how serious their problem is and the advantages of solving it.

4. *Need-payoff questions:* The final stage of SPIN selling is
    to encourage your prospect to consider just how valuable the
    right solution to their problem would be to them. The secret
    to getting results with need-payoff questions is to ensure
    the buyer identifies and specifies the benefits themselves.

You can use a similar technique as you network and as you become
involved in interviews. A position description for a role rarely
describes the key challenges facing you when you are hired. It
may set out the functional responsibilities required in a role, but
hardly ever points out the actual day-to-day challenges. These may
be related to organisational structure, people, systems, competition,
customers, finances, culture, government regulation or governance,
rather than using your technical skills.

Position descriptions usually set out the characteristics the
organisation is seeking in the new hire. For instance, one might
indicate the need for 'a leader with five years' experience in a
dynamic environment, who is strategic, resilient and calm under
pressure'. These words could be code for, 'We have big problems
and we need a strategic, resilient, and calm leader who can solve
them'. As you kick off your networking and start meeting recruiting teams, you need to follow Rackham's advice to draw out
the 'implicit needs' of the hiring organisations by using probing
questions. The more research you do and the more penetrating the
questions you ask, the more impressive you will be. Rather than
sitting back passively and simply answering questions put to you
by your network or the recruiters you meet, ask targeted questions.
This will make you a more attractive prospective candidate.

My advice in this chapter (as it is throughout this book) is to
actively approach the task of selling yourself to generate employment options. You might think that you will be perceived as too
aggressive or arrogant. You might argue that you are too senior to
need to sell yourself. You might think this kind of behaviour could
be demeaning. If so, your view is not uncommon among senior
executives. Many take the view that their accomplishments should

speak for themselves. The problem is that, with a passive approach, you will likely fail to communicate two things: first, that you are special and may bring special skills to the role and, second, that you are actually very interested in the role. Without an active approach, you are not likely to stand out. Even if you are visible and do stand out, you may be perceived to be unprepared and too passive compared to others who are more actively seeking the role. As a result, you could be overlooked and may not progress in the hiring process. By the way, if you are more junior, you could feel it is presumptuous to ask these kinds of questions. However, asking questions works better than being passive, no matter where you are in your career.

To be clear, I am not advocating aggressively selling yourself – quite the opposite. What I am saying is that you cannot afford to sit back and allow events to take their course. You are in a competitive process and, just as in any other competitive process, you need to show that you are well prepared and enthusiastic. You should have an active strategy and a clearly considered approach for achieving your goals. You must put in the work to excel in the process and differentiate yourself from the other capable people in the process.

Take the case of Simon. He was being interviewed for a senior strategy role in an international IT business. Because he had been a client of the business in a previous role, he had very clear views about the strategic opportunities for the business. Early in the interview, he was able to ask what the board of the company wanted to achieve over the next five years. Once this was explained to him, he described in detail the strategy that he believed would double the profits of the business in that time. Unsurprisingly, he provoked much more interest than other candidates who spoke in generalities, and he was offered the role.

MAXIMISING NETWORKING OPPORTUNITIES

The previous chapters have shown you how to prepare yourself to generate and explore opportunities. By now, you will have a series of hypotheses indicating where you want to explore to seek advice and validation. You are similar to an athlete who has prepared themselves, physically and mentally, to enter the competition. Now, you can begin to build your network, meeting people you know and new people as well, and seeking their advice. This is often daunting but it can also be exhilarating.

If you feel daunted, pluck up your courage and start the process. The initial group you will meet are in the first circle (your A-List) and these are people who you already know. I discussed how to handle meetings with your A-List in the previous chapter. When you move to contacts in the second and third circles (your B- and C-Lists), you will be meeting and comparing notes with interesting people who you would not have met if you were flat out at work. You will be potentially expanding your network of contacts and advisors for life. This will help you generate more opportunities as you move forward throughout your career.

Moving from planning to action requires a new mode of operation, with new discipline, new commitment and a new level of resilience. Unfortunately, you can rarely point a laser and identify the perfect role for yourself. So, now you are taking part in a numbers game, and the key is for you to keep activity levels high. You have been on the balcony, looking down on the dancers. Now you have to join the dance. Different dancers may be more or less interesting and helpful. As you expand your network, unexpected opportunities will begin to emerge. Obvious roles that you thought were 'made for you' will appear, and then disappear. Moments of elation will be followed by moments of disappointment. You are rather like the performer who has to go through multiple auditions before winning a role. Results may not come quickly, but you need to keep going. Finding a role that is appropriate for you and in which you will thrive takes time and effort. In the following sections, I set out some of the key issues you will need to consider as you build your network.

Meeting frequency – and quality

Before you can generate job offers, you must build your network. Sometimes, the perfect job may emerge quickly. But this is extremely rare. As mentioned, I ask my clients to target meeting at least 50 new people – at the rate of about five per week. As already explained, you will have prepared your hypotheses to help guide your efforts and to help others see what you want to test. If your hypotheses are inappropriate, they must be modified in light of what you discover as you do more research and learn more from your network. You do not have to limit your network to 50 new people, either. Some of my clients have met over 200 new people.

Numbers and frequency are important but make sure you are meeting the right people to help you in a concrete way. If you are a CFO, do not spend all your effort meeting other CFOs. You also need to meet chief executives and board directors, because these are the people who tend to be looking for CFOs or have friends or colleagues who are looking for CFOs. In addition, try to identify and meet role models who have made a career transition similar to the one you are facing. How did they tackle the transition? What can you learn from their strategies? What did they learn in the job-search process? Who helped them, and who might help you too?

Building your network

Once again, let me reiterate that you should seek advice, not a job. You might think you have made it clear you are seeking advice, but sometimes your message will not have been received correctly. Members of your network may introduce you by saying you are looking for a job – for example, a colleague might introduce you to someone senior, but then, when they introduce you, they mention you have lost your job. This immediately signals – even if your colleague did not intend it to do so – that you are looking for a job. Your colleague needs to introduce you as someone they are close to who would benefit from advice about a certain industry or a certain situation. It is best if they do not mention that you are looking for a job. If they do say (or imply) that you are looking for a job, their suggested contact might not agree to meet you, or they may agree to meet but then put the actual meeting off – because they've already taken the view they will not be able to help you.

In order to make sure that the person you are meeting understands you're serious about building your network, explain your networking target to them. For instance, make it clear you're seeking to meet 50 new people for advice. The challenge you face then becomes real and immediate. Introductions are no longer a 'nice to have'. Your need for assistance from them in introducing new people becomes blindingly obvious. Another approach used by one of my clients was to sum up a meeting with the following: 'I have a personal goal that each person I meet will introduce me to two new people. So, I would be really grateful if you can help me meet this goal!' By making this a clear goal, rather than something that would be good to achieve but not vital, you will make more progress. As you meet more and more people and get more practice, you will find these conversations become easier and easier.

Overcoming potential roadblocks

It is best if the person you are meeting can suggest some more people for you to meet while you are face to face in your meeting with them. If possible, ask them to arrange the connection then and there. In some places, such as Silicon Valley, where people are natural networkers and everyone is used to making personal introductions, this is easy. Networking is part of their gene pool. If you meet with someone you know, an A-Lister, this might be fairly easy. As you move to your B- and C-Lists, networking introductions are likely to be more difficult to arrange. The person you are meeting may say they need to contact the person they have in mind to obtain their approval before they introduce you. This rarely works. Too many things get in the way, and often the connection never takes place.

The best solution is, for the person you are meeting, to send an email (or a text message) to the potential contact, saying something like:

> I would like to introduce Janelle. She is a high-potential individual and she would benefit greatly from your advice. I am copying her in on this email and she will contact you to set up a brief meeting with you, if you agree. I would be very grateful if you can help Janelle.

The contact will meet you because they know and trust your network contact. They do not want to let him or her down. Only when they meet you face to face will they become interested in you personally.

Even if you use the approaches suggested, you may meet someone who says they cannot think of anyone to introduce you to. If this happens, you must treat this as your problem, not their problem. You need to get to the bottom of why this is happening, and then try to fix it then and there. Three things might be going wrong. Your contact might:

- mistakenly believe you are looking for a job, and can't think of anyone to help
- be confused or unclear about what kinds of people you wish to meet
- know something about you that makes him or her reluctant to introduce you.

A contact not being able to think of anyone suitable for you to meet is a bad sign, as is saying they need time to think and will come back to you. If they say this, they are unlikely to come back to you, even if they say they will. You need to probe what is going on and try to clarify or resolve this situation on the spot, before you leave the meeting. As you have more meetings, you will become more confident and find this easier and easier to tackle head on.

Remaining optimistic

When we first meet, my clients often ask me, 'What is the market like?' My answer is, 'Please understand that, unfortunately, there is absolutely no market for you! You are a senior executive. You have to seek out opportunities for yourself. You need to find situations where you will add value and thrive. These opportunities will emerge when your preparation meets an emerging opportunity.' I explain to them that they cannot scroll through a list of prospective jobs. A wide range of options is unlikely to be presented to them. Who knows what senior roles will suddenly emerge without warning? Not even recruiters know this.

As a senior executive, you are more complicated than a person who will be hired because of their specialised technical skills. You are different from a skilled welder, for example, with long experience in a specific technique. You are a leader who will be hired because you can manage and motivate others. If you are a senior person, lack of deep functional skills will rarely matter. The people reporting to you will do the detailed technical work. What makes you special is your ability to make wise judgements, allocate resources, plan activities, hold your people accountable, get the best out of others and negotiate outcomes. You need to show you are an effective leader who is energetic, has strong commercial acumen and has a track record of delivering outstanding results. In his LinkedIn session 'Coaching high potentials', Professor Ram Charan makes the point that 2 per cent of the talent in an organisation – and also in society - delivers 98 percent of the impact. How can you find a position where you will be able to have an impact like this? If you can find this kind of position, you will be a hero!

Also ignore the widely held belief that finding a job after, say, 55 is likely to be almost impossible. This is nonsense. In my experience, almost everybody – especially those who have held senior positions – can find a fruitful way of continuing their careers, through following the process set out in this book. Even if a suitable full-time role proves not to be available, you can always construct a portfolio career (as discussed in chapter 6). In fact, a portfolio career may be preferable for you. If you look after yourself physically, you have a good probability of living to well over 80, and may well choose to be productive in some fulfilling way, at least until you are 75.

If you're aiming to work in some capacity until 75 and are currently aged 55, you still have another 20 years of productive life ahead — or even more. If you take this view, chances are you will be productive for many years. Gone are the days when you retire to a rocking chair at 65 and then die at 66. Making the most of the remainder of your career requires a positive mindset. If you convince yourself you are about to be on the scrap heap, the chances are that you will be. Part of my role as a coach is to convince my clients that the future can be very fulfilling — provided they tackle the challenge of finding another role or another career in the way I suggest. At cocktail parties, sometimes people look at me pityingly, thinking that the outcomes of my work must be awful. I am able to tell them that virtually everyone I work with has a good outcome. That is why I like my work so much.

Let's look at another example. When Toby lost his senior role in a large retail bank, his friends told him that, although he was hugely talented and successful, they thought he would struggle to find another suitable role. They pointed out that he was a highly paid white male, aged 53, who had worked in a big bank for many years and he was also a foreigner. They thought the cards were stacked against him. Even if he did find another role, they said, he could not hope to maintain his level of compensation. The doubters were wrong. Having prepared himself well — along the lines I suggest in this book — he used the fact that he was a foreigner to his advantage. He asked his colleagues to help him to expand his network of senior executives inside and outside the banking industry. In the end, he met over 200 people. He built a strong supportive network that was instrumental in assisting him find a better role than the one he had left, at a higher salary.

If you are relatively new to a particular city and have lost your job, do not lose heart. You will be able to use the fact that you are new in town – or previously didn't have much time to meet new people – as the basis for seeking help to expand your network. You need to say something like,

> I have not lived here long and do not have an established network. Therefore, I really need you to introduce me to some senior people who might be able to provide me with sound advice and help me meet new people. In fact, I have set myself the goal of meeting 50 new people over the next three months.

I have seen this work effectively, with great results, on several occasions. People will want to help you, providing you ask for help in the right way. They just do not know how to help you until you explain your hypotheses to them and ask them who they think could provide you with good advice and counsel.

Maintaining meeting momentum

An important role of a career transition coach is helping you to maintain meeting momentum. You need a routine and a schedule, and to maintain five meetings a week. This may not sound like a heavy workload but, as mentioned earlier, probably takes about 30 hours a week, including preparing thoroughly for each meeting, conducting the meeting and then following up.

At times you will feel that nothing is going right. Promises made to you are not kept. Meetings are delayed or cancelled. Recruiters do not return calls. A technical glitch may mess up a video interview. Expectations are not met. You might feel like one of the early explorers who reached the first peak, only to find another hidden peak to climb, and then another hidden peak behind that – and all must be climbed to reach your ultimate goal. In situations like this, having a supportive confidant you can trust is helpful. In order to maintain momentum, it is also important to have the discipline of knowing you have to report in on progress on certain dates to your coach or confidant. At the same time, if you have a good coach, you will be in the care of someone who has seen all the problems you are encountering before, who knows what you are going through, and who can provide you with positive support.

You might think that the various challenges you face are unique to you. But virtually everyone going through senior career transition experiences these challenges. Be reassured that things work out in the end virtually every time, provided you keep going in the process. An experienced career transition coach or someone who has been through career transition themselves can be a vital support to you when the going gets tough. Your confidant, besides providing support to you, can also inject new ideas when your own ideas seem to be getting you nowhere. To use the fishing analogy again, they may be able to suggest better ways of fishing, or new ponds for you to fish in. This might involve suggesting meeting new people from their own networks, to help you understand the opportunities in the new ponds.

When you have started your networking, one key question keeps you on track: how many people in total have you met? That is the single most important key performance indicator for me in judging your progress. Once you have met 30 people or more, in addition to the 10 to 20 on your A-List, you are usually well on the way to finding your next role.

Keeping good records of these meetings, using Excel or CRM software (such as salesforce.com or monday.com), is vital. Once you have started to meet a series of new people, you are likely to forget the details unless you keep good records. Record everything relevant straight after the meeting, and keep separate lists for different categories of network contacts – such as executives, consultants, school contacts and recruiters. What did you learn and who will you be introduced to? When will you circle back? You should also record who introduced you, and the status of upcoming meetings. Is your meeting confirmed? This list is useful not only as you work to maintain your meeting momentum, but also as you discuss progress with your coach or support person.

UNDERSTANDING RECRUITERS

Most senior executives do not understand recruiters. As I have explained earlier in this book, you must be mindful that you and the recruiters are in very different businesses. You are in the marketing business. You are looking for a job and, for you, receiving two or more job offers is ideal. Recruiters, on the other hand, are in the risk-management business. In the best of all worlds, they will identify five excellent candidates for a role. The recruiter will probe the relative strengths and weaknesses of each, and then explain these attributes to their client.

The candidate who the recruiter believes is best for a given role is not always chosen by the enterprise doing the hiring. Beware of any recruiter who tells you that you are the preferred candidate before the final decision is made. Many slips can occur between the cup and the lip! Usually, the final choice for a role will depend on factors above and beyond the specific skills of the candidate. Good recruiters will provide their clients with advice in sorting through the candidates. But, in the end, the client needs to decide who is likely to be the best choice for the role.

Once a preferred candidate is identified, the recruiter is usually the one who does the reference checking. The best recruiters take this part of their role very seriously indeed. After the reference checking is complete, they become matchmakers, trying to ensure the preferred candidate agrees to accept the role being offered. While they are going through this process, they often try to keep the second choice for the role interested, in case the first choice drops out. If you do not hear from a recruiter for some time, they may be keeping you in reserve. Once the preferred candidate has accepted a job, the top firms may also assist with onboarding the new hire into their new role.

When I say that recruiters are in the risk-management business, I mean that a key part of the value added for their client is minimising the risk of a poor hiring decision. They must ensure there are no unknowns with a candidate for a role. These days, they check your academic and business credentials, your police record, how you behave under pressure, whether you have the work experience that you claim to have, and what others think of your growth potential. Your digital footprint may also be reviewed through social media checks. Also, any publications mentioning you might be checked for intolerance, violence, criminal activity and so on. Reference checkers will also attempt to identify any behaviours that could create reputational issues that might affect their client organisation. They will search worldwide for relevant information if you have worked overseas.

If anything keeps a senior recruiter up at night, it is the concern that their candidate is not what they claim to be. The failure to properly execute thorough due diligence on a candidate is a huge potential exposure for a recruiter. Many of the best recruiters would say reference checking is the most important part of the service they offer. It is a key part of avoiding a hiring mistake. If a new hire does not work out within, say, a year, the recruiter normally conducts another search without any additional fee.

Given this background, how should you approach recruiters while you are networking? Recruiters generally are not keen to meet you unless they think you are a good prospect for a particular role. But they will meet you if you are introduced by someone they respect. The following sections outline what to keep in mind when meeting recruiters while you are networking, and before you are involved in an interview process.

Recruiters do not want to meet you

Many senior jobseekers assume that recruiters will be keen to meet them. This is not correct. Many recruiters are inundated with requests for meetings from people they have little or no expectation of placing in a role. One recruiter's office I know of receives over 200 requests for meetings each week. It schedules only about five meetings each week with individuals who are introduced to it. Your chances of success are likely to be very small indeed if you approach a firm directly for a meeting with a recruiter.

The brutal fact is that the front office systems of recruiting firms are designed to actively discourage meetings with individuals who introduce themselves looking for a job. If you make a 'cold call', seeking a meeting with a recruiter, you will usually be asked to send in your CV. The receptionist will explain that, if you do this, a recruiter will contact you if they have any interest in you. Do not expect to be contacted. Individual recruiters in the top firms only place about 10 or 12 people in roles each year. As I have already mentioned, the low probability that you are a suitable candidate for one of their searches, combined with the low probability that you are meeting them at the right time to enter a particular process, means that you are highly unlikely to be meeting a particular recruiter at a the right time to find a role. In fact, if you are a good candidate for one of their roles, they should have identified you already.

Even if you are a great candidate for a role, a recruiter may not be willing to introduce you into a process if it is well progressed. This could be true even if you are introduced by a board member. The reason for this is that late entries can confuse the process, and cause it to derail. Moreover, the recruiter's client might well ask why you were not identified earlier in the search, thereby raising questions about the recruiter's competence.

Use your network to introduce you to recruiters

The likelihood of a successful introduction changes dramatically when you are introduced by someone who respects you and who has a relationship with a particular recruiter. Because they don't want to disappoint the person introducing you, this recruiter will agree to see you, even if they privately think it is likely to be a waste of their time. To make this happen, ask individuals you meet while networking whether they can recommend any recruiters. You want them to suggest specific recruiters, not recruiting firms. If they offer to do this, ask them to provide you with a warm introduction. The downside is that it could take a long time to meet people in your network who might help you. In addition, members of your network may not even remember that they are connected to key recruiters who you would like to meet, unless prompted by you.

The best answer, if you want warm introductions to recruiters, is to use LinkedIn. As covered in chapter 7, you can explore LinkedIn to find out who can connect you to target companies and recruiters. Suitable recruiters can be identified and introduced in three ways:

1. *Searching widely across all firms:* If you want to search all recruiting firms, enter 'executive recruiter' or 'recruiter' in the search box. You can then search your geographic area and identify any recruiters connected directly to you as a '1st connection'. If you do not have a direct connection to any relevant recruiter, search on your '2nd connections'. These are recruiters who might be introduced to you through someone you know. In fact, the real power of LinkedIn in this process is in your '2nd connections'. You may be very surprised that you are only one step away from a large number of recruiters through people you know who can introduce you. Scan through the list and identify the recruiters with the greatest number of joint connections to people you know. You may find a recruiter who is connected to 10 people who are connected to you. Often a small number of recruiters, who each have a large number of joint connections with you, will stand out. If this is true for you, look at your joint connections and identify the ones that you know best. Once you have

done this, you can decide which of your contacts would be best for you to approach.

2. *Finding connections in a particular recruiting firm:* If you know the name of a recruiting firm that interests you or has been recommended to you, enter the firm name in the search box in LinkedIn and search 'all People'. This will bring up a list of everyone on LinkedIn with the name of this search firm in their profile. You can then refine the search by location – and also by who has left the firm and who is still there. Finally, you can look at your '1st connections' and '2nd connections'. If you are searching on an international recruiting firm, you may find you are connected through people you know to 50 or more consultants in that firm, in various places around the globe. As in the preceding point, scan through the list and identify the individual search consultant in the firm with the most mutual connections with you. Then follow the same steps already outlined.

3. *Finding connections through a friend or colleague:* The best people to introduce you to a recruiter are often ex-colleagues who have also had to search for a role in the last few years. Search their list of connections on LinkedIn (assuming that they permit you to look at their connections), searching on 'executive recruiter' or 'recruiter'. Often you will find that individual friends and ex-colleagues are connected to several recruiters. If so, you can approach them to ask which recruiters they would recommend, and whether they would be agreeable to introducing you to them. If they agree, ask for them to provide a warm connection. These people often have met a number of recruiters, so they are good sources of leads for you.

Most of my clients are amazed when they find out how many connections they have to recruiters through their networks on LinkedIn. If this approach does not identify a group of recruiters who you could be introduced to, work to expand your connections on LinkedIn. You need to have at least 500 connections to gain the best benefit from LinkedIn. The more connections you have, the better — but, as mentioned earlier, only connect with people you have met.

Some career consultants will offer to introduce you to a recruiter as part of their service. As mentioned earlier, I do not believe this makes any sense. Being introduced by someone senior who has worked with you and who has an emotional connection with you is far better. I would go so far as to say that coaches who offer to introduce you to recruiters as a selling point should be treated with some suspicion. They have not seen you at work and, therefore, cannot be a credible advocate for you as an effective executive. I personally make it clear to my clients that I will not introduce them to recruiters. I tell them that they will be much more successful if they find someone who has worked with them who can recommend them from their heart to a recruiter they know. The exceptions to this are career coaches who come from roles in executive recruiting. They can be credible introducers since they have ex-colleagues who are recruiters.

Meet with recruiters only when you are properly prepared

As I have stressed throughout this book, most recruiters will not want to invest much effort in you if you are unprepared. But once you have met your A-List and have started to test your hypotheses, you will be in a much better position to meet a recruiter. You can test your hypotheses further and consolidate your thinking. You can say to a recruiter:

> I have given a lot of thought to where I can contribute most and have tested this with 15 people who know me, including some of my most senior referees. They all agree that my thinking makes sense. But they are not recruiters, so I would like to test my approach with you to see whether you agree that I am on the right track.

As a result, your conversation with the recruiter will be completely different from the conversation what would have taken place if you'd asked whether they had any jobs for you. You will have a constructive conversation about your options and how the recruiter thinks you should best move forward. Also, note that you can ask the recruiters you meet which other recruiters they would recommend. Most will be helpful. They know that each recruiter only receives a small percentage of the available work. If you can have a constructive conversation, you are likely to learn a great deal. As with any networking, your goal must be to impress the recruiter and to build a relationship with him or her. Too many jobseekers treat their meeting with a recruiter as a transaction. Your first meeting is an opportunity to build an ongoing relationship. If this happens, you have grasped an important opportunity.

I have been told by a very senior recruiter that a general rule in the industry is that the best connections tend to be with clients and prospects who are in the same age zone as the recruiter. According to him, for the best relationships, recruiters need to be within plus or minus five years of age of their clients and prospects. So, if you are 45, the recruiters you should meet should be aged between 40 and 50. This could be a factor to consider as you build your recruiter network.

As mentioned, you should have tested your hypotheses with your A-Lists before meeting with a recruiter. Keep in mind, however, that the recruiter may have a different perspective from your colleagues. For example, as I have already mentioned, unless you had previous experience as a CEO of a *public* company, a recruiter would rarely, if ever, present you for a similar role – even if you had been the CEO of a large successful *private* company. They would know you had never handled the complexity of working for a public company board of directors or had to respond to public shareholders, and that you had no experience in dealing with the stock exchange. They would consider a move like this by you to be much too risky for their client. Your own personal network might not understand this issue and might suggest that you should aspire to such a move. As with all your networking, use this advice to develop and adapt your hypotheses.

YOUR GOALS WHEN YOU MEET A RECRUITER WHILE NETWORKING

Once you have tested and validated your hypotheses, you're ready to really focus on meeting with recruiters as part of building your network. What I have in mind here is meeting recruiters to build relationships, not to seek a job. I cover how to manage job interviews with recruiters in the next chapter. Your goals when you have the opportunity to meet with a recruiter (or a senior HR executive), while you are networking, are outlined in the following sections.

Build a strong emotional connection

Before you meet a recruiter, learn as much as you can about them, their background, their education, their practice area, their career, their interests and their passions. Look up their bio on their website and check their LinkedIn Profile. Also check your research with any joint connections you have, to seek their input and advice. Too many senior jobseekers fail to do any of this basic research. As a result, their meeting with the recruiter becomes formal and administrative – and unlikely to build any emotional connection. Just telling the recruiter that you have researched their background and that you are fascinated to see their involvement in, for example, coaching football instantly differentiates you from most jobseekers. I know one US recruiter who immediately discounts you if you have not identified and mentioned that he is a one-eyed, rabid Dallas Cowboys supporter. As part of building a relationship, also mention the individuals you know who are connected to that recruiter, particularly if they have provided positive feedback about the recruiter. Tell the recruiter about this positive feedback.

Learn how these recruiters size you up

Recruiters spend their lives meeting with people and evaluating them. Most will size you up in minutes, or even seconds, using a multitude of factors: whether you are on time, how you treated the receptionist, the way you walk into the room, your handshake, what prior research you have done on them and their firm, what clothes you are wearing, what you say and how you say it, whether you look them in the eye, your mannerisms, how you sit in your chair, your LinkedIn Profile and your CV, how you respond to, 'Tell me about yourself', your gravitas, and so on. Many will be heavily influenced by your previous role and the circle of other senior executives you know. To try to learn what they think of you and who you are, explore the following questions with the recruiter when you meet them, asking diplomatically near the end of your meeting:

1. How would you describe me and my strengths?
2. What is your perception of me and my brand?
3. What do I need to do to make myself more attractive in the market?

Once you know how the recruiter sizes you up, you will be able to tell whether you are presenting yourself in a way that makes sense. Dan, for example, had a meeting with a recruiter and afterwards asked for a critique. He was told he was taking too long to answer questions, and that his answers were not clear. Dan then put together a five-minute video showing how he should have responded to the recruiter's questions, and sent it to the recruiter. He attached a message that he had taken the recruiter's criticism to heart and learned from it. The recruiter was very impressed with Dan's initiative and asked him back for another meeting! This would never have happened if Dan had not asked for feedback in the meeting, and then responded quickly and positively.

Seek their advice

It makes sense to ask the recruiter, 'If you were in my shoes, how would you be tackling my job search?' Most will respond that you need to expand your network, but they may also have some specific ideas that will help you. In addition, you can also ask:

1. Which other recruiters do you recommend?
2. Do you know of any good prospects for me to investigate?
3. Is there a particular avenue you suggest for exploring these possibilities?

You may be surprised how helpful a recruiter can be if you have a warm introduction and you show real interest in them and actually ask for their advice. One thing that you should not expect, though, is for a recruiter to introduce you their clients or to other senior people. The recruiter, who has only met you in this one meeting, will be concerned that any introduction might be interpreted as a positive endorsement of you. Since they do not know you, they are unlikely to provide any introductions.

Build a commitment to provide you with ongoing advice

Once they have met you, many recruiters will agree to stay in touch with you. Some will even suggest that you contact them, say, once a month, to bring them up to date with what you are doing. If they suggest this, ask them how they would like you to contact them. This is courteous since you should be looking to minimise the extra work you would impose on them. Whatever they suggest, it is important to gain their agreement that you can touch base in a couple of months to bring them up to date with your progress. Sometimes a recruiter will state that they will call you each month. Despite this promise, it rarely happens. It is better for you to suggest that you will initiate these calls, so that you stay in charge of the process. In some instances, recruiters have called my clients with leads to jobs even though these recruiters have not been retained to do the search. If you can form this kind of relationship, you are on the right track.

Offer to help the recruiter

Many years ago, a consulting client of mine taught me a valuable lesson. I wanted to delay a presentation because my team was not ready. He reminded me of a saying that his parents, who ran a clothing store in Greenwich Village in NYC, had taught him: 'Always bring something to the customer'. I have never forgotten this advice. I always attempt to bring an alternative possibility forward, rather than saying something is impossible. When you are meeting with a recruiter, you may be able to assist him or her with some names of individuals for roles they are seeking to fill. If you are senior, they may be looking for someone more junior. The very act of making this offer to try to help them is likely to have a positive effect. And, if you can actually provide one name (or more) that might assist them, this is likely to be a great way of moving forward and building rapport.

Thank them for their time

You are more likely to build a relationship if you recognise at the beginning of your meeting that the recruiter is putting themselves out to see you. It is amazing how many senior executives do not thank recruiters for taking the time and making the effort to meet them. One recruiter told me that only three out of 10 individuals who came for networking meetings thanked him. Not only this, but the seven who did not thank him also failed to make any effort to stay in touch or tell him if and when they found a new job. Do not make these basic mistakes! If you want a relationship, make sure you thank the recruiter when you meet, when you leave and after you have left. You cannot thank them enough. You may also wish to write a personal thank you letter, since this makes a huge impact in the age of email. Thanking them not only is good manners but also shows them you appreciate and value their advice and would welcome an ongoing relationship.

APPLYING FOR A ROLE THAT EMERGES WHILE NETWORKING

As your networking progresses, you are likely to be approached by a recruiter who has been retained to find candidates for a specific role, or you may see an advertised position that interests you. Either way, your probabilities of success will increase if you follow the guidelines outlined here.

Do not apply for a role that is too small for you

Some senior jobseekers think applying for a role will be good practice, even if it is obviously too small for them. This is generally a mistake. To start with, it makes no sense to offer to play in the junior league if you belong in the seniors. All you do is waste your own time and raise questions about the quality of your judgement and your level of confidence. As I mentioned earlier, your brand might even be diminished if you apply for a job that is too small. People may start to think you must be damaged goods, desperate, or merely parking yourself until another better role comes along.

Most recruiters will immediately see that you are too big for a given role and they will reject you. They are likely to think you will get bored, intimidate your boss, or leave the role if you are offered a better position in due course. Rejection is not good for your morale or your level of self-esteem – particularly if you believe you could easily do the job before breakfast. If approached by a recruiter for a role that is too small for you, you may need to make it clear to them that you are too senior for the job they are suggesting. If you do this, you are helping them to understand better where you fit in the market. They quite possibly will be retained in future for a job that better fits your capabilities and seniority and, if so, they are likely to call you.

Speak to the recruiting team before you submit an application

Unless you have no other option, only apply for a role once you understand what is involved and what the real challenges facing you will be. You can be almost certain that the position description does not describe the real job. It is merely the starting point in a discussion. It will describe the broad functional skill requirements and some of the attributes you will need in the position. You need to find out what is really required – otherwise, you are wasting your time and are unlikely to present yourself in the best way.

Another issue you need to clarify, if at all possible, is whether there is already a preferred internal or external candidate. Sometimes a board or management team will conduct a search merely to provide rigorous confirmation, in a professional way, that their preferred candidate is indeed the best choice. As I mention in chapter 2, if you are being compared to an internal candidate, you will usually need to be superior to them by at least 50 per cent, to have any chance of being selected. You need to decide whether it is worth your time to enter the race in this situation. Sometimes, given that many CEOs are obliged to meet diversity targets, it may be obvious that the choice of a candidate for a role is likely to be constrained. If this is the case, or looks like being the case, you need to decide whether it is worth your while to prepare your application if you do not meet these obvious, but unspoken, criteria.

So, speaking to the recruiter in advance of applying for a role will enable you to learn what the successful candidate for the role is likely to look like. This helps you to tailor your application. When speaking to the recruiter, also ask about the expected timeline for the recruitment process. If it is likely to be a worldwide search with a six-month lead time, you may take a different view about applying than if you were being involved in a shorter process. If applications don't close for a month, you do not need to rush your submission.

Your goal is to build rapport with the recruiter you have approached in order to obtain additional information. You want them to separate your application from the pile of other applications they have received so as to give you special attention. If the name of the person doing the recruiting is not provided in the advertisement, try your best to identify who they are, either through your connections on LinkedIn, or by calling the enterprise and asking who to speak to. It is worth putting real effort into this identification process. Your chances of making progress will increase dramatically if you can find out more about the job from the people involved in the recruiting process, before you apply.

Find out early what your compensation is likely to be

As I've already argued, you shouldn't take a reduction in compensation unless there is a special reason. When you are approached by a professional recruiter, they will usually check your compensation requirements early in the first conversation. They do not want to waste their time talking to someone who will not accept the role because it pays too little. If you are asked what you want to earn by a recruiter, relate your answer to your previous compensation and pick the maximum number that you can. For example, your answer could be, 'In my best year at company XX, I took home $350,000 before tax.' Set the bar as high as you can. You can always say you are willing to continue in the process and negotiate your compensation later if they say the job will pay less than the amount you specify. I have seen several situations where compensation was more flexible than initially indicated by the recruiter. Once, as negotiations progressed, my client was able to negotiate double the salary being offered, by redefining the role to create a job that was much bigger and more complex.

Unfortunately, if an HR executive or an internal recruiter in a company approaches you directly, to see whether you are interested in a particular job, they rarely indicate the compensation level unless asked to do so. Raising this issue early is best, even if you feel uncomfortable doing this. Sort it out before you invest much time in an application or in interviews. Too often, when an organisation does its own candidate search, a total mismatch arises in compensation expectations. Unless you ask early, this may not come to light until late in the process. Close to the end of your first meeting with the person who has contacted you, say something like, 'I don't want to appear as though compensation is the only driver, but I would appreciate knowing what sort of salary range you have in mind for this job.' If they ask you what you want, tell them the highest salary that you have ever received. If there is a mismatch in expectations, getting this on the table early is best for everyone. Remember – you having received a high salary in your previous role is not an embarrassment. It is a sign you are valuable!

Keep your application and cover letter short

Do not overcomplicate your application. The recruiter will be looking for a few key attributes that will keep you in the process. If they do not find these, they will reject you. Your application is merely to get your foot in the door. Make sure you find out what the recruiter is looking for when you first speak to them, and then emphasise these factors in your application and cover letter. In one recruiting process I was involved in as a board member of a school, I was looking for a senior academic who had proven commercial skills. Despite this requirement, the recruiter submitted four candidates with very limited commercial skills. The individuals might have been very competent in their own particular areas, but they did not meet my stated requirement. Fortunately for me, the fifth candidate did meet my requirement and was very impressive in other ways. She was offered the role. The other four candidates wasted their own time and mine. The recruiter had clearly struggled to find candidates that met my criteria. Presumably, he'd hoped I would be impressed by the other candidates in other ways.

Follow up to ensure that your application has been received

Many recruiting firms will send you an email to say they have received your application; however, I have seen many glitches in this process. Even if you have this email, follow up with the recruiter directly to ensure they have received your application. It is amazing what can go wrong. I have seen situations where juniors were asked to sort applications using very basic criteria – and one where my perfect candidate had his application shredded by mistake. Make sure your CV is safely in the system and thank the recruiter for taking your call. You can also reinforce your strengths and note any issues you see with the stated requirements.

For junior roles, the sorting process and initial interviews may be automated. In this situation, it is even more important to identify someone in the firm to help you prepare. Otherwise, you have a high probability of being lost in the huge numbers being processed. Do not assume the CV submission process will work. Double-check everything.

Ask others to speak up for you

If you have connections in common with the recruiter, ask your connections to drop the recruiter a note. All they need to say is that they understand you have applied for this role and, because they know you, they are willing to provide background information, if this information would be helpful to the recruiting team. They must not try to sell you. The recruiter is likely to react positively to an offer of help from someone they know. The more a recruiter can find out about you, the more they are likely to be able to identify issues and reduce risk for their client.

You can do a number of things to change your application from an administrative document to a more personal connection with the recruiter. Some people do this automatically, while others find it uncomfortable. If you are uncomfortable with this approach, realise that the recruiter is likely to welcome it. They want to know what you are like as a human being, not just what you say in a formal application letter. Time and time again, I see individuals who undersell themselves because they fail to build a relationship. Because they do not understand the job requirements and take the job description too literally, without checking, they prepare a written document that fails to hit the mark.

★★★

In this chapter, I have emphasised that you need to consider yourself to be part of an active selling process when you are networking. You have moved from planning to action, and this requires a different kind of discipline and resilience. You are involved in an activity-based process, where you are trying to meet with about 10 to 20 people you already know and 50 or more new people. I have emphasised that you are likely to sell yourself more effectively and build more productive relationships if you ask good questions (rather than talking about yourself).

You need to prepare yourself well before you meet recruiters. Part of this preparation is to meet first with your A-List to test your thinking. Once you are confident about the ideas you wish to test – your hypotheses – you are ready to meet with recruiters. To make the best use of a recruiter's time, you need to explain what you have concluded after meeting people you trust, and then seek validation of your ideas. At the same time, you should be attempting to build an ongoing relationship with any recruiter you meet, not just have a one-off meeting. A recruiter you meet now may not be able to assist you right away, but you would like them to think of you if an appropriate opportunity arises in the future.

If you are approached for a role while networking, you may be asked to submit an application. Before you do this, make sure you learn as much as you possibly can about the job and the people involved in the recruiting process before you agree to submit an application. The job description will, almost certainly, not describe the real job, so it is important to understand and evaluate, as fully as possible, the real job – including the people issues, the condition of the organisation and whether you can make a big difference – before you apply.

In the next chapter, I discuss the issues you are likely to face in an interview process and how to prepare for this. I cover the need to do thorough research. I also outline the importance of rehearsing, presenting yourself well and handling interview questions effectively. And I address how to do your best to be part of a conversation rather than a one-way interview where you are obliged to answer a series of formal questions. Finally, I discuss what to do if you are offered more than one job, which I hope you will be!

SOME QUESTIONS FOR YOU TO CONSIDER

- Are you ready to put your networking preparation into action?
- Do you have a strong list of up to 20 people for your A-List?
- Are some of your A-List super-networkers?
- Can your network introduce you to outstanding recruiters?
- How can you meet and test your thinking with these recruiters?
- Will you be able to build ongoing relationships with recruiters?
- How much can you find out about the real job before you apply?
- Have you followed up to check that your application was received?
- Do you have friends or colleagues who know recruiters and who can speak up for you?

PART IV

FINDING THE RIGHT JOB

9

Generating attractive job offers

This is the true joy of life; to be used
by a purpose recognised by yourself as
a mighty one.

George Bernard Shaw

Maximise your probability of finding an attractive job by:

- Preparing well for job interviews with recruiters
- Managing successful interviews with internal executives
- Handling multiple job offers

YOUR JOB DURING the interview process is to understand what attributes are needed by the organisation and why. After that, you must decide whether you are willing to take on these challenges and, if so, whether you are likely to be successful.

As I have already indicated, you will be much more successful in finding a suitable role by asking questions, rather than by talking about yourself. If you do good preparatory research, you will be better at asking penetrating questions. Use your networking contacts to discover more intimate information and personal insights about the people you are meeting. This will also lead to better questions, because you will have identified the issues facing the people you are meeting and the organisations you are interested in. Try to find out what they are passionate about. If you ask good questions in meetings, you will send a positive signal that you have been willing to invest real effort in understanding the role and the employer. You will show that you are perceptive, thoughtful and truly interested. All this makes you more attractive as a prospective candidate. Also, if you ask good questions, the people you meet will want to understand you better and invest energy in helping you. If you ask no questions in an interview process, even if you truly believe all your questions have been addressed, you will most likely be written off. You should never run out of questions. Ask good questions to differentiate yourself!

At all levels, but particularly at senior levels, seek to trigger a warm conversation with your interviewers. Your ability to fit the organisation is important. Try to build a relationship with the interviewers right from the start of the process. Even though it seems almost inconceivable that an important hiring decision can be made on the basis of two or three one-hour interviews, many organisations do precisely this. Some of my clients have been told they were in the top two candidates for a big role but 'just missed out' because they did not answer one of the questions well. I tell these clients they may be fortunate to have missed out on this offer, if this is how hiring decisions are made in this organisation. Having experienced this situation raises an important question for my client, however: Why did you not understand or identify this problem during the interview, and try to resolve it there and then?

In this chapter, I explain how to manage job interviews. Again, you need to take an active approach – quite the reverse from sitting back and responding to questions from the interviewer. You need to show you are well prepared and enthusiastic, with clear ways of differentiating yourself from your competition.

PREPARING WELL FOR JOB INTERVIEWS WITH RECRUITERS

How do you prepare for a job interview? Some people think they should be authentic, play it by ear, do the best they can, and roll with the punches. Being authentic is vital, but failing to prepare is almost never the best way to approach an interview. To obtain the best results, you should invest real time in preparing yourself. I often spend two hours with a client preparing for a one-hour interview. Think through the various possible approaches, and give the strategy you wish to use in an upcoming interview as much thought as possible. Consider the questions that might arise – not only likely questions from the interviewer but also what questions you will ask. Practice out loud how these might be handled. You do not have to convince the interviewer in the early interviews that you are the best candidate. Your goal in any interview must be to receive an invitation to the next stage. You need to stay in the game. That is the key requirement! You do not need to win each battle, but you do want to win the war! The longer you are in a specific recruiting process, the more you will learn about the role and what it takes to be successful. If you are a good learner, the more impressive you will be as you go on.

Your preparation might involve thinking about what risks you could take in the interview to differentiate yourself. I quoted Harry Beckwith in chapter 4: 'You cannot bore someone into buying a service.' In this regard, you should consider how you would like the meeting to progress and what initiatives you might take to make what you want happen. As a starting proposition, try to avoid being in a one-way interview. Instead, if you can, initiate a conversation by asking a key question early in your meeting. You should kick off with a question like, 'In order to make sure my answers to you are relevant, would you mind helping me understand what your board and management want this organisation to look like in five years' time?' This should permit you to start a wide-ranging conversation to understand how this goal will be achieved, and how the role you are being interviewed for will contribute to meeting this goal.

Starting a conversation can be more difficult to achieve if you face a panel interview – for example, for a government or academic role. In this situation, each panel member commonly has a pre-assigned set of questions as they work their way around the table. Diana faced this situation in an interview for a senior manager position at a university. She had been told by the recruiter that she had just scraped into the short list to be interviewed. Coming from the commercial world, and being much younger than the other candidates, she was clearly an outlier. Since she did not appear to have anything to lose, she decided to take a risk and kicked off the interview by asking the Chair to describe what attributes the panel was seeking in the candidate for this role. The Chair was surprised that she was so forthright and, after attempting to answer the question, threw it open to discussion. The panel was impressed with Diana and she found herself ranked in the top two candidates. In the end, she was beaten by an internal candidate.

When an interviewer has a series of questions that leave no room for free-ranging discussion, this is a concern. You face a big challenge if the interviewer insists on asking all the questions, and it will be almost impossible for you to determine what kinds of answers they are looking for in advance. If they ask open-ended questions, you have no context to frame your answer. The danger for you in this situation is that your answers could be way off the mark. How do you answer a question such as the following: 'You are the CFO of a large global business and you disagree with the CEO about how to explain a significant financial matter to the board. What would you do?' The correct approach, I believe, is to seek to narrow the scope of such a question and try to pinpoint the issue the interviewer is seeking to address. You could do this by asking questions to clarify the situation and to identify the issues that are likely to be important in this situation. This has two advantages: you identify the key issue that the recruiter wishes to explore, and you buy some time to think.

In most cases, you're best to initiate a conversation, rather than having a one-way interview. Ideally, you should be speaking for about 50 per cent of the time during the interview. This raises the reverse question: how do you get to the point of listening for about 50 per cent of the interview? The following sections outline my suggestions.

Find out as much as you can about the organisation

It seems obvious, but you must find out everything you can about the role and the organisation you are seeking to join. Visit a factory or store site, check its website, buy and test its products, check how well its call centre works, look at feedback from employees and ex-employees on the web, check its reputation with friends and colleagues, and research current and former employees on LinkedIn. See where its new hires have come from and their career experience. Also check with stock analysts and anyone else who might be tracking the organisation's performance. Finally, see whether any speeches or presentations are available online, and read any newspaper articles. This should start to give you a good feel for the issues facing the business, its executives and shareholders.

A thorough analysis of the organisation's website can be productive. Elton was invited to an interview for the role of CEO of a business that installed fibre optic cable. After spending some time analysing the website of the business, he identified a number of mismatches related to the way the business was described on its website and what was set out in the position description provided to him. He asked questions about these differences and, not surprisingly, the directors conducting the interview had never reviewed the company website. They were able to explain their view of what should have been shown on the website. The fact that Elton had raised these questions impressed the directors and he was later offered the CEO role.

With private companies and not-for-profit organisations, finding relevant and detailed information can be much more difficult than for a public company. In these situations, word of mouth might be the best way to try to find out what is going on. In fact, little public information being available will give you an excellent opportunity and a good reason to ask more questions in the interview. You can do this without apology because it was impossible for you to obtain relevant information about the enterprise from public sources. For instance, if very little information is publicly available, you could say in an interview, 'I have tried very hard to research your organisation. Unfortunately, as I am sure you know, very little information is available to the public. To help me understand more, it would be helpful if you could describe the current health of the business and any particular issues you face.' Owners and senior executives of not-for-profits and private companies are often proud of what they have achieved, and are usually more than willing to provide you with a comprehensive background briefing. If you ask good questions, you will learn a great deal about them and their enterprise.

Consider how to make a good initial impression

Initial impressions – those made before you even open your mouth – can be crucial. As is often pointed out, you only have one chance to make a good initial impression. If you are being interviewed for a leadership role, carry yourself and behave like a leader. How you present yourself while you are in the recruiter's office and when you are with the recruiter is important.

As Nicole Williams, a career expert at LinkedIn, argues, 'the problem with appearance is that it translates to performance. Even if your boss doesn't think that they're thinking any less of you, they will subconsciously think it'. Nicole discusses seven factors that she believes will help you make a 'brilliant first impression in a flash'. In summary, these are:

- *Grooming:* You need to look like you take care of yourself.
- *Clothing:* Make sure that what you wear is appropriate for your industry.
- *Jewellery:* Keep your jewellery subtle and don't wear things that will clank.
- *Posture:* Sit upright in the front half of your seat, with both feet on the floor.
- *Gesturing:* Talking with your hands is okay – it brings your message alive.
- *Facial expression:* Be genuine and smile often, maintaining eye contact.
- *Handshake:* Have a firm grasp, look at them in the eye and smile warmly.

Think about how to break the ice

How do you break the ice? Who speaks first? What do you say to help kick off the meeting? What pleasantries are appropriate? Your research into the recruiter may indicate some personal background to start the conversation off with. Having connections in common on LinkedIn, for example, can be a good way of kicking off a conversation. Another approach is to ask what the recruiter would like to achieve in your meeting. Then ask him or her whether they would like you to tell them about yourself. Assuming the answer is 'yes', use some form of the two-minute PEC framework explained in chapter 5.

Jeff lived in the UK and was preparing to speak with a senior executive in Singapore about a job there. Jeff could not find this person on LinkedIn and knew nothing about him, except his name – which indicated he was probably Sri Lankan. Jeff surmised that, assuming the interviewer was Sri Lankan, he was probably an avid cricket fan. And if he was a cricket fan, he probably knew the results of the recent test matches between England and Sri Lanka. So Jeff researched these results and started the conversation by reminding the interviewer of them. This turned out to be a great way of breaking the ice and building a warm initial connection!

Clarify what the role involves

I usually request that my clients prepare a list of questions to ask in an interview. Often their list is too long. In a one-hour meeting, you're unlikely to be able to cover more than half a dozen questions, if they are thoughtful. Another problem is often that the questions are too detailed and too tactical. At this stage, you do not need to know the long service leave policy of the organisation. What you do need to know is where the organisation is going and how it will get there. Therefore, focus on asking, as close to the beginning of the meeting as possible, two questions:

1. What do the board and CEO want the business to look like in three to five years? For instance, do they want to double the size of the business and, if so, how will this be achieved?

2. How will the role you are being interviewed for help to contribute to meeting this goal? In particular, is any direct

contribution from you in your function going to be important in achieving the desired goal?

Explain that understanding this future goal, and how the role will contribute, will help you be more specific and relevant when you answer the recruiter's questions. The clarity with which your interviewer answers these two questions will tell you a lot about how well he or she is prepared. If they do a poor job at describing how the role is intended to contribute to the organisation, I tend to have concerns about their competence and preparation. Do they really know much about the role? If not, how can they conduct a sensible and productive interview? The sign of a good recruiter is how well they understand the role they have been retained to fill, what it will contribute, and what issues you're likely to face as you seek to make a difference and add real value.

Ask follow-on questions

Once you understand the broad goals and how you would contribute to them, other questions will inevitably arise. These will be related to the culture of the organisation, the governance framework, key accountabilities, profitability targets, future capital expenditure plans, the capability of the current team and its potential to grow, the performance of the enterprise versus its competitors, mechanisms for future growth (including acquisitions), and so on. You might also ask what measures your boss is likely to use to assess whether you were doing a good job at the end of the first 12 months. If they can explain this in concrete terms, they are more or less articulating your KPIs. Not being able to explain this is another sign that the interviewers are not well prepared.

Belinda was a senior executive being interviewed by a young internal recruiter for a start-up technology business. Belinda was told that the company was taking 48 hours to respond to customer complaints, and was asked what she would do about this. Belinda started to probe: What kinds of complaints was the company receiving? What was the target response time? Who was responsible for responding? The interviewer could not answer any of these questions. It became obvious that the interviewer had been instructed to ask this question but had no comprehension of the issues to be addressed or what a sensible answer might involve.

You will sell yourself with the quality of the questions you ask. Good questions show you are thoughtful and well informed, and that you are interested in the role and the organisation. Good questions will launch a good conversation. Your well-thought-through questions will be a stronger way of selling yourself than by talking about your own attributes.

Reinforce that your experience is relevant

By asking these questions, you are learning a lot more about the organisation and the issues facing it. The recruiter is also learning about the way you think and how you express yourself. Most importantly, however, you are positioning yourself to be able to say something along the lines of, 'I am grateful for you explaining so much about the organisation and the challenges it faces. These are precisely the kinds of issues that I have faced and have been able to resolve in my previous role. I relish the idea of tackling them again here.' As I've mentioned, recruiters are in the risk-management business. It is music to their ears when you say that you have successfully tackled similar challenges already in a previous role.

Explain how you have contributed in the past with a story

The recruiter will likely ask you how you led your team and managed various issues in your previous role. They may also ask what lessons you learned that might help you be successful in this new role. If they do not ask this, you should ask the recruiter something like, 'Would you like me to tell you about a situation where I tackled a challenge like this?' You need to have thought about relevant stories in advance, and should have four or five compelling stories pre-rehearsed. Then you can describe, preferably in less than two minutes, a situation where you made a difference.

Ideally, use a framework such as STAR-L to explain how you contributed:

- *Situation:* Set the scene and provide any details required to tell your story.
- *Task:* Describe what your responsibility was in this situation.
- *Action:* Explain exactly what steps you took to address the issue.
- *Result:* Describe the outcomes you delivered.
- *Learned:* Explain what you learned, showing you seek to learn and develop.

If you provide a two-minute answer, you can wrap up by asking the recruiter whether more detail would be helpful. Do not try to fill a gap in a conversation where there is silence. Let the recruiter speak first. The danger with filling a silence is that your comments may not be relevant. Also, you may feel tempted to do this time and time again.

Handling questions about your development needs

As part of an interview process, you may be asked to describe your development needs. This is a tricky question because most people have development needs of some kind, depending on the situation they find themselves in! So, you will be tempted to try to think of a development need so you can answer the question. Much has been written about the 'correct' way to answer this question:

- *Some argue that you should reveal you are not perfect and expose your weaknesses:* After all, we all have weaknesses. These people would say something like, 'I know at times I am too strong, and some of my team members can be intimidated. I need to work on this; otherwise, they might think I am a bully.' Being strong is an asset in many situations, and yet you have indicated that you think being strong could a weakness. The difficulty here is that you are showing that you lack self-confidence. You seem to be apologetic about your behaviour.

- *Others argue that you should position your strengths as weaknesses:*
  For example, 'I am a strong leader and I set high standards,
  but at times this could intimidate some members of my team.'
  The problem with this approach is that a weakness in your past
  job could actually be a strength in your future job, and vice
  versa. For instance, you might think that you were too strong
  in your previous role but the people hiring for the new role
  actually want someone who is strong. The difficulty here is that
  you actually look weak to them by stating that you think that
  being a leader who sets high standards could be a weakness.

I take the view that it is better to discuss a strength, but with a twist.
In an interview, you may not know what strengths the new job
may need, and a development need in the previous role may not
matter in the new role. As a result, I suggest the following:

- *Do not indicate that you have any specific weaknesses:* You can do
  this by saying something like, '*Most people* see me as a strong
  leader but a few think that I set standards that are too high.'
  In other words, you yourself are not admitting to a weakness.
  What you are saying is that 'a few people' may believe that
  setting high standards is a weakness. The implication is that
  they are the ones with a problem. Their standards are not
  high enough.

- *Highlight that this behaviour has worked well for you:* Avoid
  being apologetic, and implying that setting high standards is
  a weakness, by saying something like, 'As you know, I have a
  track record of success and, I am proud to say, the vast majority
  of people who have worked with me admire my strength as a
  leader and support my approach.' You have not indicated that
  being a strong leader is a weakness; indeed, you have positioned
  it as a strength, and a strength that most other people respect.

The question about your development needs is asked frequently,
but what answer is expected by the person asking the question
is unclear. It could be a bit of a fishing expedition. Because you

do not know what behaviours will work best in your new job, I take the view that it is not productive for you to talk about your weaknesses. If you do talk about your possible development needs, you may look too apologetic or too weak. Therefore, talk about what *other* people might think, and keep your own opinion out of the conversation.

Discussing significant career setbacks

Most of us have suffered a significant setback at some stage in our careers. If you have had a dream run, with no bumps in the road, you should count yourself as extremely fortunate. Career setbacks come in many forms but two are worth noting here. If they are, or could possibly be, exposed publicly, these setbacks usually need to be addressed head-on in the networking and interview process.

The two most common setbacks are as follows:

- *A personal setback:* For instance, you may have suffered personal bankruptcy. Or you may have faced a situation where it was claimed you failed to carry out your executive duties, which led to adverse publicity for the business and your subsequent termination. Your reputation and brand may have taken a direct hit. In my experience, the story in the press or on social media often fails to explain the full complexity of the situation you faced. Nevertheless, many reading the story, or hearing it on the rumour mill, may assume your values or competency are suspect.

- *A corporate setback:* For instance, you might have been the leader, or one of the leaders, of a business that failed or suffered a major setback. Or, if you were a board director, you could have been faced with an important legal action against the company or the board. In both these cases, your reputation and brand could have been damaged by association with this failure or the legal action. As a result, many may be wondering whether you were asleep at the wheel or whether your judgement is suspect.

I have worked with a number of good people who have found themselves embroiled in these kinds of situations. Each has come through successfully, but the challenges involved were much greater for them because of the adverse information that was circulating. In each case, their close networks supported them and they were able to progress in their careers.

If you have been involved in a situation like this, you must be brutally honest with yourself and with others you meet. My usual advice is to ask in general terms at the beginning of your meeting, whether your contact has heard about the issue you faced. If you do not do this, and the other person does in fact know about some or all of the problem, they will believe you are hiding something. This will destroy any hope of building their trust.

Once you have surfaced the issue, I have found the best way forward is to provide a very brief description of your side of the story. Then, you can suggest that your contact seeks an independent view. You can direct him or her to someone independent and credible who knows exactly what happened and who can put your situation in perspective. Your problem is that any story you tell will be regarded as self-serving. So another, more independent, perspective is needed. If you can arrange this, anyone who is interested in understanding what happened can take the initiative to learn more. This is likely to help you make progress, assuming they are satisfied with the explanation provided by the independent third party. Many people are probably thinking that they themselves could have found themselves in your position. Importantly, not being straightforward, transparent and honest is very risky and likely to be a recipe for failure.

Confirm that you are a leader

One of the issues likely to be addressed by the recruiter is whether you are a leader. And, if so, what kind of a leader you are? A powerful way of addressing this question is to show the recruiter the feedback you received from your email requests, described in chapter 3. You can do this by working through the section in your Professional Profile that lists your leadership strengths and supports these strengths with quotes from your colleagues (as covered in chapter 4). Some of my clients have taken this section and enlarged it so that it fills a page. They take this page to meetings with recruiters and hiring teams to show them if this question is asked. Virtually all of my clients are rightly proud of the feedback they receive from their colleagues describing their leadership strengths.

Remember the First Law of Holes

Denis Healey, called by some 'the best prime minister Britain never had', spoke of the First Law of Holes: When you are in a hole, stop digging. The message here is to know when to stop. When you can see things are not going well, don't dig yourself deeper into the hole. This could be when you have made an off-the-cuff statement that is then queried by the interviewer, for example. If you do not have explicit facts to back your statement up, do not try to bluff your way through. It will not end well. Better to back off, and state that you need to check your facts. Another possibility is that you have taken too long to answer a question. If you realise this has happened, try to wrap up without delay. Then indicate that you should have explained yourself more briefly.

Ask wrap-up questions when the interview is coming to a close

Take an active stance as the interview is being wrapped up. Do more than thanking the recruiter for his or her time, and saying that you found the conversation stimulating. Based on what the recruiter has learnt about you in your conversation, ask how well the recruiter thinks you fit the role. Also ask whether he or she sees any specific issues that need to be addressed by you to improve your chances of success in the process. This gives you the opportunity to address any possible reservations or rebut any misconceptions then and there.

For instance, if the recruiter says they think you could be too big for the role, you could respond, 'I can see why you have that concern. But I can assure you that it is very clear to me that this job involves a lot of complexity and challenge. I have no doubt that the role will be very demanding and that I could be extremely effective in it. More importantly, if I was fortunate enough to obtain this role, I could be a major contributor to the future success and growth of your client's organisation.' You might think you are being too forward in asking this question about your suitability for the role; however, doing so means you avoid being told in two weeks' time that you will not be progressing to the next round, without understanding what the potential issues are, and without having a chance to deal with them on the spot. I believe most recruiters will be frank with you. Also ask about 'next steps'.

Follow up later if you failed to make a point clear in the interview

After you leave the interview, you may be concerned that you answered a particular question poorly or that you missed making a point clear. Call, or write to, the recruiter to let them know that you now think you need to clarify what you said when you were in the meeting. As I mention in chapter 8, my client Don prepared a five-minute video for the recruiter with the answer he wished he had provided. The recruiter was very impressed. Following up in this way has the advantage of getting the correct message through, while showing you are committed to presenting your best case for this particular role. It reinforces that you are tenacious and will not give in. By the way, always send a thank you note after an interview.

Rehearse in advance

None of these steps are clear-cut. Do your best to identify any possible risks or exposures in the interview process in advance. No matter what you have rehearsed, your interview will probably go in a different direction. If this does happen, make sure you have a framework that allows you to introduce some of the basic questions outlined in the preceding sections and get them addressed in some way or another. Sitting back without rehearsing and letting the recruiter take charge is obviously easier, but this is risky because the recruiter may see you as boring and lacking initiative. Instead, take the initiative rather than being too passive.

Who do you rehearse with? Your career coach or trusted support person is usually the best option. Do not forget that interviews can cover a lot of ground and be daunting, especially if the recruiter tries to explore how you behave under stress. If you are being interviewed for a senior role, influence the direction of the interview if you possibly can. If you cannot do this because the interviewer is too rigid, it may say more about the future employer than you. An experienced recruiter is more likely to challenge your thinking and your approach than someone who is inexperienced. And they are also likely to welcome a conversation rather than a question-and-answer section.

Roll with the punches

As Mike Tyson, considered by many to be one of the greatest heavyweight boxers of all time, said, 'Everyone has a plan until they get punched in the face!' A similar idea, stated less succinctly by nineteenth-century Prussian field marshal Helmuth von Moltke, is that 'No plan of operations extends with certainty beyond the first encounter with the enemy's main strength' – or, more simply, 'No plan survives first contact with your opponent'. The main point is that you need to be flexible. In this regard, remember, practice makes more perfect. You will find yourself becoming much more confident and comfortable, and more able to handle unexpected challenges in an interview once you have been through four or five of them. It is almost inevitable that you will face multiple interviews because you are rarely offered the first role presented to you.

What tends to happen is that your job target and the hiring organisation's target are not a good match in the beginning of your job-seeking process. As you meet more recruiters and learn how they operate and what questions they ask, it is easier for you to excel. As a result, the jobs presented to you and the jobs that suit you best move closer and closer, as shown in figure 9.1, as you participate in more interviews. You get better and better, and more comfortable and confident, as you go along. Also remember – just because you do not progress in a particular role, this is not necessarily a bad thing. If the recruiter is impressed with you, they may have another, even better, role available for you to consider in future.

Figure 9.1: Improving job fit as the job-seeking process continues

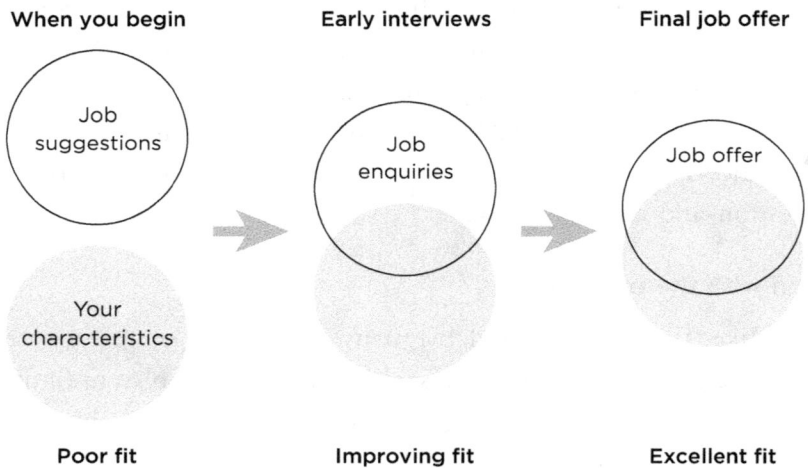

When you begin	Early interviews	Final job offer

Job suggestions

Job enquiries

Job offer

Your characteristics

Poor fit	Improving fit	Excellent fit

So, contrary to what you might think, your confidence will usually tend to increase rather than diminish as time goes by. You will see more easily where you fit. You will begin to feel more confident that you will find a suitable role. Joanne left a senior COO role in a major company when she was in her mid-fifties. She felt certain that she would never find another role similar to the senior role she had left. However, after six months, she became convinced that she should be looking for a CEO role. Two months later, she was offered an outstanding CEO role. A few years later, she went on from this CEO role to build a successful portfolio career, as a senior non-executive director with a consulting practice as an executive coach. Your early perceptions may be too negative. You need to build your network in order to begin to understand the real possibilities available to you.

MANAGING SUCCESSFUL INTERVIEWS WITH INTERNAL EXECUTIVES

If you progress from the interview with the recruiter, you will be asked to meet a variety of executives in the hiring organisation. Normally, executives in the organisation will interview between three and five preferred applicants. In this case, the recruiter will usually tell his or her client that each of the preferred candidates is capable of doing the job well. The key issue at this stage becomes fit: Will you get on well with your boss and your peers? Do you fit the role? Do you fit the culture? Do you enhance the people and team who are in place? Do you have the capacity to grow into a bigger role? Will you bring something new and valuable to the organisation? How will you behave under stress? Can we afford you? Are you a leader who can motivate people and bring out the best in them? Are you truly committed to the values and goals of the organisation? Will you work hard? Are you a problem-solver or a problem-generator? Do you have gravitas? Are you someone who can represent the organisation well in front of external stakeholders? Are you interesting? Are you fun? Will our stakeholders respect you? Will we look good if we hire you? The list goes on.

Organisations tackle internal interviewing processes in a range of ways – from formal and systematic at one extreme, to quite loose and flexible at the other. Sometimes large-scale, complex organisations insist on a series of interviews. Global consulting firms, for instance, may have as many as 10 interviews, and sometimes even more. They often present very unconventional case study problems – such as 'Can you tell me how many pizzas would fit inside the Colosseum?' – to try to determine how you think, how well you handle pressure, and how well you can explain your logic. Professional partnerships, such as law firms and accounting firms, may want you to meet a large number of their partners before they make a final decision. Other organisations will present you with a series of behavioural questions. Examples of these types of questions include:

- Can you tell me about a time you set and achieved a challenging goal?
- Can you tell me about a time when you overcame a conflict at work?
- What is your proudest professional accomplishment and why?
- Tell me about a mistake that you've made at work. How did you handle it?
- Give me an example of a difficult problem you solved. How did you do this?

Some companies, such as Apple, might spend time making sure you understand their culture before you go to a formal interview. Others, such as Amazon, want to test your ability to prepare a written document. Some put you through a series of personality tests, case studies, or ask you to attend an assessment centre. In Europe, some companies still use graphology – where your signature and handwriting is analysed, to evaluate your personality characteristics – even though no scientific basis for this analysis has been found. Some organisations try to avoid unconscious bias, while others do not care. Some send you straight to the CEO to be interviewed. Others start you with someone from HR, and you then work your way up to the CEO. You need to be properly prepared for any of these various possible approaches.

You may also be asked to complete and present a case study or similar presentation. For example, if you are a prospective CEO candidate, you could be provided with the company's strategy and financial data and then asked to present your view of the issues facing the organisation to a meeting of the directors. You could also be asked for your thoughts on how you would tackle your first 90 days. The board might be trying to determine whether your proposed approach is aligned to the organisation's strategy and values. Asking you to present this way also lets the board see you in action and helps it to understand your abilities when it comes to comprehension, prioritisation, and communication.

Given so many approaches to interviewing in-house are possible, what are the key issues for you to consider before you enter the process? Many of the recommendations set out earlier in this chapter will be relevant. Five areas are especially important, and I cover them in more detail in the following sections.

Seek to understand the interview process in advance

The best people to assist you in understanding the specific approach taken by an organisation are those who manage it, and those who have been through the process. If a recruiter is involved, they should give you a thorough briefing, outlining the process and the likely key issues. The best recruiters will actually provide you with coaching to indicate what issues are likely to be most relevant and important to the interviewers. Remember, the recruiter should want you to perform at your best. They do not want you to trip yourself up in some trivial way. If a recruiter is not involved, identify the key people on the hiring team in advance and learn what you can from them about the process. Most organisations are happy to explain their process to you and help prepare you. But you probably need to take' the initiative and ask them. If they do not volunteer to help you, make sure you ask them in advance. Again, forewarned is forearmed.

Invest real effort in preparing and rehearsing

You may have 1st or 2nd connections who have worked, or are currently working, at the company. If they have gone through the recruiting process there, they can be particularly helpful because they know what will make the difference for you and how to prepare effectively. Alice, for example, was in a process set up to hire a new CEO for a large enterprise, and she approached half a dozen board members through her contacts. Some said they would not agree to meet her since 'they did not want to give her an unfair advantage', but others agreed to meet her to provide her with some background on the role. Alice met these board members in advance of the interview process. Interestingly, as a result, she decided that she would withdraw from the recruitment process. The board members she met were not impressive, and she decided she did not want to be the CEO reporting to them! You learn a lot – some good and some bad – when you get closer to the people in an organisation.

In addition to preparing for the interviews, you need to practice for any personality or assessment tests that are likely to be required, as set out earlier in this chapter. And one final point: be careful not to over-engineer your approach and the way you handle interviews. Use your preparation and rehearsal to be confident and spontaneous – not too rigid or trying to follow a tightly constructed script!

Identify any hidden agendas

Reaching the short list of five for a role is an achievement in itself. But your probability of getting the role is still only 20 per cent (one in five). The question now is how can you move your probability – to, say, 60 per cent or more? As I've outlined in this chapter and in chapter 2, many complex issues could be at play in any senior hiring decision. You must do your best, through diplomatic questioning, to understand what the important swing factors will be.

When the board of Apple decided to rehire Steve Jobs in 1997, they did this because they realised they could not hire another conservative CEO from a traditional business. Apple was in real trouble and, although it had been offered for sale to Microsoft and Dell, both had refused to make an offer. The board decided that the only way to save the company was to find a true technical visionary to lead it. The obvious choice was Steve Jobs. Effective boards will determine the pivotal issues facing the company. Then they will seek the best person to address these and to lead the enterprise forward. They should define the job requirements in these terms.

As another example, I have seen a hiring process for a CFO where the organisation did not actually want to hire the best CFO — they wanted a CFO who would be best positioned to be the future CEO. As a result, the hiring decision revolved around what kind of CEO the board wanted in place in three or four years. They were looking for someone who would grow into the CEO role, using the CFO role as a stepping stone. Obviously, this was a much more complex decision than the one relating to hiring a good CFO. If you did not understand this before entering the final interview process, you would not be properly prepared.

Obtain subtle support from your advocates

Someone in your network may know someone in the organisation you are being interviewed by, or its recruiter. If they are respected and can validate that they know and trust you, this person may be a great help to those doing the interviewing and hiring. If this person is willing to do this, he or she could let their contact in the hiring organisation know they've heard you have applied for the role, and that they have worked with you and are happy to provide any input that would be helpful. In this way, they have made it clear that they are willing to speak in support of you. This helps to build trust in you and, from the point of view of the interviewer, is one way of reducing hiring risk. One word of warning — if your supporter's contact in the hiring organisation is the Chair or a board member, this approach may not work. Sometimes executives in organisations are very wary of apparent hiring recommendations or support coming via the Chair or the board. They are concerned that you could be too close to the board.

Ask where the board and the CEO want to take their organisation

Understand where the organisation is headed and what it will take to get there. You may have discussed this with the recruiter already, but ask the people leading the organisation this question as well. You will not only hear how the top management state their purpose and their goals, but also reinforce that you would like to be part of the team that delivers these results. Once you understand these goals, you can ask how the job you are being interviewed for will help the organisation achieve the goals, and what the challenges and risks in this job are.

Although not many people will say this out loud, a fundamental driver for anyone on the executive leadership team must be to protect the CEO from disasters and to help him or her to be successful. If you are meeting the CEO, it makes sense to ask something like, 'What must I do in this role to make you, the board and the whole organisation successful?' This sends three strong messages: first, that this role will not be all about you and your success; second, that you are looking to learn how you can contribute to the greater good; and, third, that you care about the success of the CEO and the top management. This is a much more powerful approach than suggesting the role will be good for you because you think you will learn a great deal. The hiring decision will relate to what value you can add to the organisation, not what the organisation can do for you!

Sometimes you will be asked to make a presentation to your potential boss, or to a board. Avoid death by PowerPoint! This is when you have too many slides and you put too many words on each slide. You do not need to set out all your thinking. You must keep your message strong and clear. Just use a series of talking points, with no more than five bullet points on a page. In my experience, the best presentations have virtually no words and are predominately pictures. One presentation I remember particularly well involved six slides with a series of graphics. The first slide was a photo taken in an iron works in Wales, with six men covered in black soot, each with a huge hammer. The title was, 'I come from tough stock'. The next slide was of his wife and baby son: 'I am proud of my family'. The third slide was a map of the various countries that he had worked in: 'I have deep and broad experience in ten different countries'. The fourth slide was two photos of a retail store before and after he had redesigned and refurbished it: 'I make a difference'. The fifth slide was list of five strengths that he brought to the job, with the heading: 'I can make a difference to you'. The sixth slide was a list of selected leadership strengths, taken from his Professional Profile. He also included with each strength supporting quotes, also taken from his Professional Profile. He built an emotional connection, and launched a very positive conversation. He was subsequently hired.

If you do well in this process, you increase the probability that you will be offered the role you are seeking. You may, of course, be sought after by more than one organisation. The next section discusses how you should think about this.

MANAGING MULTIPLE JOB OFFERS

Having more than one offer being discussed or negotiated increases your negotiating power. This situation could well occur if you have planted a number of seeds that lead to positive results in your networking. Be open with the various recruiters and organisations if you have received another offer or if you are expecting to receive another offer. This needs to be communicated as early as possible, not just when it is clear that negotiations are going well. Move reasonably early as a courtesy to all involved, so they are aware they are not the only organisation interested in you. You do not need to state the name of the organisation likely to make you an offer.

How to select between multiple attractive offers

If you are fortunate enough to receive more than one job offer, you need a way to help you select the role that is likely to be best for you going forward. If several competing jobs seem to meet your requirements, the next step is to refine the broad analysis set out in chapter 2. To do this simply and quickly, my clients have found it helpful to use the chart shown in figure 9.2. The idea here is to select the specific factors that are important to you and your family. The factors shown in Figure 9.2 are merely examples of what you might use. The next step is to give each factor a score out of five for each role being offered to you.

Figure 9.2: Example of process for ranking possible roles

Factors influencing your decision	Indicate your preference	Role 1	Role 2	Role 3	Comment
1. Job is in my preferred location	Boston	3	5	5	
2. Base remuneration satisfactory	$250,000	4	4	5	
3. Role level/description	Vice President	4	5	5	
4. Prestige of organisation/role	Quality reputation	5	5	5	
5. Amount of time away from home	No more than five dpm	4	4	4	
6. Likelihood of success in role	High probability	3	4	3	
7. Work will be fun	Needs to be stimulating	3	4	5	
8. Expected workload	No more than 50 hpw	3	4	4	
9. Desired autonomy in role	High autonomy	5	5	5	
10. Bonus scheme attractiveness	50% of base at target	5	4	2	
11. Opportunity to make a difference	High-impact role	5	5	5	
12. Leads to obvious next career step	Within three years	3	4	3	
13. Minimum job timeframe	Stability for five years	4	4	5	
14. Role is likely to be fulfilling	Want to help society	3	4	5	
15. Size of business	> $100 million revenues	5	3	4	
TOTAL SCORE		59	64	65	

Do not just assume that the role with the highest score is the right answer for you. Rather, use this scoring process to push your thinking. The question you need to consider is: How can I increase each of the lower scores? For instance, if the role is not in your preferred location, can you negotiate a better location or work out how to change your preferred location. In other words, use the chart to stretch your thinking, not just as a scoring methodology. If you do this the relative attractiveness of the various competing roles might change.

How to negotiate when you have emerging offers

A problem arises if you have a preferred employer you're dealing with, but they have not yet made a formal offer. Perhaps you receive an offer from a less preferred employer that needs to be accepted within three days or it will be withdrawn. If you tell your preferred future employer they must make you a firm offer within three days, they won't do this. They will not be able to respond quickly enough. You are then left in a predicament: should you take the firm offer with the less preferred employer or refuse it? If you refuse the less preferred offer, what happens if your preferred employer does not make you an offer?

To avoid this predicament, be as transparent as possible with the organisations in the process of making offers, as early as possible. If they know you are in another process, they might accelerate their process to make sure they do not lose you. You might say something like this to your preferred employer:

> I want to be totally transparent with you and wish to avoid putting you in a difficult position later. You should know that I am expecting to receive a firm offer from another organisation in a week or so. My difficulty is that I would prefer an offer from you. Therefore, I am alerting you in advance in case you might be able to accelerate your process.

Recruiters will thank you for being transparent, because this usually assists them to alert their client that they will lose you unless they move more quickly. Max was offered a senior marketing role in a global business. He had almost concluded negotiations in relation to this role when he received an approach from a small start-up business. This small business happened to be very well aligned with Max's interests and skills. He explained to the smaller business that he was about to sign an employment agreement with the global business. The small business asked him to meet its Chair that afternoon. At the end of this meeting, the Chair asked Max to meet the full board the next morning. Immediately after this meeting with the full board, Max was offered the CEO role. Max alerted the global business of this new offer, and it responded by increasing its compensation offer by 10 per cent. The small business then increased its cash and equity offer by 20 per cent. After proper due diligence, Max decided to accept the CEO role with the small business. Being transparent and having more than one offer greatly increases your negotiating clout!

As you go through more interviews and more interview processes, you will become much more comfortable with taking the initiatives described in this chapter. I am in favour of being on the front foot. You may be concerned about being seen as too pushy. However, I have never observed this to be a problem. If you do get negative feedback in this area, you can tone things down fairly easily. Again, in my experience, the problem is usually the reverse: you are tempted to be too accommodating and too passive, so as not to rock the boat or upset your interviewers. If you are a high-performing senior jobseeker, being too accommodating and too passive is not a good strategy since the recruiting team is likely looking for a person who is a good negotiator and who can take charge.

★★★

In this chapter, I have highlighted that you will not be an attractive candidate if you are passive and low energy. You being successful at selling yourself involves not only understanding what the job requires, but also building a relationship with the interviewer. However, understand that success should not involve overt self-promotion. Your future employer needs to see you as the best fit for the particular role and the person most likely to add real value. You need to work out what is required and help the employer understand that you are the best choice. To do this, you need to have joint conversations rather than one-way sessions where you are obliged to answer a series of questions without any context. You should only be speaking 50 per cent of the time. To have good conversations, be ready with good questions by doing thorough research in advance.

Your goal at each step in the process must be to progress to the next step. Seek to understand the role better as you progress through each step. As you understand the role better, you will also be working out how best to add value. Your interviewers will see you evolve and, hopefully, you will become a more attractive candidate as you understand what is required at each stage. At the same time, you will be assessing how well your values match those of the organisation and whether you are a good fit for the role and whether it is something you wish to take on.

Certain issues, such as the broad level of compensation, must be dealt with early so that you do not go through an extensive process only to find you can't afford to accept the role offered. Usually, recruiters address this issue with you at the very beginning, since they also do not want to move forward if you are unlikely to accept the compensation likely to be offered. Often, private organisations doing their own recruiting put off discussing compensation until the end of the process. Do not let this happen. Raise the issue early and you will save yourself and the hiring organisation a lot of time if the offer is likely to be unacceptable to you.

Being an active participant does not come easily to some jobseekers. As a result, they undersell themselves and reduce their chances of success. Being active does not mean being aggressive – it means applying energy and using your initiative, showing that you are an enthusiastic and passionate leader. It also means using a conscious questioning approach at each stage of the recruiting process to identify and clarify issues related to the organisation and the role. The more you can learn, the better you will perform. The final hiring decision will come down to how you stack up against the other candidates.

To help you perform at your best in the hiring process, rehearse and have a close confidant who can critique you. It is not possible to read a book such as this and then automatically perform at your best. As I mentioned earlier, skiing out in the snow is totally different to reading a book about good skiing technique. You will get better through practice and as you go through real interviews and assessments. As you get better, you will improve your chances of success. For this reason, tenacity, dedication and resilience are vital. Focus on the future and never give in. If you tackle this process the correct way, you will find a good role. I am able to look my clients in the eye and tell them this. But I also tell them that the big unknown is the time they take to find the right role. This depends on your work level and also, to some degree, on your luck.

In the next chapter, I cover the work involved in negotiating your final arrangements, and what you need to do before you start in a new role. In addition, I provide tips on how to calibrate whether you are in the right role, after you have been in the role for some months. Ultimately, of course, your goal is to be an ongoing success in any role you choose to accept.

SOME QUESTIONS FOR YOU TO CONSIDER

- Have you thought through how you would handle an interview with a recruiter?
- Who can give you some constructive feedback in terms of your grooming, posture, facial expressions and voice control?
- Have you rehearsed enough to properly prepare for a job interview with a recruiter or internal recruiting team?
- How good are you at breaking the ice, and starting to build warmth and trust right from the start of a conversation?
- How do you best answer a question related to your weaknesses and your development needs?
- If you have experienced a career setback that has received public attention, how will you handle this in an interview?
- If you've already completed some job interviews, what learnings can you take from these interviews to the next one?
- If you're likely to receive more than one job offer, how can you ensure that you are positioned to accept the offer you prefer?
- Have you carefully thought through the factors that need to be assessed as you evaluate the suitability of a specific role?

10

Thriving in your new role

If we all did the things that we are capable of, we would literally astound ourselves.

Thomas Edison

Ensure a successful transition to your new job by:

- Concluding your employment negotiations
- Preparing for your first 90 days
- Starting your new job on the right foot
- Calibrating your progress in the first year

ONCE YOU HAVE received your verbal job offer, you still have a lot to do before the hiring process is complete. First, of course, you need to wrap up the details of your job and sign a formal employment agreement. This may be a complex legal document. In this chapter, I cover several of the issues you might face as you review this agreement. You need to get your employment agreement right because, once signed, it will be difficult to change.

Even when you have negotiated your final agreement, you still have much to consider. In particular, you should prepare a 90-day plan for yourself. Doing this well will enable you to begin to contribute real value without delay in your new job. In addition, think through the practical issues you might face right at the beginning, when you arrive on the first day to start your new job. It goes without saying that it is vital you start well since people's perceptions of you and your style are formed very early.

How should you plan for the first 90 days on the job? Many senior jobseekers tend to tackle this in a superficial way. This is unwise. In this chapter, I explain the issues you should be considering, which can be surprisingly complex. For example, Geraldine was about to become the leader of a large mining services business in a developing country. The national enterprise was composed of five separate business units, each with its own profit targets. Each of these lines of business reported to her via a 'dotted line' as Country

Head, but also had a direct line of responsibility to its respective business-unit CEO in Boston. The head of each line of business believed the key reporting relationship for them was to their business-unit CEO, not to Geraldine. She had to think through a series of questions before she began this new job. For instance, at the simplest level: 'Should I start my new job by spending time with the executives who report to me in my country to understand what they do? Or should I start by spending time with my new boss and the business unit CEO's in Boston, to understand what they want? Or, is there a hybrid solution?'

Proper preparation for your physical arrival on day 1 is also important. First impressions count, and when you are a senior executive, everyone will be watching you. What you say and what you do will be noted and analysed by your team, and by others inside and outside the organisation. If you do not look and act like a competent leader from the beginning, you will miss a crucial opportunity to set the tone and communicate your expectations. I remember a highly respected orchestra conductor telling me that he had only 30 seconds, after he stepped onto the conductor's rostrum in front of a new orchestra, to show he was in charge and that he knew what he was doing. You may have more than 30 seconds, but you do not have long, particularly if you are joining an unfamiliar organisation.

You have a tricky path to tread – you must show you are confident and capable, but also willing to listen and learn. This chapter covers the issues you need to consider in your new role, and how to behave once you are there. Finally, I also provide guidelines to help you assess whether you have made the correct job decision as you settle into your role during the first 12 months.

CONCLUDING YOUR EMPLOYMENT NEGOTIATIONS

Even when you learn you are the preferred candidate, you're not confirmed in the job. The steps to confirmation will involve a series of negotiations. Until your employment agreement is signed by both you and your future employer, you have not accepted the role, and nor have they accepted you. Too many senior jobseekers accept the terms offered in the draft employment agreement without question. Possibly they are so relieved to have received an offer they want to settle the final arrangements as quickly as possible and with minimum fuss.

Don't rush to sign your agreement – instead, be a good negotiator. The way I look at it, one of the reasons you're being offered your job is because you're perceived to be a good negotiator. Work on the basis that the first offer is not the last, and actively negotiate the terms of your employment. Your new employer should expect you to do this, and should even welcome this approach. If your new employer does happen to question your desire to amend various clauses, remind them that they hired you because they wanted a good negotiator – so it should be no surprise that you wish to discuss and possibly renegotiate certain clauses in the agreement.

Eight steps need to be completed before you are ready to start your new role. You should be actively involved in each of these activities. The following sections explain each of these steps in more detail.

Negotiating compensation arrangements

Compensation can be a complex mix of base salary (cash), annual short-term incentives (usually cash), and long-term incentives (usually shares or share options or both). The payment of incentives to you will be contingent on some combination of:

- your performance
- the performance of your team
- the performance of your business unit
- the performance of your parent company or overall enterprise.

Performance can be your actual performance against budget and specified non-financial targets, or performance relative to industry benchmarks or to key competitors. Some payments may be staggered over time and they can be contingent on meeting future performance targets. Your incentives may be calculated as part of a profit pool, or related to your own performance in relation to your KPIs. The parameters might be closely measured and defined, or subject to a board decision each year. In other words, your total compensation can be calculated in many ways.

Make sure you understand the precise rules for your incentive payment program. Your future employer must be clear about how your incentives will be calculated, and you need assurance that the incentive payments are based on realistic performance targets. Don't assume you will automatically be able to meet the hurdles for payout of the incentives. You may find it impossible to hit the targets because of factors outside your control. To avoid this problem in your first year, try to negotiate a guaranteed payment of your short-term incentive. Alternatively, attempt to negotiate a sign-on bonus. This will protect you if the specified incentive hurdles are not met by you in the first year.

Start-ups and private equity businesses usually pay relatively low base salaries. To make the package more attractive, they provide shares or share options that will become valuable if the company meets its three- to five-year profit goals. The payout may be contingent on listing on a stock exchange, or on all or part the company being sold. If more than 50 per cent of the shares are sold, this will involve a 'change of control'. Be clear about the rules for receiving the long-term incentives or equity payouts. If a change of control occurs early, make sure that this triggers your full incentive or profit-sharing payout if you decide to leave then. Remember – working around the clock for a low salary to make someone else rich, and missing incentive payments just because control changed earlier than expected, makes no sense!

The longer-term incentives or equity participation will commonly not be paid to you if you leave the company before predetermined dates or specified transactions take place. Make sure you understand the rules related to these. The requirements set out in the offer letter may be too onerous for you to accept. If you cannot understand the compensation arrangements, ask your accountant or lawyer for advice. Tax rules are complex and you would be well advised to understand the exact tax arrangements related to the various proposed payments before you commit to them. You might be able to reduce your future tax commitments if you structure the arrangements appropriately. If you are accepting an overseas role, the tax arrangements are likely to be particularly complex and you must obtain the best advice.

Understanding your future career path

You may feel that discussing your future development opportunities with your future employer before you join the organisation is presumptuous. You might believe that discussing where your career might head, so early on, is premature. But, in fact, this is the perfect time to start this discussion. Some big questions you should raise, at least in general terms, are:

- What is your organisation's philosophy regarding the continuing development of your executives and how are decisions made?
- What sort of development programs does your organisation offer? Who attends these programs and how are participants selected?
- Do opportunities exist to attend advanced educational programs, such as Harvard's Advanced Management Program? How would this be decided?
- Can employees obtain financial assistance and/or time off for further study? How much support is provided? How is it decided who will participate?

Remember, even if you are 50 years old, you still have – on average – at least 25 years of useful productive life ahead, assuming you wish to remain an active contributor. Therefore, it is important that you continue to learn. Ascertain how your future employer thinks about and invests in developing its people to move further in the organisation. As noted in his biography, Steve Jobs argued, 'It doesn't make sense to hire smart people and tell them what to do; we hire smart people so they can tell us what to do.' Part of your job is to get smarter and many smart employers will help you do this. If you do not discuss your future career path during the hiring process, you will miss the opportunity to plant the seed early that ongoing development is very important to you.

Completing assessment testing

From time to time a hiring decision is contingent on completing psychological or other tests, such as cognitive abilities, knowledge, work skills, physical and motor abilities, personality, emotional intelligence, language proficiency, and even integrity. The tests could be online or a psychologist may spend several hours interviewing you. You may need to participate in an assessment centre exercise. Whatever the approach, make sure you practise before you take the tests. You will find a great number of practice tests available online. If the organisation testing you does not share your results with you, this is unacceptable. You may decide that this is a deal-breaker since it is vital for you to know what issues have been raised in your testing.

How each employer uses the results of these tests is up to them. Low scores are not necessarily a knockout. In fact, I have worked with individuals who have scored very low on certain tests – say, numeracy – but have still been offered a senior role. One thing to remember is to be totally authentic. Some tests 'red flag' your results if you are providing inconsistent or conflicting answers, and this can result in you being knocked out of the process.

Obtaining references

Many recruiters will tell you that reference checking is the most important part of the hiring process. Some organisations use recruiters to check references, while others do it themselves. Some carry out superficial checks, and others are detailed and conscientious. One recruiter I know takes over one hour for each reference-checking interview. Others take much less time. The more senior the role you are being considered for, the more likely it is that the reference checking will be intensive.

The process may also involve a series of informal checks, and these can lead to problems even when the formal reference checking is strongly supportive. Donald, for example, had completed the whole process involved in being selected for an important position on the executive leadership team in a major public company. As a final check, the CEO mentioned Donald's name to the company Chair. That night the Chair met an old university friend at the airport, and asked him whether he knew Donald. The Chair's friend said he had known Donald at university, 20 years earlier, and felt that he was not trustworthy. That was enough for the Chair to reject Donald without any further discussion. Given the rigorous and highly successful reference-checking process Donald had gone through, this decision seemed totally unfair. But this kind of thing can happen.

Your references may be checked when you reach the short list of two or three, or when you are the final preferred candidate. It is important to understand what approach is being taken. If you are one of, say, three candidates being reference checked, you still only have a 33 per cent chance of being selected for the role. In this case, it is best to make your referees aware that they may be called on multiple times, depending on the outcome of the process you are in. Also, you should consider speaking to the person doing the reference checking to alert them that you are concerned about drawing too heavily on your referees. In some cases, you may need to say you're not willing to approach your referees until you are the preferred candidate for the role. Overuse of your referees can be a real issue if you are asking very senior people with tight schedules to provide references for you.

The six key issues being checked in most senior reference checking are:

1. your claims in your CV, particularly your personal achievements, your impact, and your pattern of success

2. your capacity as a leader, your authenticity and integrity, your strategic skills and track record in execution of strategic plans

3. your ability to handle stress and remain calm under pressure, your commercial acumen and judgement, and your wisdom and balance

4. your ability to work effectively in the role with the current team, and your desire and ability to develop and energise people to be their best

5. your attitude, commitment and drive, growth potential, and the functional skills where you are likely to need support

6. whether the referee would be happy to hire you or work with you again, and their view of your suitability for the new role.

If you are asked for a list of referees, ask what kinds of referees the organisation or recruiter would like to contact. Your preferred referees will, of course, probably be the same as you selected for your panel from your A-List. But showing you have a range of possible referees, rather than just two or three especially supportive people, will also give you an advantage. Ask the person doing the reference checking who they would like to speak to. A wide range of people is possible – for instance, individuals who have worked for you, or previous bosses, board directors, key customers, or consultants or advisors who have provided advice to you. Consultants who have worked with you might be accountants, lawyers, management consultants or other specialists. Do not offer your peers as referees unless you have a special working arrangement with them. Peers see you in planning and resource allocation meetings and usually cannot comment firsthand or in depth on how you lead and manage your people.

If you have worked for or with someone who may provide a poor reference or a reference that is less than flattering, make sure you signal this in advance to the reference checker and explain why this referee and their reference may be problematic. Sometimes you have worked with someone where an important disagreement has occurred. Sometimes you have had questions about someone's integrity that made it difficult for you to be forthright with them. Sometimes you have been obliged to work for someone who is extremely controlling and micromanages you. Sometimes you have had to take a strong position with an external consultant or supplier who was not providing adequate service. If one of your referees might have issues with you or the way you worked, this is not necessarily a knockout, and could actually be the reverse! Those doing the reference checking do not expect every referee to provide perfectly supportive feedback on you. In fact, if this happens, the person checking your references may suspect your referees have been rehearsed. Make sure you offer individuals as referees who have seen you at work over an extended period. A new boss who took up their position three months before you left is unlikely to be suitable. Referees who do not know you well will be superficial and, if they are honest, will not be able to provide authentic or thoughtful feedback.

Once you understand the kinds of individuals the reference checker wishes to contact, provide some suggested names and ask which would be most suitable. Usually, two or three referees will be selected from your list. Make it clear that you must obtain the referees' approval before the recruiter contacts them. Brief your referees to provide them with an overview of the job. Also, tell them what you have told your future employer and the recruiter about your strengths, and why you are keen to accept the offer. If your selected referees have not already seen your Professional Profile, you should explain the contents and offer to send this to them. Follow up with your referees after they have provided their reference. Find out what issues the recruiter raised with them and how your referee responded. Also make sure you thank your referees for their help and generosity. If you have asked your referees to assist you more than once, ensure that you brief them on the status of your job search and indicate whether you think you might need their assistance again in the future.

Completing your employment arrangements

Your employment arrangements are set out in a formal employment agreement. This is usually prepared by specialised employment lawyers for your employer. These can be complex documents, sometimes running to 20 pages or more. I have seen some as long as 100 pages. Review your draft document carefully and understand precisely what the various clauses mean for you. I have seen documents which, even when read very carefully, remain incomprehensible! Use AI, as a starting point, to help you identify issues in the Offer Letter. You should consider whether you need professional advice from lawyers or accountants. Of particular interest to you should be the proposed probationary period, the termination arrangements, the non-compete requirements, the construction of any short-term and long-term incentive programs, and the ownership of any intellectual property contributed by you. Commonly, your offer may state that you will participate in a short-term and long-term incentive plan. However, the details of these plans are usually set out in other policy documents and may change from year to year. If your targets are related to future incentive payments, you need to understand exactly what is involved in meeting these targets, and decide how feasible meeting these targets will be. While these plans may change in the future, obtaining copies of current incentive arrangements will provide you with the details on how these incentives might be calculated. Again, professional advice might be required.

Negotiate any terms you disagree with. Review probationary periods, non-compete requirements and termination clauses carefully. While non-compete arrangements are often legalistic and appear extremely onerous, in many countries your employer will find it difficult to enforce such arrangements. Most courts are not sympathetic to arrangements that appear unreasonable. Despite this, it makes sense to try to limit these restrictions. You do not want to be severely restricted from finding another job if your new role does not work out. As a practical matter, employers will often permit you to join a competitor as long as you commit to, first, not exploiting proprietary intellectual property; second, not attracting away key employees; and, third, not taking away their clients during a specific period of time.

You may be tempted to cut corners or save money by not seeking professional advice. This approach might be appropriate with simple agreements, but failing to obtain professional advice could be risky with legal contracts at a senior level. Something that looks trivial may hurt you later. For example, Ted signed an employment agreement with a private equity firm. This set out the requirements for being allocated equity each year over the next five years. Certain profitability levels, to be achieved each year, were set out in detail. Ted failed to meet the goals in years three and four but far exceeded the total cumulative goal by the end of year five. Because of the way the agreement was drafted, he only received three-fifths of the equity that he would have earned if the agreement had taken into account the cumulative performance across the five years. If he'd received better advice, he would have earned nearly 70 per cent more shares in the business.

While you are in this negotiation phase, you have maximum negotiating ability. Once you accept the employment arrangements, they will normally be difficult to renegotiate (unless your new employer clearly needs you more than you need them). Therefore, it is important to sort out all the detail of your arrangements – including class of airline travel, entertainment allowance, telecommunications costs, computer equipment, car allowance, parking, fees for industry associations and funding for further study and personal development. Make sure these payments are tax effective. Many of these items can attract various fringe benefits taxes (depending on where you live), so be clear as to whether you or your future employer is responsible for these taxes. One additional idea, as one of my clients reminds me, is to 'negotiate your way out on your way in!' In other words, work out your outplacement arrangements when you negotiate your other arrangements. This helps to ensure you will be looked after at the right level, if you are ever asked to leave your new employer in the future.

Using your probationary period to your advantage

Many employment agreements stipulate that new employees will be 'on probation' for six months, and sometimes longer. This means that the employer has the right to terminate you without cause during this period with, say, one week's notice. However, remember that your new employer is also on probation during this period. This means you can leave for any reason during this period with one week's notice. The advantage for you here is that, if a better offer is made to you during the probation period, you are under no moral or other obligation to stay with the organisation you have just joined. At the same time, I always remind my clients they should do everything in their power to leave graciously and gracefully. You need to leave well, as discussed in chapter 1. In some instances, your early departure may actually be good for your new employer. For example, perhaps you have made considerable progress in your role in the first six months and a different kind of person, maybe a more junior internal candidate, could fill your role from then on. If so, your move could be a win–win for everyone involved.

Take Fynn, for example. He had been Chief Information Officer (CIO) of a complex business unit in the subsidiary of a large bank. He had a great track record of success but was made redundant in a reorganisation. He accepted a deputy CIO role in a national electricity utility, even though it was one level lower than his previous job. Three months later, he was offered a much larger role in a federal government department. He accepted this larger role but negotiated a three-month transition so he could move on from his role in the electricity utility with minimal disruption. In fact, it was clear his deputy could now be promoted into the role he was vacating. So, it was an excellent outcome for all involved.

Unfortunately, the probationary period does not always work out well even if you do an outstanding job. Audrey is an example here. Audrey obtained an excellent position as country CEO of a global infrastructure business. The parent company was headquartered in Europe. During her first six months, she successfully negotiated three major new contracts. Her win rate had never been achieved in her country by this business before. Despite this, at the six-month point, she received a call to say she would be terminated. It turned out that the previous country head had become available. This person had a good reputation with the management of the parent company and they wanted to bring him back. The parent company agreed that Audrey had been an exemplary employee and arranged for her to receive a generous payout rather than the one week's notice that was in her agreement. Most probation periods turn out well, but you need to realise that this is not always the case, even if you perform well.

Deciding your start date

Starting without delay after your employment agreement is signed is tempting, and you may be asked to do this. Don't, unless you have no other choice. Take at least a month before you start in the new organisation. This will give you time to rest, learn more about your job, think about how you will contribute and plan the vital first 90 days. You can also have some informal meetings with your new boss and some of your key direct reports during this intervening month. This will allow you to get to know more about your colleagues personally, and their families. Concentrate on building personal rapport at the beginning, rather than spending your time on what needs to be fixed and how to meet budgets. The business issues can be tackled once you join the organisation. If you build personal rapport, your colleagues will respect you. They will see that you are keen to build relationships, to learn about them and their families, and to understand the culture of the organisation.

This break between jobs may be the last time you will be able to arrange a decent time away from your job for a while. Make the most of it!

Thanking everyone who helped you

Once your new role is finalised is the perfect time to thank everyone who helped you along the way. Contact each person on your A-, B-, and C-Lists to tell them the good news! You need to decide the most effective way of doing this. Ideally your messages should be personalised, via phone, email or personal letter. Your thank you message should also go to any recruiters you met, even if they did not find you this role. Near the date when you begin your new job, you could also post a message on LinkedIn, thanking everyone who assisted you and saying how pleased you are to be joining your new employer. Let everyone know how grateful you are for their help in making this new career move happen. People remember when you thank them. Particularly when they do not expect it, or when they believe they didn't actually do very much to help you.

Many jobseekers forget to thank their network or are much too cursory. As a result, they miss an important opportunity to build ongoing emotional connections and relationships. You never know whether one of the people you thank will provide you with an opportunity in the future, or whether you may need to call them to help you solve a problem. Of course, as well as thanking them, you may be able to immediately help them in some way. This will have an even more dramatic and memorable impact. As I discuss later in this chapter, it's smart to keep reinforcing and building your network even after you have secured your new role. This thank you message is the first step.

Getting this detailed administration out of the way is a big relief for you and your future employer. You will now be in a position to begin to think about, and plan, how you will approach your new role in more detail.

PREPARING FOR YOUR FIRST 90 DAYS

A new role can be a great opportunity, but it can also involve considerable risk. In a new position, you lack established working relationships and do not have a detailed understanding of the role or the work environment. As I mentioned earlier, I always think it's worth assuming the situation you face will be more difficult and more challenging than you expect. Don't be fazed by unplanned challenges. But be aware, if you fail to build positive momentum during your first 90 days, you are likely to face an uphill battle from that point forward. Professor Michael Watkins, author of *The First 90 Days*, writes that the first 90 days in a new role is crucial for your subsequent career. According to Watkins,

> Lots of my research shows that what you do early on during a job transition is what matters most. Your colleagues and your boss form opinions about you based on limited information, and those opinions are sticky – it's hard to change their minds. So, shape their impressions of you to the best of your ability.

This is consistent with the work done by Daniel Kahneman, who shows in *Thinking, Fast and Slow* that early impressions skew subsequent perceptions. For instance, as I mentioned in chapter 3, research shows that university examiners are heavily influenced by how well a student answers the first question in an examination. If the teacher marks your whole examination sequentially, they will mark you higher on subsequent answers if you do well on the first one. The reverse is also true. You will be given lower marks on subsequent questions if you do poorly in your answer to the first question. Given this phenomenon, it is important that you launch successfully and that the first 90 days go well for you.

In thinking about the first 90 days, it can be useful to think in terms of three 30-day periods: the first 30 days focusing on learning about the organisation and its people, the second 30 days focusing on the marketplace, customers and other stakeholders, and the third 30 days planning the way forward and obtaining approval for your plans.

What factors should you think about as you plan your first 90 days? I cover the key aspects to consider in the following sections.

What situation will you be facing when you join the organisation?

Assess the situation and identify issues you may face at each level:

- *At an organisational level:* Is the organisation small or large, global or local, running well or in trouble, in a growth market or a mature market, profitable or stressed, in a strong market position or under competitive attack, confident or scared? Is its purpose clear? Are its systems effective? Is the governance of high quality? Are its values clear and well communicated? Do they walk the talk? In other words, what shape is your organisation in?

- *At the human level:* Are the board and the CEO well respected and effective? Are the employees highly competent? Are they engaged or demotivated? Is the culture positive? Are good people staying or leaving? Is the senior leadership team well regarded and are people in the organisation happy? Do they understand and believe in the purpose of the organisation?

- *At a personal level:* Will individuals who aspired to your job be reporting to you? Are they likely to be supportive, demotivated or attempting to undermine you? If this is an issue, can it be resolved with the CPO before you join? How competent are your team members? Are they likely to welcome you or be concerned about their futures?

Getting a clear calibration of all these dimensions before joining the organisation will often be impossible. Sometimes you are not told the full story or you will even be misled. But you would do well to find out what you can as you plan for your first 90 days. Know what you are getting yourself into and be as prepared as possible.

Consider Alison. She joined a respected national business as Chief People Officer, reporting to the CEO. It soon became clear that one of her direct reports believed he should have been given her job. He was a friend of the CEO and began to undermine Alison by communicating various concerns about her and her management style directly to the CEO, behind Alison's back. He also expressed concerns to his peer group about Alison's capability, without involving Alison. Instead of dealing with the issue directly with Alison, the CEO sat on the problem and allowed the situation to fester. In the end, Alison's position became untenable and she resigned. Could Alison have foreseen these problems and taken steps to minimise this risk before she joined?

How urgent is the need for change in your area?

You need to have a view on what actions are urgent and what actions can wait until you have a better grasp of the opportunities and options available. When a business is sailing smoothly, urgent change is not usually required. You have the luxury of taking your time to listen and learn, and to consider your options. In this situation, it makes no sense for you to initiate radical action without deep consideration. Of course, radical action may be required if you were hired to trigger transformational change but, even then, it is best to take your time to think, plan and gain wide buy-in to the way forward you will be proposing.

In some rare situations, you may find yourself facing the need for radical and immediate change. After the global financial crisis (GFC), for example, a great number of businesses were in significant trouble. They needed to roll over debt, but new debt was hugely expensive or not negotiable at any price. Many businesses faced the possibility that they would not survive. You may be made aware, during the recruiting process, that your new business is in crisis or under financial stress, and that action may be required by you immediately after you join. If so, you should consider whether you are willing to join a business in this condition. What are the risks for you and what are the possible rewards? How might your brand be affected if the business fails? Will others question the quality of your judgement for joining a troubled business? If you do decide to join the business, your focus will then need to be on how to minimise the impact of these risks.

Jon, for example, had been a CFO in a major bank, and left his job to become the CFO of a leading national agribusiness. Soon after he arrived, the GFC occurred. The business he had joined was in trouble because some important banking covenants were breached. Fortunately, because of his banking relationships, he was able to renegotiate the arrangements and help the business trade through this difficult period. In this case, his banking know-how and relationships proved to be vital.

Sometimes the situation is even more complicated. Vanessa was hired as the CFO of a national logistics business just before the GFC hit. As a result, her first major job was to try to negotiate new debt to replace a major bank loan that was about to roll over. A few weeks later, the CEO was terminated. The Chair of the board became acting CEO while the search for a new CEO was conducted. Vanessa's whole world had changed in four weeks. Fortunately, Vanessa proved to be up to the task and proved her resilience under extreme pressure and substantial uncertainty. As a result of her work, a year later she was promoted to run a large, complex subsidiary of this logistics business. After that, on the basis of her work during the GFC and afterwards running the subsidiary, Vanessa was given the CEO role at a major publicly traded business. Unexpected things happen! Will you be prove to be flexible and resilient?

How will your success be measured?

Find out how, and how quickly, your success will be measured. What goals does your boss intend to set for you, both short and longer term? Your goals should be clear and must be more than short-term financial results. The financial results you deliver will be the outcome of your ability to lead and motivate your team to achieve important outcomes. Specific financial outcomes should be a measure of your success in managing your business, not the goal of your job. Your KPIs should be structured to measure your longer-term management success. Will you be helping to build a great organisation? Can you improve the engagement scores of your team? Can you improve customer service and can you lift the net promoter score achieved by your team? Will the 360 feedback you receive show you are an effective leader who is respected? Many good businesses have been damaged or destroyed by focusing too intensely on short-term financial results. Ideally, your goals will have been made clear during the recruiting process, and agreed with you. But situations change and your goals may be modified by the time you take up your new role. Make sure you clarify and confirm your goals again after you have joined. If the suggested goals are not appropriate, consider how and when to attempt to renegotiate them.

Take the example of Gary. He accepted a role as country manager of a fintech company in South-East Asia. The business had grown rapidly over the past five years but had never made a profit. Because of COVID, the business had recently begun contracting severely. Gary understood he was going into a challenging situation. However, he thought he could stabilise the business in the short term and then rebuild it over the next few years. After Gary took up his position, he was told by his regional head that the private equity investors who owned the business wanted him to make the business profitable within 12 months. His initial review indicated this was impossible, but Gary's boss didn't want to hear this. Gary had a young family and needed this job. The question he faced was whether he should either:

- try to convince his boss and the private equity investors that making his business profitable with 12 months was impossible, and they should look to develop more feasible longer-term goals, or

- go along with the impossible revenue and profit goals and deal with the problem at the end of the financial year, with an almost certain probability that he would have failed to make the business profitable.

In the end, Gary took a revised five-year plan to the board and this was approved. A number of initiatives were agreed for the first year and the budget for the year was adjusted to make it more realistic.

Ideally, you should be aspiring to make a strong positive difference and to create a legacy when you accept a senior role. This could happen in many ways. You might have big ideas that change the direction of the business. Or you might make the business better. For instance, improving the culture and safety performance is crucial in many businesses. In addition, your ability to build strong community support for your organisation is likely to be vital, as is improving the ability of the business to meet regulatory guidelines and governance requirements. Remember that good financial results are likely to be the result of leading your people well. It is dangerous, and likely to be damaging, to focus on financial performance alone. The questions for you will be: What factors will be used to assess your performance? How will these factors be measured? And how can you influence these choices so that you can deliver great results, hopefully above and beyond expectations?

How should you manage risk?

In any new situation, you will face not only opportunities but also risks. Professor William Sahlman, in his classic article, 'How to write a great business plan' (which I also mention in chapter 6), says, 'One of the great myths about entrepreneurs is that they are risk seekers. All sane people want to avoid risk.' With this in mind, consider what exposures you might face in your first 90 days and, indeed, the first 12 months. The conversation with your boss should address how you can minimise the possible downsides and maximise the upsides. He or she should be helping you understand your possible exposures and working with you to consider ways to address these. This is worth a special conversation with your new boss before you start since you will need him or her to protect you if something goes wrong. How can you obtain a commitment from your boss that he or she will protect you and develop you while you are learning during the first 90 days?

Alina joined a medium-sized business in a new role and assumed she would be welcomed with open arms. After all, she was an acknowledged subject matter expert in her field. However, she struck problems almost immediately. One of her peers felt that Alina was encroaching on her area. This peer pushed back on many of Alina's ideas and attempted to undermine her credibility. This situation should have been foreseen by Alina's boss, and action should have been taken before Alina arrived to address this potential problem. Also, Alina herself should have considered this possibility and identified that these problems might occur. Did she ask the right questions during the recruiting process and did she prepare properly in advance of starting work?

Plan to identify and address issues – some expected and some unexpected – that might confront you during the first 90 days. Carefully consider how you will tackle the first 90 days before you begin your new job. Start with some informal meetings with your new boss and other key people before your formal start. You can test the ideas in your 90-day plan during these meetings. These meetings will not only help you to prepare more effectively in advance but also communicate that you are serious about starting on the right foot. How can you make sure that you understand what might go wrong and work out how to avoid these problems before you begin?

STARTING YOUR NEW JOB ON THE RIGHT FOOT

Everything rarely goes smoothly and exactly to plan. As I have already mentioned, it is wise to assume that the situation you face in your new role will be more challenging than you expect (perhaps even as challenging as the widely used graphic illustrated in figure 10.1). The key is to be adaptable and to try to foresee challenges. Depending on the nature and magnitude of the challenges that do arise, and your experience, you may find the new job daunting or exhilarating.

Figure 10.1: You will likely face more challenges than you expect

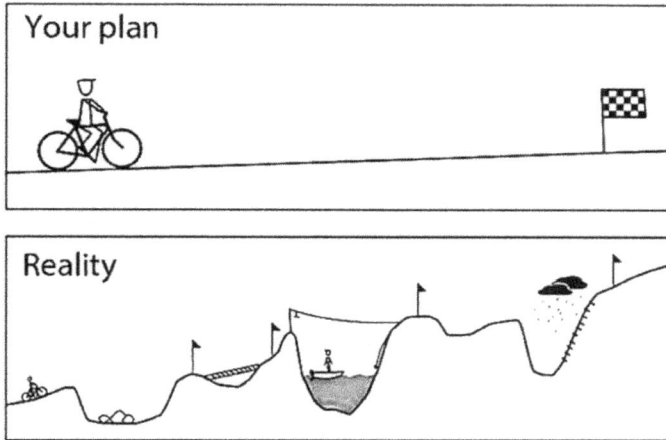

New CEOs almost universally state that the job is much more challenging than they ever imagined. As I mentioned in the Introduction, according to Dan Ciampa in his *Harvard Business Review* article 'After the handshake', 'one-third to one-half of new CEOs – whether they're hired from outside or from within – fail within their first 18 months, according to some estimates'. The reason seems to be, according to Ciampa, that newcomers misread the political situation or overestimate the organisation's willingness to abandon old behaviours. At the same time, boards and key executives fail to grasp the complex nature of CEO succession or set one-dimensional expectations of the new leader. In my experience, executives below CEO are usually more successful at holding their jobs, but some do leave. If the original recruiting process was sound, a failure to stay in the role is usually more related to problems with your fit with others in the organisation, rather than anything to do with your own functional capabilities and competence.

What kinds of actions can you take to maximise your probability of success? Some of your success will be related to how you begin. How do you start on the right foot? The following sections outline the actions I believe are vital if you are to succeed in your role in a new organisation.

What can you learn from successful teachers?

As you think about your first day at work, think back on some lessons from great teachers you have known. How do they ensure that their pupils have a happy first day at school, and thereafter? Michael Linsin, founder of Smart Classroom Management, has set out a series of steps to help teachers maximise the likelihood of having a positive impact on day one. He suggests that the first impression of the students will be critically important and will likely define how the class operates for the rest of the year. He argues, 'It can either set you on a path to a rewarding school year, or throw you into a ditch from which you may never recover.'

Some of his teacher strategies might help you think about how to present yourself when you start on the first day of a new job. Three of his recommendations for teachers taking their first class of the year are:

1. *Connect directly person to person:* Linsin recommends that you should stop each student at the door as they enter your classroom. You should look each student in the eye, say hello, and introduce yourself with a smile. 'This simple act puts nervous students at ease and sends the message that you care about them. It's also a quick and easy way to begin building rapport and reciprocal kindness.'

2. *Share a personal story about yourself:* Linsin suggests you should not jump straight into teaching. Instead, he advises you to share a funny or quirky story about yourself that shows your personality. This could include providing some interesting background about yourself and your family. He makes the point, 'Your likeability is crucial to effective classroom management and nothing breaks down walls, creates ready-made leverage, and draws students into your circle of influence faster or more powerfully than telling a story.'

3. *Show that you value excellence:* When you start teaching, your first lesson needs to set the standard that you wish to attain all year. It is the most important class of the whole year. 'You're setting the bar of expectations exactly where you wish it to be.'

You are not a teacher, but you are (or will be) a leader and a coach. As you consider how you might handle your first day at work, these three thoughts from a leading teacher are worth considering. The question, of course, is how to translate this story into your particular situation?

Ten prerequisites for success in a new role

Ten actions will help you be successful once you are onboard and in your new role. Some seem obvious. Even so, they might be difficult to achieve as a result of multiple demands on your time and your energy. Also, the various communications you receive from others higher in the organisation may not always be clear, and may even be confusing. What seems straightforward before you begin may be much more complicated after you are actually sitting in your new role.

Ask for help

Most people around you, especially those who hired you, will want you to be successful in your new role. If you do not know something, ask for help. Often your formal induction will be administrative and at a very high level, concentrating on the basics you need to know in order to function. These days, handovers can be brief or non-existent. The person who had the role before you may have already moved on. It is vital that your boss invests the time to explain what it will take to deliver outstanding results.

Some organisations make accountabilities clear from the beginning, outlining what decisions you are accountable for, what decisions you may make an input into but are not responsible for, and where others will make decisions without your input. In one global electronics company, for instance, country level marketing decisions are made at head office and not in individual countries. Some companies have complex matrix organisations (with solid and dotted-line reporting) and your precise accountabilities are unclear. Decisions in these organisations usually have to be socialised and generally take much longer than in smaller, less complicated organisations. One of my clients told me he could take decisions in his new role, in a small company, in six weeks that took over nine months in his prior role in a large, matrix organisation with all sorts of checks and balances.

Again, good communications with your boss will be vital. In addition to this, your secret weapon could be your EA (Executive Assistant), if you have one. He or she can explain how things really work in your new organisation. A common issue for many new senior employees is being scheduled to attend too many meetings. Make sure you have thinking time blocked out in your diary by you or your EA so that you have time to think and are not forced to attend back-to-back meetings. Finally, find a mentor within your new organisation. Sometimes this is a wise person who is not part of the formal hierarchy. They can help you understand the culture of the organisation and what you need to do to be perceived in a positive light.

Ironically, the challenge for you is not so much when the culture is radically different. You can see this clearly and, if you understand the differences, act accordingly. The real problems tend to arise when the culture you are joining is similar to the one you left, but not quite the same. Then, you may not pick up the subtle differences. For instance, although you were told when you were hired that the business wanted to grow, you find, after you arrive, that all the real measures of success relate to cost control. (See the section 'Understand the new culture', later in this chapter, for more on this.)

Denise, a successful CEO in a number of large complex retailers, was very open with her team. Every four weeks she sat down with her direct reports and encouraged feedback on what she could do more or less of, or otherwise change. She came up with a plan of action for herself with them, and benchmarks for her performance under various headings. She then reviewed these benchmarks with her team at each meeting to see whether she was modifying her behaviour in the way previously agreed with them. The huge advantage of this approach was that everyone was involved and feedback – whether favourable or critical – was instant. Denise's personal improvement effort gathered momentum and became a catalyst for a combined team improvement effort.

Avoid preconceived, easy answers

A new person in a senior role can often assume that what needs to be done to address the problems in their area is obvious. They take the view that they have all the answers and the previous person in the role did not really know what they were doing. This is not uncommon when a manager is transferred from another country or from another business. However, you should avoid imposing your answers without properly understanding the situation and the options for action. You can lose the respect of your team and others in an organisation if they see you shooting from the hip and providing superficial solutions to (what they perceive to be) tough, complex problems. If they believe you will not listen or do not think issues through, they may be less willing to debate issues with you or to point out defects in your thinking. They may start to exhibit passive-aggressive behaviour.

Australian General Sir John Monash, who built a reputation as a great military and peacetime leader, wrote in his letters during World War I, 'I always tell my staff: "I don't give a damn for your loyalty when you think I am right. The time I want it is when you think I am wrong."' One new CEO from overseas complained to me once that the people reporting to him in his new role would tell him, metaphorically, that a house was burning down in his street, but they would not tell him that the property on fire was actually his own house! Why was this happening? Something was wrong with the culture and transparency of the organisation! When you first arrive, deliver some early wins. Identify what these will be and then get on with them. Then you have more time to think before making radical change elsewhere. You can initiate these more radical changes after you know more and have thought the whole thing through properly and have tested your thinking.

Build broad relationships early

It is tempting to bury yourself in the numbers and in reading background documentation when you first arrive. This is a mistake. You should be investing in building relationships with people above you and below you, as well as your peers and other stakeholders – including clients. Your relationship with your new boss will be paramount. Ask your new boss who you should meet and what issues you should discuss with them. Ismail was hired as the CFO of a large public corporation. We decided that one way he could build relationships was to visit each board member in the first two weeks to ask what improvements they would like to see in the board papers. The board members made a number of suggestions and Ismail delivered these changes in the board papers at his first meeting with the board. Unsurprisingly, the board was impressed with Ismail's positive attitude and his responsiveness. His relationship with the board members went from strength to strength.

It is vital that you receive feedback sooner rather than later if something is not going well. The philosophy explained in *The One Minute Manager*, by Ken Blanchard and Spencer Johnson, can be a key to your success. Their approach is to communicate one-minute goals, one-minute praisings, and one-minute reprimands. Waiting until 90 days have passed before you obtain feedback doesn't make sense. Ask for quick weekly one-to-one meetings with your boss to learn and develop. Be aware that you cannot expect your boss to change his or her behaviour to suit you. You need to be the one who figures out how to adapt to the way your boss operates. Most bosses hate surprises, so you should do your utmost to make sure that he or she has timely and reliable information, and early warnings of potential problems. An important question you need to resolve is how to get back on track if something goes awry.

Your relationship with your boss can sometimes be a problem. Perhaps you were given to a great deal of freedom by your previous boss and then you find your new boss is a micromanager. In this case, your new boss needs to build trust in you and then step back to give you more freedom. Otherwise, this controlling approach is likely to lead to significant difficulties. Dave was the CPO in a national dairy business. He was frequently away, visiting dairy operations across the country to ensure that the people in each facility were being listened to. A new CEO was appointed and wanted Dave to be in the next office to discuss people issues face to face. He wanted Dave to be available 'on demand'. He could not understand why Dave was not immediately available when he wanted to speak to him. When Dave returned from one of his trips, he was terminated. Are you listening carefully enough to your boss?

This problem often occurs for you if you are brought in to run a family business. The family, despite all sorts of promises in advance of your arrival, cannot bring themselves to delegate decisions to you. The problem is likely to be even worse if one of the relatives of the owner reports to you. They can compare notes on your performance over family dinner! Be very careful to understand in advance how you and the family owners will work together if you decide to accept a role like this.

Deliver what you promise

Promising a great deal and then failing to deliver will create huge problems. In a new role, you are not aware of all the things that could go wrong because you are new to the organisation. You do not know how good the other people are, whether the systems work, whether accountabilities are clear or overlap, who to trust to keep their promises, who insists on signing off decisions, how long they take to provide sign-offs, and so on. In one corporation I know of, meetings often had more finance executives than operating executives. As a result of the risk-averse attitude of the finance people, decisions were slowed right down – and operating executive frustration levels were high. In short, be careful about what you promise and when you say you will deliver – until you can be sure of how things actually work. Make sure your boss signs off on any significant promises so you have someone senior supporting you and protecting your back.

New CEOs often take dramatic steps to reduce expectations when they arrive in a new role. They slash previous earnings projections and state that the business goals are unrealistic and need to be rethought. Plans need to be redrawn. This gives them more room to manoeuvre going forward. You may know the old joke about the outgoing CEO handing the new CEO three envelopes: 'Here are three envelopes. Each time something goes wrong, open an envelope.' Something went wrong, so she opened the first envelope. It said, 'Blame the previous Chair'. Then something else went wrong. The second message said, 'Blame the previous CEO'. Then a third thing went wrong. This time the third message was 'Buy three envelopes'. Make sure you don't get to the third envelope. And never mistake intense activity for progress or impact. You and your team could be spinning your wheels even though you see yourselves as working very hard. The key is to make sure you are working on the right priorities and delivering tangible results that have impact. Reports are one thing. Positive actions that are taken as a result of a report are quite another thing! You need to deliver the latter!

Understand the new culture

New cultures can be difficult to understand; however, failing to work out how to operate in the new culture could be disastrous for you. As Watkins highlights in *The First 90 Days*:

> *When new leaders act in ways that are inconsistent with the culture, they risk triggering an organisational immune system attack. This increases their vulnerability to making bad calls and contributes to a vicious cycle that ends in failure.*

The cultural differences between the big-end of town and start-ups should not be underestimated. Andrew Maitland, who has worked in large and small companies, kindly prepared the information in table 10.1 for me. Andrew makes the point that anyone who says they are an 'entrepreneur' but who works for a large company probably does not really understand what true entrepreneurs need to do to survive!

Table 10.1: Different challenges: Corporate leader versus start-up leader

	Corporate leader	**Start-up leader**
Financial management	Optimise financial results	Conserve, so as to stay in business
Risk management	Identify/mitigate/manage risks	Take risks to survive and grow
Problem resolution	Detailed analysis prior to action	Action, then problem resolution
Time frame	Long-term strategic horizon	Short-/immediate-term horizon
Hiring decisions	Past achievement focused	High-energy, initiative focused
Taking advice	Professional consultants	Leverage company network
Governance	Minimise risk	Maximise opportunity
Investment decisions	Hurdle rate methodology	Invest to attract capital
Decision-making style	Generate broad consensus	Leader takes charge
Project time frames	Multi-year perspective	Multi-week perspective
IT systems complexity	Major, highly complex legacy systems	Simpler, single-purpose systems

Other cultural differences can be subtle and, in some ways, much more challenging. When the cultures are similar but not exactly the same, the differences may be difficult to identify and calibrate.

But these subtle differences may trip you up. To try to understand the culture of a new organisation, and its peculiar subtleties, listen a lot and speak a little – at least at the beginning. As the old saying goes, you have two ears and one mouth for a reason! As mentioned earlier, seeking out a thoughtful and experienced mentor who can help you understand 'the way we do things around here' makes good sense. Keep in mind, too, that reminding others of the way you did things in your previous job makes no sense at all! Finally, do not forget that what is written down in the policy statement may or may not be the way things really work. Do people actually walk the talk? You'll likely only determine this once you are embedded in the new organisation.

When it comes to subtle cultural differences, it is worth knowing about Rebecca. Rebecca headed up a offshore business for a major global business headquartered in the United States. The business was in the top 20 corporations worldwide, and she was in the top 100 executives in the business. As such, she was provided with an expert coach from head office for two weeks a year. This coach shadowed everything she did during that two-week period. After one visit, Rebecca was told that she would not be recommended for a promotion to the US business unless she changed her behaviour. The problem, as explained to Rebecca, was that she remained silent for about six seconds before answering a question. This was too long – she needed to respond within three seconds if she wanted to be perceived as top management material in the US. Only an experienced senior US coach would have picked up a subtle behaviour such as this. Do your best to watch out for subtle cultural differences – they may be more important than you think!

Rebuild and mobilise your team

Rebuilding your team is a delicate issue. You have inherited a team that has the advantage of a great deal of relevant knowledge about the business. On the other hand, you may need to make changes to add more energy and drive, or you may need a team that is committed and loyal to you and your goals rather than to the old regime. You would rather not be told that your idea was tried five years ago and will not work, for example. The key issue here is not so much the need to make change in the team but the timing of this change. The most common approach is for the new executive to observe how people work and take their time in making changes.

The danger is that you will take too long. One of my clients started in a senior CFO role and found that his predecessor had asked his direct reports to assemble raw financial data. The previous CFO liked data and he liked controlling the message to the top! He would assemble the data he received and decide what recommendations to make to the CEO and the board. My client did not want data from the team he inherited – he wanted recommendations. It soon became clear, however, that most of the team he inherited could not adapt to this changed requirement. So the need for a substantial upgrade in the team was quickly obvious. You should be in a position to decide what to do with your team well before the six-month mark. Good people will applaud you when you identify and deal with obvious underperformers.

Make the complex simple

Great leaders have a way of getting to the heart of matters. They see through the complexity and distil the key elements. I remember the CEO of a major bank with the lowest cost to revenue ratio in his country. He told me that, after the GFC, his bank had needed to cut its costs by 20 per cent, even though he headed up the most efficient bank in the country. His rationale was that the other competitive banks were in trouble and would be forced to cut their costs drastically. So, if he did not cut the costs of his bank, it could become the high-cost bank. This was a simple but very dramatic and consequential decision.

Many will accuse you of being too simplistic when you try to get to the heart of complex situations. Work hard to identify the crucial elements – often known as root-cause analysis – rather than being superficial. This is where proper evidence and deep questioning is required. Also, this is when you need an ability to frame the problem and the solution in a way that is persuasive and compelling. This is hard to do – otherwise, top management consultants, who generally make a living from doing this, would be out of business by now! As Richard Branson said,

> *When you're first thinking through an idea, it's important not to get bogged down in complexity. Complexity is your enemy. Any fool can make something complicated. Thinking, simply and clearly, is hard to do.*

Use your strengths to differentiate yourself

In chapters 3, 4 and 5, I talked first about understanding what makes you special, and then how to communicate this. You will have given this a lot of thought, so build on what you learned. You were selected for your new job because of your perceived strengths and the value they could bring to the organisation. In your new role, you are likely to do better if you can differentiate yourself and be known for the strengths you bring. Above all, stay true to yourself. As Confucius said, 'The cautious seldom err.' You need to take risks, but they should be measured risks.

Amelia, a very competent and experienced senior executive, was offered the choice of two roles by a leading global technology-based business. One option was to join its head office team in California and the other was to run one of its new businesses in her home country. I recommended the latter option. I thought it would be easier for Amelia to excel and differentiate herself running her own business on her home territory, even though this appeared a riskier and more challenging role to her. My view was that, at the head office, Amelia would be one of hundreds of highly competitive, capable people who would understand the corporate culture much better than she did. They would know infinitely better than her what it took to excel. In the corporate headquarters, even though she was exceptional in many ways, she risked becoming just one of an exceptional group. In her home country, however, she could be a unique resource for the global business.

In another situation, Harry, who had been a partner in a big four accounting firm, had the choice of moving to another firm in a similar role or joining an engineering consulting firm in a business development role. This engineering firm needed more senior, non-engineering commercial expertise to broaden its relationships with the CEOs of its clients and prospects. Again, my advice was against the obvious choice – in this case, I advised my client to join the engineering business, where he could bring new valuable skills and could differentiate himself. This turned out to be a good decision for him because he brought new value to the engineering group, and was seen as a real asset.

Maintain and build your network

You have invested a great deal of effort and time in building your network between your last job and this one. Many senior executives ease off on networking once they are in the new role. This is natural, given the day-to-day pressures you will face. However, if you do ease off completely, you will be missing a great opportunity to keep expanding your knowledge and influence. As I mentioned in chapter 7, Professor Charan has pointed out that networking can be an exponential multiplier of knowledge, effort and impact. One phone call to the right person can solve a problem that might take months if you tackled it from first principles. The challenge you will face in your new role is that your work will expand to fill the time available. As a result, you are unlikely to allocate time to networking, and your network will stagnate.

One way of overcoming this problem is to arrange lunches at your office with an interesting guest, such as a leading academic in your field. (Executive search firms are experts at arranging these kinds of lunches.) You can invite a range of senior people to these lunches and discuss issues that are of interest to them. This allows you to meet new people in a way that provides them with learning and stimulation, without a huge investment of your time. Most people are keen to learn more and welcome an opportunity such as this. This initiative might also help you and, therefore, your employer to perform better. Another option is to join a group that arranges lunches or education events each month. Whichever way you to decide to grow your network, you will need to invest time and effort.

Beware of burnout

Pace yourself. Burnout creeps up on many executives. Individuals who suffer from burnout are often over-achievers who believe they can push through, even though they are feeling diminished. When they are affected by burnout, executives may feel that part of them has gone into hiding. Challenges that were formerly manageable start to feel insurmountable. Burnout is the opposite of engagement. The engaged employee is energised, involved and high performing. The burned-out employee is exhausted, cynical and overwhelmed. Burnout is usually characterised by three factors: first, feelings of exhaustion; second, increased mental isolation from your job and your colleagues; and, third, feelings of negativism or cynicism related to your work. The net result, at best, is reduced professional effectiveness and motivation. At worst, you could suffer severe psychological damage.

You might suffer burnout if you experience chronic workplace stress and fail to manage this. As Dr Monique Valcour, executive coach and professor at the United Nations, points out, 'You can't overcome burnout simply by deciding to pull yourself together'. Rebounding from burnout and preventing its recurrence requires three things: replenishing lost energy and emotional resources, avoiding further resource depletion, and finding or creating new resources to assist you and support you going forward.

If you have taken on a role that involves conference calls with colleagues in North America, Asia and Europe, for example, it is tempting to work around the clock. These are the kinds of situations where you might start to suffer from burnout. You need to be able to recognise this early, and put protective strategies in place.

Getting the 10 things outlined in the preceding sections right does not, of course, guarantee success. But if you can manage your way through the challenges you face with these ideas in mind, you will do better than most.

CALIBRATING YOUR PROGRESS IN THE FIRST YEAR

One last thing to consider is how you will decide whether your new job is the right one for you once you have settled in. Unfortunately, not everyone in a complex organisation is in the right job. As you gain more experience in your organisation, ask yourself these questions about your role:

- Am I starting to wonder whether I am in the right job?
- What needs to change to improve the situation and how can this be achieved?
- Should I set a deadline for making measurable progress? If so, when?
- How visible should I be about my concerns?
- Who should I discuss these concerns with?

Also ask these questions about yourself:

- Is my reputation and brand at risk if I stay? Or if I leave?
- How will I explain an early departure to recruiters and others?
- Am I putting my family or those important to me at risk if I leave and cannot find another role quickly?
- Am I letting my team down, particularly if I have brought people in on the basis that I will be their boss? If so, what do I do?

There are no right or wrong answers. In my experience, it usually makes sense to bring things to a head, rather than allowing troubling situations to drift. Liam called me after only three months in a job in a big business owned by private equity. He told me his team was under-resourced and he was very worried he was not able to do good work. He feared he would be fired before the end of his probation period. He was having trouble sleeping. I suggested that he should hang in for a while to see whether things improved. Maybe things would be easier as he became more experienced in the role and learned his way around the business? He agreed to do this. At the six-month mark, Liam called me again and told me he could not sleep at all and thought he might have a nervous breakdown. My recommendation this time was to resign the next day. Liam did this. He was told by his boss how sorry he was because, he said, Liam was doing such a great job! Despite what his boss said, there is no doubt Liam made the correct decision. Within three months, he was offered three better jobs – because it was well known in the industry that any competent person who could survive for six months with his previous private equity employer was likely to be a superstar.

In his presentation 'Leadership: Five skills to focus on' (available via LinkedIn), Professor Charan makes the point:

> *It is the high-potential leaders who create the future, who create new value. High-potential leaders are different from high-potential individuals. High-potential leaders are a magnet for other talent. They stretch other talent. They expand the potential of others.*

He goes on to discuss how you find high-potential leaders, how you develop them, and what skills to focus on. Finally, he discusses three tests to use to decide, as a high-potential leader, whether you should stay in your organisation or leave. These are important tests, whether you consider yourself a high-potential leader or not. I outline the three tests set out by Professor Charan, and add my own comments, in the following sections.

Have you stopped growing or contributing?

Are you growing in your experience and capabilities in a way that will help you progress? As I outlined in chapter 2, one of the key tests for you when considering a role was whether you could make a big difference through adding substantial value, and whether you would be permitted to do this. Another key question I also suggested in chapter 2 was, 'Where will the job lead?' You need to keep revisiting these questions. If you begin to take the view you are not able to make a significant continuing contribution, you should be starting to think about next career steps.

Isabelle, for example, joined a business owned by an overseas group to become head of mergers and acquisitions. It looked to be an exciting role, and the CEO reinforced with Isabelle that she could help transform the company. Isabelle identified over ten possible acquisition targets during the next five years. She was highly commended by her colleagues for the quality of her work. But her board did not accept any of her acquisition recommendations. It turned out the foreign owners of the business where she worked did not want to increase the financial exposure of their business in this country. They were not comfortable buying any additional businesses there. Isabelle realised that her job was leading nowhere and resigned. The question she can ask now, of course, is: 'Should I have understood that my contribution was not being valued much earlier and, if this could not be rectified, resigned then?'

Is your boss helping and coaching you to succeed?

Is your boss actively taking positive steps to care for you and to maximise your chance of success? Professor Charan asserts that if your boss does not give you feedback, does not seem to care about you, or your relationship with him or her is not good, you should consider moving on. This tends to be easier said than done because it is possible that your boss might change, or maybe you could change bosses by moving to another part of the organisation. But the underlying idea makes sense. A key issue is whether your values are aligned with those of your boss and also with those of the organisation. After you have been in the organisation for several months, you will be able to judge this better. Not all organisations walk their talk!

Sam was made country head of a business that he then moved from losses to profits within one year. His boss, who had been the previous head of the country that Sam now managed, was now living in Europe. He was clearly irritated that Sam had built a more successful business than he had been able to do when he led the business before Sam. Sam was contacted by his boss up to 10 times a day, questioning and second-guessing Sam's decisions. Sam explained to his boss that he could not function effectively in his job with this level of intervention. He also discussed the issue with the Global CPO. Nothing was done because Sam's boss was a significant owner in the international group. Sam and I decided that he should resign in three months if his boss's behaviour did not change (realising that any significant change was rather unlikely). As a result, Sam started preparing an exit plan.

Is the overall business growing or declining?

It is usually much easier to excel in a business that is growing. You should carefully evaluate your position if you start to feel the business is plateauing or in decline. Professor Charan points out that signs will emerge that the business has begun to decline. For instance, maybe it becomes clear to you that the top management do not know what to do. Maybe they have lost their ability to energise the business. Maybe their only solution appears to be to keep cutting costs. As a result, the company's market value, reputation and brand are beginning, ever so slowly, to decline. 'In a declining company, that does not show any turnaround, it's not a great place for you to be', says Professor Charan. Again, whether to stay or go is not always a clear-cut decision for you. You may believe you can be part of the answer to the problems in the business. The question for you is how hard will it be to turn things around? How long will it take? And what real role can you actually play? Remember – it is much easier to be effective and to look good in a growing organisation than in a contracting one. Also remember the old saying in the consulting profession: 'You cannot cost-cut your way to business success'. Beware of situations where cost-cutting is deemed to be the answer to the question of how to succeed.

Phil was the country head of a successful multinational. His business was strong and the culture of his team was positive. The future in his country looked bright, although it was a small part of the total global business. As a result of problems faced in other parts of the business, Phil was told to find a way of cutting his costs by 10 per cent. In his view, this would damage the future success of his business. When he pushed back, the group finance team accused him of not being committed to the success of the total business and of being too weak. Phil then faced the dilemma of what to do. Should he try to protect his business for the longer term or follow the instructions of the group? If he followed their instructions, he would improve the short-term performance of the business in his country but would damage its longer-term prospects.

Ultimately, you are responsible for your career and for your own destiny. Often the situation is muddy and difficult to assess. You need to be brutally honest and ask yourself: Have I stopped growing in my job? Is my boss failing to help me succeed? Is the business that I am working for in decline? If the answer to any of these questions is 'yes', you have some serious thinking to do. Often, obtaining independent advice is best. Just talking things through with someone who is independent and who asks good questions can help you to distil the issues you face. You may then be able to see the way forward with more certainty.

★★★

In this chapter, I have covered the period from when you receive a verbal offer until you are established in your new role. You may be surprised at how many things there are to consider. Active, thoughtful consideration and planning in advance can make a huge difference between your success and failure. I fully recognise that every situation is different. Therefore, the broad advice here needs to be considered in the light of the specific situation that you face. These general ideas are intended to provide you with a useful framework to analyse your own particular situation and work out a good way forward, while avoiding potholes.

You may think I am over-engineering the problem. But my experience shows that these strategies work. It is surprising how many complex issues can hit you indiscriminately when you are negotiating and launching into a senior role. I recently received a text message from a new CEO that merely said, 'I thought my new job title was CEO, but it is really Firefighter!'

When I took on my first CEO role, I was surprised how little time there was for 'productive work'. HR problems, legal and governance problems, and communicating with my board absorbed an amazing amount of my daily working time. I wish I had known more at the time about how to plan in advance and how to identify the issues that were likely to cause trouble. I would have been much more effective. The advice in this chapter should help you negotiate the key elements of your job in a way that not only sets you up for short-term success but also helps you succeed longer term.

SOME QUESTIONS FOR YOU TO CONSIDER

- Do you understand all the elements in your offer letter?
- Is your new organisation committed to career development?
- Can you assess the health of your new enterprise in advance?
- Do you understand the specific challenges you will face?
- What is the best way to build trust with those in your new team?
- Have you developed some early trusted relationships?
- Are you working to connect effectively with key stakeholders?
- Have you taken steps to evaluate if you have the right job?
- Are there clear signs the role is not right for you?
- If so, have you prepared a plan B?

Conclusion

The process set out in this book works. My frameworks are designed to guide your thinking. I have explained how to think about the challenges you will face, and provided specific examples and checklists for you to follow. As you begin your thinking, concentrate on what makes you special. Focus on your pattern of achievement, your leadership strengths and what attributes other people respect you for.

DON'T UNDERSELL YOURSELF

Remain positive and active. Do not hold back. Take the lead. You can lead in most situations, as long as you know where you are trying to go. Some of my clients ask whether they will seem too pushy. I don't think so, but in any case, why not take a risk? Even though some of my clients initially worry about overselling themselves, this is not a problem when they begin networking. In fact, more often than not, they are told the reverse by their colleagues – that they are actually underselling themselves.

The risk of underselling yourself is much greater than the risk of overselling yourself. But remember that you need to sell yourself by asking questions, not by talking about yourself. If you try the questioning approach set out in this book, you will gain experience as you expand your network. You will become more confident and compelling as you go along. At the beginning of your networking process, you might seem to be applying a huge amount of energy and seeing virtually no results. You seem to be walking out with the tide and it just keeps going out. Then – usually when you have met 30 or so new people – the tide turns and people begin approaching you. That is when you know the process is beginning to deliver results.

ALWAYS AIM HIGH

Stretch yourself and aim high. It is easy enough to lower your sights later if you really have been too ambitious. But it is not easy to change others' perceptions if you aim too low at the start. Instead, think big – aim for the stars and be happy to hit the moon! Plenty of people, including recruiters, will be urging you to aim low. Don't buckle to that pressure, even when the going gets tough. It is amazing how things work out if you do not give in and keep the process moving forward.

The process set out in this book is a marathon, not a sprint. The problem for many people is they fail to prepare. Their preparation for this marathon is equivalent to a brisk walk twice around the block. You must prepare, and invest in this preparation in an active and positive way. Resilience is key. Never lose sight of what makes you special. Remember the work of Carol Dweck, the professor from Berkeley who developed the concept of a 'growth mindset' (covered in chapter 3). Individuals with a growth mindset see their setbacks as a learning experience. Those with a fixed mindset believe setbacks show that they have reached their limits. You need to do all you can to maintain a growth mindset.

DO THE WORK – BECAUSE IT WORKS – AND STICK TO IT

This book is, of course, a reference guide. Your challenge is to bring these ideas to life for yourself – to make them sing for you. This is easier to do if you have someone you trust working with you. A good professional career coach will be extremely helpful to you – to provide direction and perspective, test your thinking, help you rehearse, and provide encouragement if something is not working well. If you do not have the luxury of professional help, this book will assist you to lift your job-search skills and your approach to a higher level. Use it as a reference guide and a reminder at each stage in your transition process. It contains all the practical ideas you need to manage the process of seeking out and securing your ideal job.

Also remember the advice of Daniel Kahneman in *Thinking, Fast and Slow* – that, statistically, a series of setbacks should be followed by a success. If this does not happen, you need to double back to investigate the root cause of what is going wrong. You may need to fish in a different pond! Do not hesitate to go back over the material in this book and revise your ideas as you progress through the chapters. This should be a living document.

TURN NETWORKING INTO BUILDING LIFELONG RELATIONSHIPS

I received a joint text from two previous senior executive clients recently. After working with me about 10 years ago, both have gone on in their careers to a series of very senior roles. They mentioned that they had been talking together about the source of their various jobs. Their combined text message to me was very simple and clear: 'Recruiters: 0; Networking: 8.' Networking works!

As you know, I advise expanding your personal network to include at least 50 new people. The idea of starting this process can be daunting. But it is actually relatively easy if you tackle the process in the right way. As your network expands, you will substantially improve the probability of success in your job search. Remember the three concentric circles – your ABC Network – from chapter 1. You need to generate warm introductions from circle to circle. Trusted colleagues and acquaintances are key to you doing this successfully. LinkedIn will be a secret weapon that helps you see who is connected to whom. Both will help you make warm connections from circle to circle.

As mentioned earlier, one of my clients received four job offers from contacts in their third circle. All four of these prospective employers were introduced to him by a single contact in the second circle. What was extraordinary was that he had never met this person in the second circle. How could this happen? It was quite simple really. A person in the first circle, who was a great admirer of my client, had provided a glowing recommendation to the person in the second circle. This recommendation was so strong that the person in the second circle recommended my client to four people in the third circle, sight unseen. This shows the power of the transfer of trust. If you connect with the right people, who trust you and truly believe in you, amazing things can happen.

THE SECRET OF SUCCESSFUL NETWORKING IN TWO SIMPLE WORDS

Part of successful networking and transferring of trust is always saying two simple words: 'Thank you'. Never forget to do this. In addition to saying thank you, another way to transfer trust is to work out how to do someone you have met a favour, in reciprocation for their help. Remember, you are trying to build relationships for life, not just have one-off meetings. It is always good to help others, and you can never be sure when they will help you – it could be now or much later. That is why this process depends on you meeting people. The more quality people you connect with, who have significant networks, the better. Do not overthink who you should meet. But, if you can meet super-networkers, this will be particularly good. They have large networks and will find it easy to introduce you.

This book is written to help and inspire you as you plan and prepare for your next role. I've had a long career in advising senior jobseekers in finding new roles. But, my one-on-one time is limited. So, I have set out in this book what I have learnt over the past 25 years. It should give you the guidance you need to move forward. If you believe I have left something out, or need to explain something more clearly, please drop me a line. If you find the information in this book useful, let me know that too – especially if something works well for you. Now you are ready to launch yourself and aim high! Go for it, and shoot for the stars! I hope this book helps you to change your life. Good luck!

William Cowan
www.buildingawinningcareer.com

Appendices

A. Example description of a single role in a detailed CV
B. Example of a one-page Board CV
C. Example of a more junior CV for a graduate
D. Example of a one-page description to test a business idea
E. Example cover letter

Appendix A: Example description of a single role in a detailed CV

DETAILED EMPLOYMENT HISTORY

United International Banking Corporation   **Jan 2003–Dec 2020**

UIBC is a global bank, headquartered in Singapore. It has 80,000 employees around the world. UIBC has a strong, consistent record of growth, internally and through acquisitions.

**SVP, Customer Experience & Service
Innovation, Consumer Division**   **2016–2020**

Reporting to Chief Product Officer, to transform Consumer Division's way of working to be customer journey led and "agile" and to build a culture of innovation, collaboration and value creation.

Member of the Senior Leadership Team. Responsible for 100 people based in four countries. Annual expenditure budgets of $20M.

Key Challenges:

- Influencing stakeholders to actively participate in a customer and data centred approach for business decision-making in the face of them losing control.

- Driving collaboration and agile ways of working across organisation silos where predominant approach was waterfall.

- Changing annual investment plans for pre-defined projects to an "agile" investment process to enable faster progression of insight led initiatives.

- Driving culture of using customer and data insights to identify new product development/improvement opportunities.

- Morph from a risk-averse method of high predefinition and justification of projects to a test and learn mentality that quickly validates the desirability, feasibility and viability of ideas.

Selected Achievements:

- Baselined service design for Everyday Banking & Consumer Finance.

- Operationalised two cross-functional agile squads to uplift customer/staff experience and business performance.

- Developed customer and data-led strategy to regain service leadership.

Appendix B: Example of a one-page Board CV

Genevieve Hamdell
PPE, Oxon; MAMP; FAIM; GAICD

M: +66 426 055 888   E: ghamdell@telenet.com.au

Passionate about building stronger & more competitive enterprises in the Asian century. Seeking to introduce world-class business capability, based on digital technology.

Senior Corporate Profile – 15 years' experience as Senior Executive in Major Global Corporates

Proven business builder – Significant line experience including expense budgets of $200M, teams of 1500 staff across geographic locations; annual revenues of $500M in dynamic, complex environments.

Significant Asian experience – Built regional services business in India, Philippines, Hong Kong, Singapore, and Thailand that delivered $170M of benefits annually to United International Corp.

Transformational leader – Empowered teams and created substantial shareholder value in services-based businesses – delivered 10% EBIT improvement plus a substantial profitability turnaround.

Relevant Board Skills – 15 years' experience on various Boards and Committees

- **Strategic insight in technology-based businesses**
  - Recognised for asking strategic questions & offering commercially astute strategic insight.
  - Proven capacity to find innovative solutions in complex, dynamic environments.
  - Cares deeply about customers and leveraging technology for competitive differentiation.

- **Positive influencing skills**
  - Track record of successfully collaborating across boundaries/geographies/cultures.
  - Built high performing teams in diverse geographies/cultures/regulatory environments.
  - Deeply interested in talent development and positive performance management.

- **Rigorous approach to governance**
  - Understands productivity drivers with experience in offshoring/outsourcing/technology.
  - Has led large, complex businesses bringing operational discipline and focus on outcomes.
  - Managed in highly regulated environments; deep understanding of risk and compliance.

Senior Executive Career

United International Corp. – 2008–2013 – SVP, Global Shared Services
The Far East Group – 2006–2008 – Chief Executive Officer and MD
XMCC Corp – 2004–2005 – VP, Media Solutions; VP, Solutions Sales & Marketing
Hammel Lawyers – 1999–2004 – Director, Marketing and Strategy (incl. merger activities)

Non-Executive Director Experience

Government Solicitor – 2013 to present; Member, Audit Committee
Chief Executive Women Council – 2013 to present; Chair, Marketing & Comms Committee
University of Malaysia – 2007 to present; Chair, Building and Grounds Committee
The Far East Group – 2007–2008
Diversity Council – 2000–2010; Chair, Membership Committee

Appendix C: Example of a more junior CV for a graduate

Gerald Russell

E: geraldrussell@icloud.com   M: + 67 488 777 333

BCom, Edinburgh --- Financial Accountant at CityXX --- Rifleman in UK Army (Reserves)

PROFESSIONAL OVERVIEW

Completing degree – BCom at **Edinburgh University** in 2021.

Part-time roles – Financial Accountant at **CityXX Consulting** & Rifleman (Reserves) in **UK Army**.

Passion – Want to add value by helping organisations solve important business problems and grow.

Signature strengths – 1) Working at intersection of technology & commerce; 2) Building trust quickly within teams, and 3) Applying a diverse set of experiences & skills to solve complex problems.

KEY ACHIEVEMENTS at CityXX Consulting Group – Financial Accountant   2016–Current

CityXX helps companies implement & capitalise on their investment in advanced business software. My role ranged from processing transactions & preparing financials, through to complex systems accounting design.

- Introduced process improvements for cost tracking & revenue recognition to improve pricing decisions.
- Guided & tested customisations to support more accurate pricing model & subscription billing platform.
- Updated financial reporting models & systems to support Group's growth in new regions & sectors.

KEY ACHIEVEMENTS at UK Army (Reserves) – Rifleman   2018–Current

Riflemen are skilled soldiers who fight enemies at close quarters in all phases of warfare. Expert with a variety of weapons. Role relies heavily on skilled tactics, first-aid proficiency & effective teamwork.

- Provided emergency assistance to isolated flood-affected communities.
- Successfully acted as point of contact for evacuees & supported air & land convoys providing aid.
- Supported Police in enforcing lockdown measures to reduce community spread of COVID-19.

KEY SKILLS

Organisational skills:

- Proven analytical and problem-solving skills
- Critical and creative thinking

Functional skills:

- Excellent verbal and written communication skills
- Can multi-task, work independently, or in a team

EDUCATION

Edinburgh University, Bachelor of Commerce – Accounting/Economics   2016–2020

Glasgow Grammar School   2012–2015

PERSONAL INTERESTS

Hiking, AFL, Brazilian guitar, History

Appendix D: Example of a one-page description to test a business idea

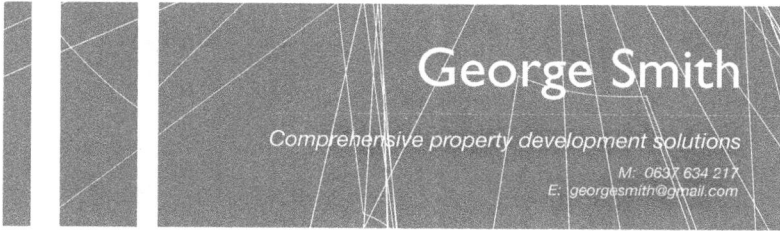

George Smith

Comprehensive property development solutions

M: 0637 634 217
E: georgesmith@gmail.com

Creating substantial value in property development

George has over 20 years in senior roles creating successful property developments with end values of over $2b.
His track record combines strategy, negotiation and business acumen.

George will work with you to **transform the value of the project**
- Identifying and acquiring property
- Creating high value strategic objectives
- Capacity to communicate effectively
- Focus on outcomes considering financial and risk management

5 steps in successful development:

Creating the Vision	Acquiring Suitable Land	Delivering the Infrastructure	Marketing the Project	Selling the Product
Concept Highest & best use Feasibility	Sourcing Deal Structure Negotiation	Cost Effective Solutions Time Control Team Management	Market Research Market Positioning Communicate Benefits	Builder Relationships Community Relationships Customer Focus

In a sound career George has a track record of:
- Building a successful development business with strategic acquisitions
- Negotiating with vendors and authorities to deliver vision and objectives
- Formulating marketing strategies to ensure the product is desirable to the target market.

Appendix E: Example cover letter

William F Rowe
Mobile: 0421 000 632; Email: wfr1963@outlook.net

12 July 2021

Mr James Smith
Executive Recruiter
London, UK

Dear James,

Group Chief Financial Officer – your ref: 178FR

I refer to our recent telephone discussion and confirm my interest in this senior position.

As you can see from my attached résumé, I am a leader who has added significant value in a variety of senior roles. My achievements have been widely acknowledged inside and outside the businesses where I have worked.

My signature strength is my ability to build high performance teams that deliver outstanding results. I am particularly proud that these results have been both significant and sustainable.

Based on your description of the requirements for the role, I believe my strengths are highly relevant and that I can make a major contribution to the future success of the business. For example, I have:

- Been highly effective in close partnering with four CEOs, to provide leadership and support to senior management teams;
- Developed and implemented successful growth and profit improvement strategies in three different businesses;
- Delivered a series of complex business transformations, and have led the successful integration of five major acquisitions;
- Provided thought leadership to two Boards on four acquisition strategies and capital raisings, including managing investor relations and governance matters; and
- Developed and implemented robust financial policies and effectively leveraged technology to deliver quality management information in five businesses.

I look forward to hearing from you in due course concerning my application. Please do not hesitate to contact me on 0421 000 632 should you wish to clarify any aspect of my background.

Yours,

William F Rowe

Further reading

BOOKS

Beckwith, H (2012), *Selling the Invisible: A Field Guide to Modern Marketing*, Little Brown.

Bennis, W (2009), *On Becoming a Leader*, Basic Books.

Birkman Fink, S & Capparell, S (2013), *The Birkman Method: Your Personality at Work*, John Wiley & Sons Inc (US).

Blanchard, K & Johnson, S (2015), *The New One Minute Manager*, HarperCollins Publishers.

Blainey, A (2009), *Marvelous Melba: The Extraordinary Life of a Great Diva*, Ivan R. Dee (US)

Bolles, R (2021), *What Color is Your Parachute? Your Guide to a Lifetime of Meaningful Work and Career Success*, Random House US.

Bridges, W & Bridges, S (2017), *Managing Transitions: Making the Most of Change*, John Murray.

Carnegie, D (2017), *How to Win Friends and Influence People*, HarperCollins Publishers.

Charan, R, Drotter, S & Noel, J (2010), *The Leadership Pipeline: How to Build the Leadership Powered Company*, John Wiley & Sons Inc (US).

Chu, K (2019), *100 Lunches with Strangers*, Kaley Chu Publishing.

Coleman, H (2020), *Empowering Yourself, The Organizational Game Revealed*, AuthorHouse (US)

Cuddy, A (2015), *Presence: Bringing Your Boldest Self to Your Biggest Challenges*, Orion.

Dreyer, B (2020), *Dreyer's English: An Utterly Correct Guide to Clarity and Style*, Random House UK.

Dweck, C (2017), *Mindset: Changing the Way You Think to Fulfil Your Potential*, Little Brown.

Gladwell, M (2001), *The Tipping Point: How Little Things Can Make a Big Difference*, Abacus (2001)

Hunt-Davis, B & Beveridge, H (2020) *Will It Make the Boat Go Faster? Olympic-winning Strategies for Everyday Success*, Troubador Publishing.

Kahneman, D (2012), *Thinking, Fast and Slow*, Penguin UK.

Minto, B (2021), *The Pyramid Principle: Logic in Writing and Thinking*, Pearson Education UK.

Rackham, N (1995), *SPIN Selling*, Taylor & Francis Ltd.

Rath, T (2007), *StrengthsFinder 2.0®*, Gallup Press.

Sinek, S (2010), *Start with Why: How Great Leaders Inspire Everyone to Take Action*, Penguin UK.

Watkins, M (2013), *The First 90 Days: Proven Strategies for Getting Up to Speed Faster and Smarter*, Harvard Business Review Press.

Zinsser, W (2016), *On Writing Well: The Classic Guide to Writing Nonfiction*, HarperCollins Publishers.

ARTICLES

Ahrendts, A (2015), 'How I hire: My guiding principles', LinkedIn Pulse.

Aquino, J (undated), 'How to practice a speech', Cool Communicator blog.

Botelho, E, Powell, K, Kincaid, S & Wang, D (2017) 'What sets successful CEOs apart', *Harvard Business Review*.

Brooks, A (2019), 'Your professional decline is coming (much) sooner than you think', *The Atlantic.*

Burrier, D (2010), 'Create a Nelson Mandela brand', *Harvard Business Review.*

Capowski, G (1994), 'Anatomy of a leader: where are the leaders of tomorrow?', *Management Review.*

Casciaro, T, Gino, F & Kouchaki, M (2016), 'Learn to love networking', *Harvard Business Review.*

Christensen, C (2010), 'How will you measure your life?', *Harvard Business Review.*

Ciampa, D (2016), 'After the handshake', *Harvard Business Review.*

Dewar, C, Hirt, M & Keller, S (2019), 'The mindsets and practices of excellent CEOs', McKinsey & Company.

Drucker, P (2005), 'Managing oneself', *Harvard Business Review.*

Elberse, A (2013), 'Ferguson's formula', *Harvard Business Review.*

Gillogly, B (2020), 'Watch Ford's Willow Run plant churn out a B-24 every 55 minutes', Hagerty.

Goldman, D (2000), 'Leadership that gets results', *Harvard Business Review.*

Granovetter, M (1973), 'The strength of weak ties', *American Journal of Sociology.*

Gruber, P (2013), 'What do the Oscars mean for you and your success', www.peterguber.com

Linsin, M (undated), 'Five essential strategies for the first day of school' Smart Classroom Management blog.

Lovallo, D & Kahneman, D (2003), 'Delusions of success', *Harvard Business Review.*

Mohr, T (2015), 'The confidence myth and what it means for your career', LinkedIn Pulse.

Okamoto, R (2017), 'Five ways to introduce yourself perfectly in 20 words or less', LinkedIn Pulse.

Peters, T (1997), 'The brand called You', Fast Company.

Rutledge, B (2011), 'Cultural differences: Monochronic versus polychronic', The Articulate CEO blog.

Sahlman, W (1997), 'How to write a great business plan', *Harvard Business Review*.

Shinagel, M (2013), 'The paradox of leadership', Harvard Professional Development blog.

Uzzi, B & Dunlap, S (2005), 'How to build your network', *Harvard Business Review*.

Valour, M (2016), 'Steps to take when you're starting to feel burned out', *Harvard Business Review*.

VIDEO

Cuddy, A (2012), 'Your body language may shape who you are', TED Talk.

Charan, R (2018), 'Leadership: Five skills to focus on', LinkedIn Learning.

PODCASTS

Preparing Yourself to Manage Your Job Search in the Most Effective Way – William Cowan with Bob Gerst:

www.buzzsprout.com/803141/12723735

Index

www.ingramcontent.com/pod-product-compliance
Lightning Source LLC
Chambersburg PA
CBHW071316210326
41597CB00015B/1250